Digital Virtual Consumption

Routledge Studies in Innovation, Organization and Technology

RIOT!

Digital Virtual Consumption

Edited by Mike Molesworth
and Janice Denegri-Knott

Routledge
Taylor & Francis Group

LONDON AND NEW YORK

First published 2012
by Routledge

2 Park Square, Milton Park, Abingdon, Oxon OX14 4RN
711 Third Avenue, New York, NY 10017, USA

*Routledge is an imprint of the Taylor & Francis Group,
an informa business*

First issued in paperback 2016

Library of Congress Cataloging-in-Publication Data
   Digital virtual consumption / edited by Mike Molesworth and Janice
Denegri-Knott.
      p. cm. — (Routledge studies in innovation, organization and
technology ; 23)
   Includes bibliographical references and index.
   1. Digital electronics—Social aspects.   2. Technological
innovations—Social aspects.   3. Information society.   I. Molesworth,
Mike.   II. Denegri-Knott, Janice, 1977–
   HM851.D5454 2012
   303.48'33—dc23
   2011049633

ISBN13: 978-0-415-52929-7 (hbk)
ISBN13: 978-1-138-20307-5 (pbk)

Typeset in Sabon
by IBT Global.

Contents

Figures and Tables

FIGURES

TABLES

1 Introduction to Digital Virtual Consumption

Janice Denegri-Knott and Mike Molesworth

A decade ago we were leading a seminar on interactive media strategies with a group of undergraduate marketing students. The setting for observation was the then very new *Habbo Hotel*. We spent much of our time observing the pixilated avatars that were congregated in a series of chaotic rooms, moving about, nervously reacting to other guests' attempts to make contact with them. Nothing new there. Our students quickly grew tired of what seemed to be repetitive and cumbersome exchanges between Habbo users, until one our students made the discovery that the poorly pixilated furniture was actually for sale, and not only this, that they were desirable commodities. Even today, with some incredulity we digest news that virtual world residents have paid £216,187 for Planet Calipso Virtual Space Station or that more than half the US population plays some sort of videogames.

Why, we can ask, would somebody buy a chair they cannot physically sit on or a planet they cannot physically visit? Why do some grown men and women spend so much of their leisure time consuming videogames or participating in online communities? What meaning do consumers make of their time engaging in such activities? What characterizes this kind of consumption and how might it be different from other types of consumption (and indeed how might it be similar)?

The collection of chapters in this book deals with such preoccupations. The defining theme is consumption, both in terms of the consumption of digital virtual spaces like videogames, the online stock market, Woot and Second Life, as well as the consumption of objects within and about those spaces. However, this is not a book about online shopping. To us, consumption invites an analysis of how market resources—consumer goods, services, and technologies are just that, resources—both symbolic and material, through which all sorts of broader projects are negotiated by individuals and communities in view of substantiating a moral undertaking—to be a particular kind of person, to organize, and to support a particular type of community. Simply put, the essential capacity of consumption is both to make sense of who we are and the groups we belong to and to actualize socially agreed ideals or provide a space to subvert socially convened scripts.

This may sound counter-intuitive; after all, the study of consumption has been wedded to an analysis of material culture and the all too physical processes involved in acquiring and appropriating goods. That impetus to acquire and use, however, is often the result of seeking a material actualization of what is first imagined, of what Shields (2003) has called 'the virtual,' the 'almost there.' Virtual is understood here, as Shields (2003) does, as both real and ideal and entwined with our perception of reality. It is what we imagine, it is what 'is almost there' but isn't yet. Key to this analysis is Shields's insistence that the virtual (what we imagine) is real, but ideal compared to the material that is real and actual. Rather than place the ideal and the actual as opposites (unreal versus real), they may more usefully be compared to what is ideally possible and what is actually probable. It is important to note that this book is not about virtual consumption, not even about celebrating 'consumption light' or de-material consumption of the kind that has a supposed ever so light environmental footprint. While other texts may celebrate the potential of wasteless consumption promised by digital consumption as in the consumption of code, this book reminds us of the ever-present material. The title of the book is purposefully not digital consumption, or virtual consumption, although both of these terms are also commonly used to describe what we mean by digital virtual consumption (DVC). For us, virtual consumption is located in the consumer imagination at large and has a long history, whereas digital consumption better describes specific technical and socio-cultural arrangements that define a user's experience in a specific computer mediated environment, be it *eBay*, Second Life, or iTunes. That analysis to us, which is limited to what happens on the screen and surgically removes consumers from their everyday life, is misconstrued and perpetuates, unwittingly, a problematic severance between our digital and offline selves and lives. It fails to acknowledge that the consumer subject arrives, already with a particular moral code or subjectivity, a particular intentionality or way of seeing, which is not solely a product of DVC, but rather their being in a particular socio-historic milieu and embedded in complex webs of relationships on and off the screen. It also downplays the necessity of material stuff and processes in supporting emerging consumption practices.

To understand DVC we draw on Rob Shields's (2000, 2003) theorization of the digital virtual as liminoid space—somewhere between the imagination and the material, and under the control of the individual's desire to engage with them. As Shields (2000, 2003) puts it, the ontological stature of the digital virtual as an 'in-between' place allows experimentation beyond normal consumer subject positions dictated by material resources and properties, and the physical makeup of the individual. DVC differs from virtual or imaginary consumption—daydreaming or fantasizing in other words, where a reality is summoned in the mind of the individual—inasmuch as the object of consumption is experienced as owned and used within the parameters of digital virtual spaces created from servers, networks, and digital processors (owned, run, and maintained at a cost and usually for a profit by commercial organization), and audiovisual equipment (bought or leased by consumers). However, these materialities of apparently non-material spaces are not what are experienced in use; rather they are manifestly absent (see Law, 2004). In DVC the object of consumption seems to lack material substance so cannot be used in material reality, but is also free from the limitations of what is probable such that the ideally possible is made present and can be experienced. For example, a digital virtual car cannot drive its owner to work or the shops but also needs no fossil fuel, finance agreement, or warranty plan in order to be experienced; a digital virtual home will not keep its owner warm and dry or allow food to be prepared, but it may defy space or planning limitations as it is built and furnished; and a digital virtual magic sword cannot cut material flesh, but it may render its owner's avatar invincible in battle in a digital virtual space (see Chapter 2, this volume).

In these digital virtual spaces the normal rules of materially real quotidian life are suspended, providing a performative matrix for experimenting with different modes of practice. In fact the potential for individual change is such for Shields (2000, 2003) that it supercharges the potential for transformation present in the liminal—not as a space to manage societal change through the rites of passage that once characterized transitions in life (starting school, starting work, getting married, having children, retiring, etc.) but smaller, individual, liminoid change through personal and often private experimentation. In DVC the possibility of experimentation and transformation remains largely wired into commodities and consumer experiences, themselves already liminoid, but also germinates the possibility that the more transgressive modes of practice, which are blocked in the materially real because they are too difficult to actualize or because they are taboo, can be enacted in the digital virtual.

In this sense DVC opens up another theatre on which consumption, with both its potential for further alienation and positive transformation, can be enacted. This potential to actualize all sorts of imaginings makes it a fertile terrain to document just how collectively and individually, what on digital virtual spaces becomes significant to consumers (see Chapter 2, this volume). It is therefore not surprising to find that much of the time our contributors are dealing with communities (Kozinets, Ross, Jacobs, Martin), personal relationships (Venkatesh and Behairy; Denegri-Knott, Watkins, and Wood; Vicdan and Ulusoy), individual desires and fantasies (Myers, Molesworth), individual self-realization (Zwick), means of sustaining and supporting digital virtual communities in games (Ross, Óskarsson), virtual worlds (Martin), consumption centred communities (Kozinets), and auction houses (Jacobs).

MAKING SENSE OF AND MAKING SENSE WITH

One of the reasons that DVC may be compelling is its steady supply of novelty and difference. The domain of material consumption as contributors to this volume have intimated has become a bit too known, too desperately the same to incite interest. The promise of novelty, in terms of goods, experiences, and social arrangements, seems infinite. With novelty and newness comes the requirement to make sense of these experiences and objects, to assess their use value, their significance, the in-game structures regulating MMOR, the socio-cultural conventions that operate in digital virtual worlds and games, and the kinds of shared knowledges and conventions that dictate behavior even in forum based communities and online auction houses. This book sheds lights on these sense making efforts.

Conceptually, too, we are yet to understand the kinds of systems of signification or meaning that allow us to make sense of digital virtual goods. To begin with Vili Lehdonvirta (Chapter 2) offers us a history of the digitization of consumption where he explores the sources of value for digital virtual goods. He argues that digital virtual goods like materially real objects fulfill the same symbolic and functional needs, with the added advantage that they are a bit more honest, relying less on the symbolic value of branded symbolic goods.

In Chapter 4, David Myers puts forward an eloquent argument for understanding digital virtual goods within games as impermanent things or infinite durables that can never be used up. Like other consumer goods, they must always have a minimum of functionality, but unlike other consumer goods digital virtual goods within games are of seemingly infinite duration, so we consume without ever using up the object of consumption. However, the games through which these digital virtual goods are consumed, at least our desire to play them, is corroded over time because repeated play reduces the initial novelty its semiotic system first aroused. We must move onto the next game. This kind of logic is also present in Mike Molesworth's discussion of videogames as shopping, Melinda Jacobs's study of Woot-offs, where consumers are anxiously waiting for future items to be listed, and Vicdan and Ulusoy's analysis of the constant re-creation of avatars on Second Life. Here too we see an always future oriented consumption, where novelty is the number one value to be consumed.

Not only do digital virtual goods need to be worked out, but also the very social arrangements, rules, shared understanding, and knowledges that structure specific digital virtual consumption destinations. Part of this stems from the liminoid, potentially transformational nature of DVC that works something like a sandbox for working out new socio-cultural arrangements. Rob Kozinets's (Chapter 7) candid reflection on his 1999 paper on virtual communities of consumption reconsiders this potential for transformation arising from consumers' multimodal relationships as helping produce some kind of long standing social gain. Curiously, even the most commodity-centered discussion over time can transform into a more meaningful, personal, and community centered engagement.

Other transformations of course abound. On the one side there seems to be gamefication of consumption, but also a transformation of games into commodity consumption as well as collectivization of consumption. Melinda Jacobs (Chapter 11) shows us how a coming together of games structures and consumer culture produces a distinct form of consumerism or consuming as gameplay on the American wholesale outlet Woot and its Woot-offs. During a Woot-off items once sold are removed and others put up for sale. Jacobs suggests this obstacle has created a consumerist disposition where there is a desire to establish what is being sold next; this too has created a community that works together in order to accelerate the unveiling of the next good put up for sale. Sandy Ross's (Chapter 10) six-year engagement with Final Fantasy XI (FFXI) reveals the emergence of collective forms of consumption, where collective rather than individual wealth is encouraged and where a new type of market morality is performed in constructing a quasi-utopian project. By looking at how collective wealth is accumulated by linkshells (guilds) she examines how guild members collectively impose limits to individual desires and create a collective sense of what should be desired and who has a rightful claim to consumption. These limits to consumption are important because they produce stability that enables game play and individual consumption dreams and the affective or emotional requirement to maintain networks of fictive kinship and social ties of linkshell alive.

The emphasis on a communal or collective interest can also be found in Jennifer Martin's chapter on Second Life's gift economy and role of freebies (Chapter 13). As she writes, it is not uncommon for Second Life residents to encounter all sorts of free digital virtual goods, from trinkets to fully furnished homes, which fulfill all sorts of objectives, from expressing generosity, enticing recipients to become future paying customers to socializing newbies into the Second Life economy.

So clearly, consumers need to work out what such objects mean and become socialized into proper consumption as we see in the Woot, Second Life, and FFXI cases; these experiences, too, fulfill another related: to consider DVC in light of their materially real everyday life. Some chapters in this collection offer glimpses of those moments of reflection, when individuals reconsider their consumerist proclivities and the nature of their desires. Others narrate the ways in which consumers re-enact well known consumer scripts, but perhaps in ways that are perceived to be more successful than in the materially real. Handan Vicdan and Ebru Ulusoy (Chapter 12) explore how consumer creativity is deployed to construct multiple virtual selves not so much to impress fellow Second Life inhabitants but rather to experience being 'someone different.' They see this as a continuous process of re-construction, which goes beyond the purely symbolic to include an immersive, embodied, highly sensual experience where consumers are constantly asking themselves about the way they are and how they behave. So, although playful and recreational, DVC offers opportunities for meaningful reflection. This reflective capacity seeps through assessments of what is to be deemed personally valuable digital virtual possessions, as Janice Denegri-Knott, writing with Rebecca Watkins and Joe Wood (Chapter 6), discover through their interviews with owners of digital virtual goods. In the absence of a solid material object, transforming digital goods into meaningful possessions is more obviously centered on the purposeful contemplation of what has been invested in the process of adapting, changing, storing, and re-materializing digital virtual possessions. These kinds of reflections, as we will see in the following chapters, emanate from the inevitable tension between individual and collective imaginations and the constraints of material reality.

RE-ASSERTING MATERIALITY

Throughout this volume we are constantly reminded of the conceptual pitfalls of reproducing a duality between what is physical or material consumption and what is digital virtual. Such analyses would have us believing that somehow DVC is a domain of its own, where bodies and their limitations are abandoned and where the mind can run free, and reality is dematerialized. In his chapter Magaudda (Chapter 8) re-asserts the weight of materiality in our analysis of DVC by focusing on the intimate relationship between DVC and material objects in how consumers consume digital music. Drawing on practice theory, he makes a case for re-asserting the role of the material in shaping consumers' experiences. As he puts it, within the context of DVC materiality still matters, and a lot. It is necessary then not to forget about the weight of the material in shaping and making sense of an emerging consumer culture.

Whereas DVC represents a liminoid space between what is imagined and what is actually real, this liminality implies not only that the material and the symbolic are strictly interwoven, but also that it is impossible to think of DVC without making reference to the changing forms of materiality in social life and to how this materiality contributes to shaping possibilities and constraints of DVC (Magaudda, Chapter 8). For instance, Vicdan and Ulusoy tell us in their chapter how present the corporeal body is in consumers as they craft their digital virtual selves in Second Life, even when it seems absent. The body is there when consumers want to overcome their bodies by feeling their body through their avatars like embarrassment for being a newbie or for standing too close to others. We find consumers reflecting on the need to find somewhere desolate to carry out their transformations, feeling embarrassed by their avatars' nakedness and attempting to make their avatars more like themselves and themselves more like their avatars. Similarly, Denegri-Knott, Watkins, and Wood in their chapter on how digital virtual goods are transformed into meaningful possessions (Chapter 6) document how consumers find more stable and visible instantiations for what they perceive to be ephemeral and fragile digital virtual possessions.

The material is also very present in the analysis of macro considerations, or the socio-historic conditions that prefigure a certain attitude or the social imagination of users who find themselves using computers, videogames, and smart phones to achieve all sorts of socially convened goals. That is, the discourses that structure our field of action as we move about in the materially real are present too in DVC, even when they are subverted. Looking at the broader political and historic context is important because it prefigures a certain predisposition to become a certain kind of person, who will be immersed in DVC in a particular way. Drawing on Foucault's critique of liberalism and neoliberal forms of government, Zwick (Chapter 9) argues that online investing has become a key site for the production of an entrepreneurial subjectivity, a certain type of individual or consumer self based on insecurity, competitiveness, individualization, and inequality. In that analysis, although DVC made it possible for consumers to act out as self-enterprising online investors, the online investor was more of an outcome of a distinct neoliberal form of government.

The immediate context of DVC is important too. The backdrop to DVC, the necessary work carried out before the consumer is able to engage in DVC, is often overlooked. So not only do we have to be attendant to the material, technological artifacts that make up DVC but also the filial relationships that do their part in socializing users into accessing technology in a certain way. In their chapter, Venkatesh and Behairy (Chapter 3) illustrate the many ways in which young consumers display a degree of autonomy in deploying a wide range of acquired skills, and these are executed with autonomy but embedded within a relational context. It seems then that DVC is tempered by a range of familial relationships, which are manifest in some form of computer instruction.

CONCLUSIONS

In summary, this collection of chapters charts a more nuanced trajectory of the ways in which DVC is incorporated into everyday life, sometimes with surprising effects. This is then not so much about isolating DVC as a distinct terrain one escapes to, but rather seeing DVC as a space to transform and be transformed with, about working out the meanings and uses of digital virtual goods investing our imaginative prowess in transforming them into objects of desire, and in the process become equipped with a new range of skills, competencies, and knowledge through which we can make sense of ourselves and our place in our social milieus. At the least, even when DVC is more obviously structured by market type relations, it too can be transformed to support meaningful relationships with ourselves and others. If anything, DVC offers us opportunities to become a different kind of consumer.

REFERENCES

Law J. 2004. *After Method: Mess in Social Science Research.* Routledge: London.
Shields R. 2000. *Performing Virtualities: Liminality On and Off the "Net."* Available at http://virtualsociety.sbs.ox.ac.uk/events/pvshields.html [accessed on 4 May 2005].
Shields R. 2003. *The Virtual.* Routledge: London.

Part I

Contexts and Perspectives

2 A History of the Digitalization of Consumer Culture

Vili Lehdonvirta

INTRODUCTION

It is frequently argued in sociology that consumption has become a central part of life in contemporary post-industrial societies, also known as "consumer societies" (Baudrillard, 2002). More recently, the rapid diffusion of information and communication technologies (ICTs) in everyday life has inspired discourses on "information society" (Castells and Himanen, 2002). There is a relative dearth of scholarship addressing the intersection of these two major paradigms. The purpose of this chapter is to examine how information society interacts with consumer society in a broad range of processes that can be termed the *digitalization of consumption*.

For a long time, studies on information technology consumption focused on the consumption of the technologies and devices themselves. Researchers focused on such questions as how many households have Internet access and what kind of people use mobile phones most frequently. But the adoption of digital technologies in everyday life has also had a profound influence on the way we consume other goods and services. Products are increasingly examined, compared, purchased, and paid for on the Internet and through mobile services. Consumption-related information is disseminated and discussed on blogs and forums. Consumers self-organize on social networking sites and take active roles in production processes through crowdsourcing and other technologies. One of the most striking developments has been the rise of digital virtual consumption: millions of people around the world are now spending billions of euros per year on virtual items, characters and currencies in online games, social networking sites, and other digital hangouts (Lehdonvirta and Ernkvist, 2011).

The method of this chapter is to trace a brief history of different phases in the digitalization of consumption. The story is structured around a distinction among the sites, processes, subjects, and objects of consumption, and the analysis draws on three theoretical approaches to consumption in the social sciences: economistic, structural, and hedonistic. This allows the chapter to provide some answers to the questions that one encounters when looking back on the history of digital consumption: What is the difference between buying a book online versus buying it from a brick-and-mortar store? Why are some people so attracted to seemingly non-existent virtual items as to be willing to pay real money for them? Does this economization and consumerization of online interactions represent a failure of the higher ideals that many had for the digital world? I conclude the chapter with a discussion of how the digitalization of consumption and especially digital virtual consumption bear on the big question of consumer society: reconciling markets with environmental sustainability.

APPROACHES TO ANALYZING CONSUMPTION

The consumer theory of modern mainstream micro economics posits that each consumer has a set of *preferences* that determines which goods and in which quantities they choose to purchase from the market within the constraints of their budget (Jehle and Reny, 2001). Economics does not present a theory of where consumer preferences come from, however. It is assumed that preferences are something that exist prior to and independently of their possible satisfaction: they are "latent wants" that become realized in the act of consumption (Campbell, 2004: 37). In sister disciplines such as marketing and management studies, the source of these wants is commonly located in notions of "basic human needs" borrowed from psychology and physiology. According to a classic marketing textbook, "[n]eeds are the basic human requirements. People need food, air, water, clothing, and shelter to survive. People also have strong needs for recreation, education, and entertainment" (Kotler, 2003: 11). Following the ideas of Maslow, these needs are moreover thought to adhere to a hierarchy of importance that determines the order in which they must be satisfied (Kotler, 2003: 196).

Sociologists have criticized the idea of all consumer behavior emanating from a set of inborn needs (e.g., Baudrillard, 2002; Belk, 2004; Campbell, 1998; Slater, 1997: 133–136). In extreme conditions, it is clear that physiological needs can predict consumer behavior. But the wants that people pursue in more affluent societies can be seemingly pointless or even counterproductive from a physiological or psychological perspective. Any consumption decision, such as the purchase of virtual items, can always be explained after the fact as the pursuit of a suitably abstract need, such as the need for self-actualization. If the only evidence for such an abstract need is the behavior it is supposed to explain, then the theory is a simple tautology.

Whatever the source of consumer preferences, in the economistic approach to the study of consumption, it is assumed that their fulfillment is the source of well-being (Jehle and Reny, 2001: 5). Key analytical concerns in this approach are such issues as transaction costs, entry barriers, and other hurdles that may prevent consumers from exercising their choice to the fullest possible extent. When analyzing the digitalization of consumption from this perspective, the main question is whether it helps or hinders the fulfillment of consumer choice.

Outside economics and marketing, consumption is examined and theorized in the works of sociologists, anthropologists, and cultural theorists. With some simplification, it is possible to identify two major perspectives from this sizeable literature: *consumption as social signification* and *consumption as a hedonistic project*. I refer to the former as the structural approach to consumption and the latter as the hedonistic approach. If economic consumer theory assumes that consumers behave according to their preferences over goods, then the structural and hedonistic approaches provide substance to that theory by explaining where those preferences come from. At the same time, some of the theories also question the economic theory's behavioral assumption, positing that consumers are driven not so much by their own rational calculations as they are by the positions they occupy in social structures.

The structural approach to analyzing consumption focuses on the use of goods as tools for communicating and constructing social bonds and distinctions. Generally speaking, consumers are seen as communicators who use commodities to express social status, class distinctions, group memberships, and identity positions (e.g., Bourdieu, 1984; Simmel, 1957[1904]; Veblen, 1997[1899]). Commodity flows also demarcate, structure, and strengthen social relationships (e.g., Mauss, 1990; McCracken, 1990). In contrast to the economistic view, "needs" and "necessities" are not seen as objective truths but as culturally defined categories (Bauman and May, 2001: 147–162; Belk, 2004). Increasing affluence and the continuous introduction of new goods into society results in classificatory shifts, where goods that were previously considered luxuries are redefined as decencies and eventually as necessities (Belk, 2004: 71–72). Digital technologies are currently undergoing such a shift. For example, the mobile phone that used to be a luxury of top executives is now an everyday necessity for Finnish and Japanese teenagers (Rantavuo, 2006; Wilska, 2003). In Finland, broadband Internet connection has been declared a basic right.

In the structural approach, the satisfaction derived from goods is primarily linked to their use as markers and only secondarily related to their physical consumption (Douglas and Isherwood, 1978). An extreme example of this is the accumulation of collectible objects, which can be completely "useless" and non-functional (Baudrillard, 1994). Even if the collected objects were once useful in some way, when they enter the collection they are no longer used in their original purpose (Belk, 1995, 2004). Although collectors frequently describe the thrill of the hunt for collectible objects, Belk (1995) argues that the hunt is, in the end, usually a highly competitive game of status seeking.

At the same time, Belk (2004) acknowledges that the collector's single-minded pursuit can also be seen as highly pleasurable romanticism: noble saving of objects that few others appreciate. This position brings us to the hedonistic approach to consumption, which focuses on the emotional pleasures and experiences of consumption. For Campbell (1989, 1998, 2004), consumption is not so much a means of constructing identities as it is a means of *exploring* one's self-identity. As consumers expose themselves to different goods on the marketplace, they learn about their own identity by monitoring their own responses to different choices and products. For Campbell, consumption is less about acquisition and more a quest of exploration to become as acquainted with one's inner self as possible.

A problem with Campbell's theory is that it assumes that consumers have one "true" self-identity that they explore. Others, such as Featherstone (1991), posit that consumption is a vehicle for daydreaming. Featherstone argues that urban everyday life is *aestheticized*: overflowing with imagery that can evoke dream-like and pleasurable aesthetic sensations. He invokes Baudelaire's concept of a *flâneur*—a gentleman strolling the streets to experience the sights and sounds of the city—to describe the contemporary consumer. The majority of the processes of consumption take place inside the strollers' imagination in response to what he experiences. Featherstone also describes a more active citizen of the city of consumption, reminiscent of the dandies of the same period as the *flâneur*. The dandy fashions life as an artistic project that consists of the creative mixing of consumption styles and a pursuit of ever new hedonistic experiences.

Critical thinkers such as Baudrillard (2002) suggest that markets have long ago hijacked the sociological and hedonistic processes described above. Marketing produces a continuous flow of new images and signs to be used in daydreams and social distinction games. Baudrillard uses the term *commodity-sign* to describe the products of this economy. Although from an economic perspective it would seem that consumers "prefer" each successive generation of signs to the previous one, for Baudrillard it is not clear if this cycle results in any actual increases to well-being. What is clear, however, is that each new turn of the cycle consumes another portion of the planet's natural resources.

Awareness of the detrimental effects that consumer culture is having on the environment is increasing, and related changes can be seen taking place in advertising and public discourse: an increasing emphasis on ostensibly "green" products and services as signals of cultural competence, and the re-casting of some highly resource consuming activities and products as unfashionable and ignorant choices. Silvestro (2009) outlines two perspectives to these changes. A hopeful view sees the green consumption boom as "responsible consumerism [. . .] a change in values and an improvement of capitalism" (Silvestro, 2009: 281). A more cynical view sees no reason to doubt that consumers' choices remain nothing but moves in a game of social signification and distinction. "Green" goods are, after all, usually more expensive, exclusive, and difficult to maintain (Haanpää, 2007).

SOCIOLOGICAL ANALYSIS OF INFORMATION TECHNOLOGY CONSUMPTION

Many sociologists have examined how technical appliances are used in social signaling. For example, empirical studies show that socio-economically disadvantaged people tend to consume new technologies less than socio-economically advantaged people (Hsieh et al., 2008; Räsänen, 2006, 2008). One explanation for this is that working class people lack the necessary education and spending power to enter the digital age. But a more Veblenian interpretation is that higher classes are drawn to novel and expensive gadgets because of the gadgets' ability to create social distinctions (Yoshimi, 2006: 76). From a cultural perspective, new technologies are often associated with an array of new advertising images. Successive generations of hardware promise new varieties of freedom, creativity, and adventure that enter consumers' daydreams. In this sense, new technologies are no different from new types of sneakers or new varieties of washing powder.

But besides being consumption objects themselves, digital technologies have also had a profound influence on the consumption of other goods and services. We can thus distinguish between two kinds of analyses: analyses of digital technologies as consumption objects, and analyses of the consumption of other goods and services through digital means. Today, consumption practices that involve or make use of digital technology are numerous. For the purposes of analysis, it is useful to break down the concept of consumption into smaller elements. Ritzer (2001) suggests that we examine how digital technology bears on the *sites, processes, subjects,* and *objects* of consumption. The subjects of consumption are the consumers themselves. The objects of consumption are the goods or services being consumed. In the following sections, I will trace a brief history of the practices and discourses of digital consumption, starting with changes in the sites and processes of consumption and ending with transformations in the subjects and objects. At the same time, I will provide analyses of these changes using the three perspectives outlined in the previous section.

CHANGES IN THE SITES AND PROCESSES OF CONSUMPTION

The consumer Internet boom that started in the mid-1990s prompted retailers to start building facilities for online shopping. The basic model of online retailing was the same as the existing modes of remote retailing, mail order catalogs, and TV shopping, and is utilized most of the same infrastructure: huge warehouses for stock and logistics, mail and delivery companies for distribution, and credit cards for payment. Advertisers and other public discourse highlighted the economic benefits of this new mode of shopping (Underhill, 2000). Shopping at online stores is available at any time from any place with an Internet connection. It can be fast and efficient compared with the process of selecting from a mail order catalog and relaying the order to an operator over the phone. Web search tools enable much more efficient price comparisons than traditional modes of shopping do. Thus, although the digitalization of the retail process introduced a whole world of new problems in the form of computer related problems and glitches, it realized certain clear advantages in the areas of convenience and availability.

At the same time, online shopping has been criticized for failing to provide the sensual and social benefits of traditional brick-and-mortar retail. Underhill (2000: 218), writing in the late 1990s, identified "three big things that [physical] stores alone can offer shoppers": "touch, trial or any other sensory stimuli", "immediate gratification"; and "social interaction": the company of other shoppers as well as interactions with shop staff. According to Underhill (2000: 218), online shopping is more about "orderly, planned acquisition of goods" than the "sensual, experiential aspects of shopping." Others were even more pessimistic about the ways in which the digitalization of shopping sites changed the social aspect of consumption. Ritzer (2001: 150) saw online shopping sites as "dehumanized and dehumanizing worlds in which satisfaction from human action and interaction is all but impossible." Friends, shop assistants, and other human beings are totally eliminated from the process, and consumers enter their own computer generated "dreamworld" of consumption. As social controls are eliminated, consumers are increasingly vulnerable to the online shopping sites, which are moreover always available and therefore harder to escape from. At the same time, local brick-and-mortar markets are presumably out-competed by the self-service digital markets, so that shopping loses its function as an activity for strengthening social ties between local community members. Further, the acquisition of "useless" goods merely for the purpose of using them as social markers may also decrease.

Some commentators have highlighted a more positive transformational aspect of digital shopping sites: their ability to provide a far wider selection than it is possible to find even in the largest superstores or mail order catalogs (Anderson, 2006; Underhill, 2000). For example, while a typical large bookstore offers a selection of 100,000 books, *Amazon.com* has an inventory of 3.7 million book titles (Anderson, 2006). A similar situation prevails in several other industries and product categories. The massive selection is made possible by the low cost of listing products in an online store as well as efficient searching and browsing features that allow customers on the Web to find what they are seeking.

A consequence of the huge selection is that consumers' purchases can be distributed over a much wider range of products than what was previously possible, a *long tail*, enabling greater divergence and fragmentation in tastes and styles. According to Anderson (2006), this allows consumers much greater freedom to express their preferences, not being constrained by their local retailer's selections. This is obviously an advantage from the economic perspective, but it also has cultural implications. Anderson contrasts manufactured "hit culture," engendered by limited shelf space, with a new "niche culture," where consumption patterns reflect the true diversity of tastes in society. Anderson believes that this postmodernist "niche culture" is morally superior because it reflects people's tastes in a "purer" way. He suggests that it allows shoppers to realize "the true shape of demand in our culture, unfiltered by the economics of scarcity" (Anderson, 2006: 9).

Featherstone (1998) and Denegri-Knott and Molesworth (2010a, 2010b) connect digital consumption sites and processes to the hedonistically oriented consumption literature. Featherstone's early analysis describes the online world as a supercharged cityscape where the *flâneur* does not have to wait until the next street corner to experience a new vista; he can simply click a hyperlink and be instantly transported. At the same time, however, the trip through the city loses its narrative structure, and it becomes impossible to make sense of the experience in the traditional way.

Denegri-Knott and Molesworth's (2010a) detailed analysis of *eBay* reveals how the site's massive selection of goods is being used by consumers to stimulate imagination and fashion daydreams. In support of this notion, they note that the majority of purchases in online sites are only taken as far as the checkout stage and cancelled just before any money is spent. Far more people stroll around the digital shopping arcades than actually spend money on them. From an economic perspective, this may sound as if digital shopping sites are failing to fulfill consumers' needs. But from a hedonistic perspective, this observation suggests that digital shopping sites have psychological significance that goes far beyond their economic impact. Even if the first wave of digitalization led to a "rationalization" of the sites and processes of consumption, people quickly discovered how to adapt them for their hedonistic aims.

CHANGES IN THE CONSUMER

Since mid-2000s, there has been much enthusiastic discussion under such rubriks as *remix culture, Web 2.0*, and, most recently, *social media* (Benkler, 2006; Hietanen et al., 2007; Lessig, 2004; Scoble and Israel, 2006; Surowiecki, 2005; Tapscott and Williams, 2006). The basic claim in these discussions is that certain new technologies and, more importantly, new ways of designing online services have led to a radical empowerment of the consumer. Technologies and design techniques such as blogs, RSS feeds, tags, social networking, Web applications, Creative Commons licensing, and peer-to-peer networking have permitted users to emerge from uninformed shoppers into discerning connoisseurs, from passive consumers to active producer consumers, and from isolated individuals to "carrot mobs."

The first new digital consumer was arguably the "pirate" that got involved in the distribution of digital goods. Starting from 1990s, peer-to-peer file sharing programs "empowered" users to duplicate and distribute software, music, movies, and digital books to each other in a very efficient manner outside the official distribution channels and schedules. This gave rise to an ongoing conflict between "file sharers" and the entire copyright industry. Although many authors writing about Web 2.0 and social media would probably not associate illegal file sharing with participatory web culture, it is clearly one of the first instances of digital technology radically changing the role of consumers in a market. In the traditional copyright regime, the production of new information goods, especially cultural content such as music and movies, is based on large investments in production and marketing, which may later be recouped by monopoly profits made possible by copyright. In contrast, the political agenda of file sharers, as expressed by the Pirate Party of Sweden (which holds two seats in the European parliament), involves scaling back the copyright regime in favor of free private copying and "culture-sharing." This goal is exemplified by the file sharing hub Pirate Bay.

Another change in the consumer can be seen in the value appraisal part of the value chain. The Web has been a platform for people to express their opinions and experiences regarding products since its popularization in the mid-1990s, but only the latest wave of the so-called Web 2.0 techniques has allowed that information to be organized, ordered, and filtered in ways that make it highly usable to individual consumers (Scoble and Israel, 2006). As a result, consumers now have more powerful means and varied angles at their disposal when they seek to assess and compare the value of information goods (Benkler, 2006). Social networking and mobile communication technologies have also permitted individual consumers to self-organize in ways that improve their traditionally weak bargaining position against vendors. For example, in China, groups formed for the purpose of *tuángòu* or team buying use their market power to negotiate lower prices with vendors (Montlake, 2007). The participatory wave of Web technologies has enabled online shopping to regain much of the sociability that the first wave of online retail was criticized for lacking.

Finally, a third change is that the digital consumer can also assume a more active role in the production side of the economy. New technologies allow users to move from passively experiencing goods to actively participating in the experience, appropriating the goods to new uses, and combining and altering the goods to create entirely new experiences. For instance, new software for editing videos, sampling music, and touching photographs (often acquired from peer-to-peer networks without paying for a license) has enabled suitably skilled participants to create a "remix culture" on the basis of industrially produced cultural products (Lessig, 2004). Open-source software and Web application mashups are somewhat analogous phenomena in other fields of production.

Another set of technologies that transforms consumers into producers is known as *crowdsourcing*. Crowdsourcing entails outsourcing tasks traditionally performed by employees or contractors to a large group of people (i.e., a crowd) through the Internet (Howe, 2008). Most early examples of crowdsourcing are extensions of marketing campaigns (Kleemann et al., 2008). But in other cases, companies approach the crowd as a genuine source of ideas and productivity rather than as potential customers. For example, *Amazon* used crowdsourcing to identify duplicate product pages on its massive e-commerce site. It developed a website where people could look at product pages and get paid a few cents for every duplicate page they correctly identified. Other tasks that companies outsource to anonymous Internet users include market research, data input, data verification, copywriting, graphic design, and even software development (Lehdonvirta and Ernkvist, 2011). A market study estimated that over the past ten years, more than one million workers have earned $1–2 billion via crowdsourced work allocation (Frei, 2009). The new consumer who participates in processes of production has been called a *prosumer* by consumption scholars (Collins, 2010; Ritzer and Jurgenson, 2010).

A set of values, manifesting as the guiding principle of the digital consumer's actions, can be found implicit in much of the literature sketching the digital consumer. These values are clearly not the values of appropriation, accumulation, and exclusivity, as found in the traditional status games of consumption, but are more akin to the *hacker ethic* articulated by Steven Levy (1984): sharing for the benefit of others, using technology to improve the world, and valuing people based on their mental abilities rather than on their material possessions. The digital consumer is portrayed as an enlightened, post-materialistic consumer, in comparison with which the petty status games of the material consumer seem very last century. Benkler (2006) believes that participatory technologies lead to "a more critical and self-reflective culture." Collins (2010) calls his version of this notion the "prosumer culture."

How enlightened is the digital consumer, really? It is true that social media tools such as *Facebook* are frequently used for laudable purposes, such as organizing "carrot mobs" or consumer groups that use their collective bargaining power to persuade companies to invest in environmentally friendly practices (Leivonniemi, 2008)? Negative word of mouth about unethical businesses also spreads fast on online networks. But at the same time, new trends and fads also propagate on the Net at unprecedented speeds. Users collect points, friends, likes, mentions, comments, coins, and badges, and they compare themselves with their peers. Processes of social comparison are no longer limited to physically proximate individuals: Online social networkers can compare their status and possessions with people who come from widely different strata of society (Ariely, 2009). In the end, it is not necessarily so that digital consumers have become less materialistic; it is simply that their material has become more digital.

CHANGES IN THE GOODS BEING CONSUMED

A third aspect of the digitalization of consumption is change in the objects being consumed. The first goods to be digitalized were information goods, such as music CDs and newspaper articles (Shapiro and Varian, 1999). Their value is based on the *information* they contain: a rendition of Beethoven's ninth symphony, for example, or the information that Osama bin Laden is dead. Digital information has the peculiar property that it can be shared with other people without losing any of its fidelity—or, as economists say, digital information is *non-rivalrous*. It is also hard to stop people from sharing digital information—or, as economists say, information is *non-excludable*. Because of these properties, digital information goods like MP3 files are radically different consumption objects compared with material information goods like CDs.

Digital information goods make poor collectables. Every copy of a digital good is indistinguishable from the original. There are no first pressings or limited editions, no old and new copies, no second-hand or new, only perfect mint. There is no scarcity: Everyone can have everything. For the same reasons, digital information goods are also not as effective in structuring social relationships. They cannot be used as status items to distinguish rich from poor. They can, however, be used in the same way as fashion items to build distinctions through taste: You can have any music file you like, but do you know which one is the right signal in your network this season? Partly because of these shortcomings in digital information goods as consumption objects, marketers have developed a new variety of digital goods known as *virtual goods*. Although digital information goods are well established in literature, this newer concept is much less explored. It is thus worth describing its history in some detail.

Both digital games and online communities have for a long time included features that simulate economic activity and trade: play money, simulated shopping malls, and numerous kinds of virtual goods ranging from clothes to furniture (Lehdonvirta et al., 2009). For individuals immersed in these games and environments, these virtual goods and currencies have probably always been personally important. Yet they have not attracted the attention of consumption scholars, probably because they did not directly involve the spending of money.

This detached nature of virtual economies began to change when players started to exchange game assets for real money. Around 1999, some players of so-called massively multiplayer online games (MMOs) started to put their game goods on auction in the recently launched e-commerce sites like *eBay* (Castronova, 2005; Huhh, 2008). Perhaps surprisingly, they soon received bids from other players. When an auction was completed, payment was carried out using ordinary means, such as check or money order. The two players then met up in the game, and the seller handed the auctioned object to the buyer. This way, an exchange value measured in US dollars or Korean won could soon be observed for virtual goods ranging from characters to gold nuggets (Lehdonvirta, 2008). The biggest publicly reported player-to-player trade is the 2007 sale of a character in the online game *World of Warcraft* for approximately 7,000 euros (Jimenez, 2007).

As trade volumes increased, what started as a player-to-player phenomenon soon attracted commercial interest. Professional players, known as "gold farmers," began to play the games for profit rather than pleasure, harvesting massive amounts of game assets and selling them to wealthier players on online markets. By the mid-2000s, this activity had grown into a whole industry that is now estimated to employ as many as 100,000 game laborers in digitally connected low-income countries such as China (Lehdonvirta and Ernkvist, 2011). Virtual goods are now also among the most sought-after commodities among cybercriminals (Krebs, 2009). They hack into players' game accounts, steal the enclosed items and currencies, and sell them on electronic marketplaces for a profit (Lehdonvirta and Virtanen, 2010).

Before long, game publishers and online community operators took note of this phenomenon. Instead of charging users a subscription fee or showing advertisements, they realized that they could generate revenues by selling virtual items to their users. This business model first became popular in Korea, China, and Japan (Nojima, 2008; So and Westland, 2010; Wi, 2009) and, around 2009, broke into mainstream Western online business (Lehdonvirta and Ernkvist, 2011). For example, American game developer Zynga makes relatively simple simulation and nurturing games that anyone can play for free on *Facebook*. Their hit game *Farmville* has at best claimed more than 90 million active players. Those players who wish to advance faster in the game's virtual economy can buy items such as virtual tractors and tractor fuel. So many players do that Zynga expects to earn $1.8 billion from its games in 2011. In total, approximately $7 billion worth of virtual items and currencies were sold by publishers in 2010. More virtual tractors are sold in a day than real tractors in a year.

Even though virtual goods are digital, they are rivalrous and excludable by design. A virtual tractor cannot be copied without the game operator's cooperation. You can take a screenshot of it and send it to your friend, but the result is comparable to a photograph of a conventional tractor—just an image that bears none of the functionality of the original. In this sense, virtual goods are much closer to material goods than to what we conventionally think of as digital goods. In fact, empirical studies suggest that consumers use virtual goods for the very same purposes as they use material goods: to seek fulfillment to needs, real or imagined (Lehdonvirta, 2009a, 2009b; Martin, 2008); to communicate and construct social distinctions, bonds, and identity positions (Lehdonvirta, 2009b; Lehdonvirta et al., 2009; Martin, 2008); and to stimulate and pursue hedonistic fantasies (Denegri-Knott and Molesworth, 2010b).

Unlike digital information goods, artificially scarce virtual goods make great collectables and status items. The latest development in the market is that digital music and e-book publishers are trying to make their products resemble virtual goods. For example, a company called Kindlegraph has developed a technology that allows authors to make copies of their e-books unique by signing them. Has technology completed a full circle to arrive at where it left from? Not quite: Compared with paper books, these new virtual books retain the benefits of weightless digital distribution.

Denegri-Knott and Molesworth (2010b) put forward a slightly different view of virtual consumption. They propose a taxonomy where virtual goods reside in a liminal space between the consumer's imagination (where consumers daydream about consumption) and the realm of material consumption (where daydreams are actualized). Because virtual goods are clearly more tangible than mere figments of imagination, they cannot be said to reside in the consumer's mind. Yet Denegri-Knott and Molesworth (2010b: 110; emphasis added) argue that they are not part of the material world of actual consumption, either. They argue that virtual goods "lack the material and sensual texture of the consumer goods of material consumption, [. . .] cannot fulfill physical needs and *cannot be used.*". They moreover point out that many virtual goods exchanges do not involve real money at all; many sites allow users to engage in complex consumption-like acts without charge. Thus they put forward a taxonomy of three "realities" and proceed to provide an analysis of the functions of virtual goods in the consumer psyche.

I disagree with the notion that virtual consumption needs to be placed in a separate realm from "ordinary" consumption (Lehdonvirta, 2010a, 2010b). Being material has never been a hallmark of an actualized consumption. Going to the cinema, purchasing a digital music file, or gambling are all examples of actual but intangible consumption. To be precise, there is no such thing as completely immaterial consumption: Even virtual goods physically manifest as magnetized regions on a ceramic platter inside a server computer and are made perceptible to the user by bombarding their eyes with photons. Nor is spending money a necessary feature of actualized consumption. Many products and services are funded through other models than direct consumer payments, such as when advertising-funded newspapers are distributed for free. Quantitative consumer researchers observe not only the spending of money, but also the spending of time and attention.

I also disagree with the suggestion that virtual goods cannot be used. Even if one discounts social and hedonistic uses such as using a virtual item as a gift or using it to seek sexual stimulation, many virtual items also have functional or "utilitarian" uses. Denegri-Knott and Molesworth (2010b: 110) point out that these functional uses are limited to the virtual environment: A virtual good "lacks material substance and cannot be used in material reality (a digital virtual sword cannot cut; a digital virtual car cannot be used to transport its owner)." It is implied that this limitation makes the usefulness somehow less real or less important. I have provided several arguments against this position elsewhere (Lehdonvirta, 2009b: 75–80). They can be summarized as follows. First, the usefulness of a material consumer good is often similarly limited to a very specific context, such as the garden (sprinkler, tree trainer) or the kitchen (egg separator, can drainer).

These uses do not necessarily stem from some deep human need, but from the problematization of everyday life by marketing. Second, there is no reason to posit that material contexts are always primary to computer-mediated ones. For a person whose hobbies and friends are online, virtual goods can be more tangible and useful than a car or a garden tool. In fact, I would suggest that on the Internet, material goods are not real. On the Internet, the veracity and ownership of a virtual good can be ascertained, whereas doing the same for a material good is very difficult. The majority of sports cars being bragged about by anonymous Internet conversants probably do not exist outside their ostensible owners' imaginations.

A better way to define consumption is through the practices and beliefs of consumers. After all, consumption is a culturally defined category and not an intrinsic feature of any site or object. Among some audiences, virtual goods are being used in the same ways as others would use material goods. In some cases they may be used as stand-ins for or "simulations" of material goods, as Denegri-Knott and Molesworth suggest, to allow the consumer to fantasize about an expensive car, for example. But as more and more aspects of life, from friendships and family to work and leisure, are played out in part through mobile phones, social networking sites, console games, and online communities, virtual goods turn from stand-ins to the real things and the actual objects of consumption.

CONCLUSIONS: DIGITALIZATION OF CONSUMPTION AND THE FUTURE OF CONSUMER SOCIETY

In the preceding sections, I showed that the digitalization of consumption consists of changes to the sites, processes, subjects, and objects of consumption. From this brief history, a picture of three distinct waves of digital consumption emerges: the online shopping wave, the participatory consumption wave, and the virtual consumption wave. In the first wave, brick-and-mortar stores were partly replaced and partly augmented by digital consumption sites and digital processes such as mobile payments. These news sites and processes had the effect of extending the scope of consumption in multiple ways: extending the temporal and geographic availability of consumption, as well as the selection of available goods. From an economic perspective, this makes consumption more "convenient." From a hedonistic perspective, it provides consumers with immense dreamworlds in which to fantasize about consumption.

In the participatory consumption wave, the subjects of consumption, the consumers themselves, are transformed by new information sharing and collaboration possibilities. The subjects are also offered new roles in economic processes, so that their status can change from simple consumers to participants or even prosumers. However, it is not clear at all that this represents an "improvement of capitalism" rather than an acceleration of it. Despite changes in discourses, the social logic of distinction and status competition is still very much apparent in the subjects' actions. This penetration of consumer culture into digital spaces can be seen as a failure of some of the higher ideals that some held for the digital world (Lehdonvirta, 2010a).

Yet some striking changes can also be seen in the objects of consumption. These new objects, digital virtual goods, have only recently started to enter mainstream consumption. They are used in very similar ways as material consumption objects are used: to communicate and construct social distinctions, positions and bonds, and to pursue hedonistic projects and daydreams. Within the digital environments in which they are embedded, they can also be used as tools to solve problems, real or artificial, in the same way as material goods are used in other environments. In contrast to material goods, virtual goods give up any pretense of catering to some physiological human need. In this way, they are often more "honest" than some of the material goods of the consumer society, which continue to be marketed on the fantasy that their value is tied to some basic needs rather than to daydreaming and culturally defined games of signification.

These changes together make up the digitalization of consumption. What bearing, if any, does this process have on the big question of consumer society—reconciling market economy with environmental sustainability? The digital consumer may be somewhat better positioned to take collective action and steer society away from crisis, but so far there is no indication that this in itself is enough. Indeed, the digital consumer may be even more susceptible to "virally" diffused consumption trends that lead to wasteful resource use. Digital sites and processes of consumption, insofar as they extend the scope of consumption and facilitate manipulative marketing practices, can likewise be expected to abet hyperconsumption. At the same time, it must be noted that there are also research projects and government programs that seek to enlist the help of manipulative technologies, such as serious games, to change consumer behaviors toward more sustainable patterns (Yamabe et al., 2009).

Perhaps the most significant environmental potential is in the digitalization of the objects of consumption. The digital hardware and networks that are used to access virtual goods and other digital consumption objects are by no means free of resource consumption. On the contrary, it has been estimated that information and communication technologies (ICTs) account for 2 percent of global carbon dioxide emissions, approximately the same share as aviation (Gartner, 2007). However, the environmental impact of digital virtual consumption does not increase as a function of the number of virtual goods purchased. This is a key difference to material consumption, where each additional unit purchased represents a direct increase in the environmental footprint. In virtual consumption, each additional good represents at most an additional row in a database. Moreover, the disposal of virtual goods does not leave behind waste that needs to be stored or recycled. Publishers can create short-lived disposable virtual goods that keep the spending cycle going without increasing the environmental burden in any way. Virtual goods also do not involve physical transportation, either of the good to the consumer or of the consumer to the consumption site.

If continuous consumption is a necessary aspect of contemporary society, either because it has become a crucial form of signification in our culture or simply because our economic model requires it, then directing excess spending to virtual consumption instead of material consumption could help reconcile this social fact with the limitations of physical reality.

REFERENCES

Anderson C. 2006. *The Long Tail: Why the Future of Business Is Selling Less of More.* Hyperion: New York.

Ariely D. 2009. *Predictably Irrational: The Hidden Forces That Shape Our Decisions.* HarperCollins: London.

Baudrillard J. 1994. The System of Collecting, in *Cultures of Collecting,* J. Elsner and R. Cardinal (eds.). Reaktion: London; 7–24.

Baudrillard J. 2002. Consumer Society, in *Jean Baudrillard: Selected Writings* (2nd ed.), M. Poster (ed.). Stanford University Press: Stanford; 32–59.

Bauman Z, May T. 2001. *Thinking Sociologically* (2nd ed.). Wiley-Blackwell: Oxford.

Belk RW. 1995. *Collecting in a Consumer Society.* Routledge: London.

Belk RW. 2004. The Human Consequences of Consumer Culture, in *Elusive Consumption,* K. M. Ekström and H. Brembeck (eds.). Berg: Oxford; 67–86.

Benkler Y. 2006. *The Wealth of Networks.* Yale University Press: New Haven, CT.

Bourdieu P. 1984. *Distinction. The Social Critique of the Judgement of Taste.* Routledge: London.

Campbell C. 1989. *The Romantic Ethic and the Spirit of Modern Consumerism.* Macmillan: Oxford.

Campbell C. 1998. Consumption and the Rhetorics of Need and Want. *Journal of Design History* 11(3): 235–246.

Campbell C. 2004. I Shop Therefore I Know That I Am: The Metaphysical Basis of Modern Consumerism, in *Elusive Consumption,* K. M. Ekström and H. Brembeck (eds.). Berg: Oxford; 27–44.

Castells M, Himanen P. 2002. *The Information society and the Welfare State. The Finnish Model.* Oxford University Press: Oxford.

Castronova E. 2005. *Synthetic Worlds: The Business and Culture of Online Games.* University of Chicago Press: Chicago, IL.

Collins S. 2010. Digital Fair: Prosumption and the fair use defence. *Journal of Consumer Culture* 10(1): 37–55.

Denegri-Knott J, Molesworth M. 2010a. "Love It. Buy It. Sell It": Consumer Desire and the Social Drama of eBay. *Journal of Consumer Culture* 10(1): 56–79.

Denegri-Knott J, Molesworth M. 2010b. Concepts and Practices of Digital Virtual Consumption. *Consumption Markets and Culture* 13(2): 109–132.

Douglas M, Isherwood B. 1978. *The World of Goods.* Basic Books: New York.

Featherstone M. 1991. *Consumer Culture and Postmodernism.* Sage: London.

Featherstone M. 1998. The Flâneur, the City and Virtual Public Life. *Urban Studies* 35(5–6): 909–925.

Frei B. 2009. *Paid Crowdsourcing: Current State and Progress toward Mainstream Business Use*. Available at http://bit.ly/smartsheet_report [accessed on 1 June 2011].

Gartner 2007. *Gartner Estimates ICT Industry Accounts for 2 Percent of Global CO2 Emissions*, 26 April. Available at http://www.gartner.com/it/page.jsp?id=503867 [accessed on 15 March 2011].

Haanpää L. 2007. *The Colour Green: A Structural Approach to the Environment-Consumption Nexus*. Publications of the Turku School of Economics, A-7:2007. Turku School of Economics: Turku.

Hietanen H, Oksanen V, Välimäki M. 2007. *Community Created Content: Law, Business and Policy*. Turre Publishing: Helsinki.

Howe J. 2008. *Crowdsourcing: Why the Power of the Crowd Is Driving the Future of Business*. Crown Publishing Group: New York.

Hsieh JJ, Rai A, Keil M. 2008. Understanding Digital Inequality: Comparing Continued Use Behavioral Models of the Socio-Economically Advantaged and Disadvantaged. *MIS Quarterly* 31(1): 97–126.

Huhh JS. 2008. Culture and Business of PC Bangs in Korea. *Games and Culture* 3(1): 26–37.

Jehle G, Reny P. 2001. *Advanced Microeconomic Theory* (2nd ed.). Addison Wesley: Boston, MA.

Jimenez C. 2007. The High Cost of Playing Warcraft. *BBC News Online*, 24 September. Available at http://news.bbc.co.uk/2/hi/technology/7007026.stm [accessed on 28 July 2010].

Kleemann F, Voß GG, Rieder K. 2008. Un(der)paid Innovators: The Commercial Utilization of Consumer Work through Crowdsourcing. *Science, Technology and Innovation Studies* 4(1): 5–26.

Kotler P. 2003. *Marketing Management* (11th ed.). Prentice Hall: Englewood Cliffs, NJ.

Krebs, B. 2009. The Scrap Value of a Hacked PC. *The Washington Post Security Fix*, 26 May. Available at http://voices.washingtonpost.com/securityfix/2009/05/the_scrap_value_of_a_hacked_pc.html [accessed on 15 March 2011].

Lehdonvirta V. 2008. Real-Money Trade of Virtual Assets: New Strategies for Virtual World Operators, in *Virtual Worlds*, M. Ipe (ed.). Icfai University Press: Hyderabad; 113–137.

Lehdonvirta V. 2009a. Virtual Item Sales as a Revenue Model: Identifying Attributes that Drive Purchase Decisions. *Electronic Commerce Research* 9(1): 97–113.

Lehdonvirta V. 2009b. *Virtual Consumption*. Publications of the Turku School of Economics A-11:2009. Turku School of Economics: Turku. Available at http://info.tse.fi/julkaisut/vk/Ae11_2009.pdf [accessed on 1 June 2011].

Lehdonvirta V. 2010a. Online Spaces Have Material Culture: Goodbye to Digital Post-Materialism and Hello to Virtual Consumption. *Media, Culture and Society* 32(5): 883–889.

Lehdonvirta V. 2010b. Virtual Worlds Don't Exist: Questioning the Dichotomous Approach in MMO Studies. *Game Studies* 10(1). Available at http://gamestudies.org/1001/articles/lehdonvirta [accessed on 1 June 2011].

Lehdonvirta V, Ernkvist M. 2011. *Knowledge Map of the Virtual Economy*. World Bank: Washington, DC. Available at http://www.infodev.org/en/Document.1076.pdf [accessed on 1 June 2011].

Lehdonvirta V, Virtanen P. 2010. A New Frontier in Digital Content Policy: Case Studies in the Regulation of Virtual Goods and Artificial Scarcity. *Policy and Internet* 2(3).

Lehdonvirta V, Wilska T-A, Johnson M. 2009. Virtual Consumerism: Case Habbo Hotel. *Information, Communication and Society* 12(7): 1059–1079.

Leivonniemi, S. 2008. Netissä levinnyt kuluttajaliike toi ryysiksen Juttutu-paan. *Helsingin Sanomat*, 27 September. Available at http://www.hs.fi/tulosta/1135239785972 [accessed on 1 June 2011].

Lessig L. 2004. *Free Culture: How Big Media Uses Technology and the Law to Lock Down Culture and Control Creativity*. Penguin: New York.

Levy S. 1984. *Hackers: Heroes of the Computer Revolution*. Anchor Press/Doubleday: New York.

Martin J. 2008. Consuming Code: Use-Value, Exchange-Value, and the Role of Virtual Goods in Second Life. *Journal of Virtual Worlds Research* 1(2). Available at https://journals.tdl.org/jvwr/article/view/300/262 [accessed on 1 May 2010].

Mauss M. 1990. *The Gift: The Form and Reason for Exchange in Archaic Societies*. Norton: New York.

McCracken G. 1990. *Culture and Consumption: New Approaches to the Symbolic Character of Consumer Goods and Activities*. Indiana University Press: Bloomington, IN.

Montlake S. 2007. China's New Shopping Craze: "Team Buying." *MSN Money*. Available at http://on-msn.com/norTFF [accessed on 1 June 2011].

Nojima M. 2008. 人はなぜ形のないものを買うのか 仮想世界のビジネスモデル [Why Do People Buy Immaterial Goods: Virtual World Business Models]. NTT Publishing: Tokyo.

Rantavuo H. 2006. Kamera kännykässä: kuvien käyttö henkilökohtaisessa viestinnässä, in *Vaurauden lapset: Näkökulmia japanilaiseen ja suomalaiseen nykykulttuuriin*, K. Valaskivi (ed.). Vastapaino: Tampere; 111–132.

Ritzer G. 2001. *Explorations in the Sociology of Consumption: Fast Food, Credit Cards and Casinos*. Sage: London.

Ritzer G., Jurgenson N. 2010. Production, Consumption, Prosumption: The Nature of Capitalism in the Age of the Digital "Prosumer." *Journal of Consumer Culture* 10(1): 13–36.

Räsänen P. 2006 Information Society for All? Structural Characteristics of Internet Use in 15 European Countries. *European Societies* 8(1): 59–81.

Räsänen P. 2008. The Aftermath of the ICT Revolution? Media and Communication Technology Preferences in Finland in 1999 and 2004. *New Media and Society* 10(2): 225–245.

Scoble R, Israel S. 2006. *Naked Conversations: How Blogs Are Changing the Way Businesses Talk with Customers*. Wiley and Sons: New York.

Shapiro C, Varian HR. 1999. *Information Rules: A Strategic Guide to the Network Economy*. Harvard Business School Press: Boston, MA.

Silvestro M. 2009. Political Consumerism: An Extension of Social Conflict or a Renewed Form of Economic Collaboration?, in *The ISA Handbook in Contemporary Sociology*, A. Denis and D. Kalekin-Fishman (eds.). Sage: London; 278–290.

Simmel G. 1957[1904]. Fashion. *American Journal of Sociology* 62(6): 541–548.

Slater D. 1997. *Consumer Culture and Modernity*. Polity: Cambridge.

So S, Westland JC. 2010. *Red Wired: China's Internet Revolution*. Marshall Cavendish: London.

Surowiecki J. 2005. *The Wisdom of Crowds*. Anchor Books: New York.

Tapscott D, Williams A. 2006. *Wikinomics: How Mass Collaboration Changes Everything*. Portfolio: New York.

Underhill P. 2000. *Why We Buy: The Science of Shopping*. Touchstone: New York.

Veblen T. 1997[1899]. *The Theory of the Leisure Class*. Project Gutenberg. Available at http://www.gutenberg.org/etext/833 [accessed on 1 June 2011].

Wi JH. 2009. *Innovation and Strategy of Online Games*. Imperial College Press: London.

Wilska T-A. 2003. Mobile Phone Use as Part of Young People's Consumption Styles. *Journal of Consumer Policy* 26(3): 441–463.

Yamabe T, Lehdonvirta V, Ito H, Soma H, Kimura H, Nakajima T. 2009. Applying Pervasive Technologies to Create Economic Incentives That Alter Consumer Behavior, in *Proceedings of the 11th International Conference on Ubiquitous Computing.* ACM: New York; 175–184.

Yoshimi S. 2006. Consuming America, Producing Japan, in *The Ambivalent Consumer: Questioning Consumption in East Asia and the West,* S. Garon and P. L. Maclachlan (eds.). Cornell University Press: London; 63–84.

3 Young American Consumers and New Technologies

Alladi Venkatesh and Nivein Behairy

INTRODUCTION

Young consumers today are thoroughly engrossed in technology. From television to the Internet, videogames to personal computers, pagers to mobile phones, they demonstrate competence in a whole range of technologies at home, at school, and in the wider social world. We find that the *Facebook* generation is as comfortable socializing online with friends as they are meeting in person (Ito et al., 2009; Livingstone, 2006). As early adopters and innovators, they are in many ways the defining users of digital media (Satofuka, Kantola, and Kono, 2009; Subrahmanyam, 2003). Clearly, the younger segment is exhibiting certain self-directed and networking behaviors and initiatives, which are the focus of our current study.

Researchers are beginning to recognize the emergence of new technologies as a major transformational force (Simakova and Neyland, 2008). There is no question that we are in the middle of a digital revolution (Denegri-Knott and Molesworth, 2010). In particular, young consumers are gaining attention in the context of technology adoption and use (Boyd, 2007; Hansen and Hansen, 2005). Recent trends indicate that they are exhibiting certain socially oriented networking behaviors in their consumption of new media (Turkle, 2005). Although our intuition is reasonable and supported by recent literature, an important question remains as to how these tendencies are manifested in technology consumption and use.

Central questions underlying this study are: (1) What is the nature of young consumers' involvement with new technologies in their everyday life? (2) How are the socially oriented and networking initiatives of young consumers expressed through this involvement? (3) What are some policy implications of young consumers' digital behaviors?

THEORETICAL BACKGROUND AND FRAMEWORK

Children and Technology Use

Our main interest is to examine how young people are assimilating technology in daily life. For example, Greenfield and Yan (2006) have shown that children do not simply participate passively in technology use, but create virtual worlds on their own terms and are therefore, indirectly, coconstructors of technological environments. Similarly, Subrahmanyam's (2003) investigation of teenage online communications shows that the two goals of technology-related research are to understand how the digital worlds are "created by teens" and how "children are shaped by the worlds the technologies create." With this background, we shall now proceed to examine some underlying conceptual issues.

Because young people's involvement with information technology and media is oriented toward their interactions with their social groups and friends, a certain level of self-directed initiatives is required in order for them to establish social networking relationships and engage in technology use. These self-directed behaviors indicate a certain level of relational autonomy that, according to Mackenzie and Stoljar (2000), "is premised on the conviction that persons are socially embedded and their identities are formed within the context of social relationships." It thus includes the ability of young consumers to develop an understanding of the technology on their own with and without external guidance, to be self-reliant in gaining the necessary knowledge and accepting some level of responsibility for their actions. In sum, self-directed behavior becomes a crucial developmental milestone that occurs during childhood and adolescence (Steinberg, 2002).

Adolescent Behavior and Consumer Research

In the field of consumer research, Roedder-John's (1999) review of children's socialization along with Cook's (2000) work is certainly an important reference point for our present study and indicates "relational" aspects of their identity formation. In some related research, Carlson and Rossbart (1988) and McNeal (1999) examined the extent to which parents encourage direct independent consumption decisions by children while Peracchio (1992) examined children's decision-making roles.

Based on the above discussion, the key aspects of children's self-directed behaviors are: (1) young consumers' ability to act on their own, while given the social context, employing a relational mode of behavior; (2) developing ones' self-identity based on self-motivated actions and reasoning; and (3) young consumers' creative explorations.

RESEARCH DESIGN AND METHODOLOGY

Given that the aim is to examine children's use of computers (and other electronic devices) and the impact these technologies have on their daily lives and construction of their worldviews, an interpretive research approach was considered most appropriate (Turkle, 1995, 2005). That is, the purpose of this research is to generate theoretical ideas based on inquiry into

Table 3.1 Respondent Pool by Age and Gender

Age	Males		Females	
Category	Name	Age	Name	Age
8–10	Justin	8	Sonia	9
	Sean	10	Alexandria	
Late Childhood	Matt	10		
11–13	Gunner	12	Chelsea	11
	Michael	12	Rachel	11
	Tyler	12	Samantha	13
Early Adolescence	Ross	13		
	Ken	13		
	Hunter	13		
14–17	Andrew	14	Hailey	14
	Joe	16	Ashley	14
Last Adolescence	Jordon	16	Jennifer	16
	Steve	16	Chole	17
18–19	Won	18	Julie	18
	Kenneth	18	Christine	18
Early Adulthood	Vincent	19	Jeevitha	18
			Devina	19

the existing world of practice using grounded theory methods (Strauss & Corbin, 2008) and not test existing theory, In other words, theoretical sensitivity based on empirical analytics rather than theory testing using hypotheses is the core of grounded theory.

Data for this study were gathered using McCracken's (1988) long-interview procedure as well as through direct observation of computer use. A sample of 31 young consumers was included in the study. Age (ranging from 9 to 19 to encompass late childhood, early adolescence, late adolescence, and early adulthood) and gender (male/female) were factors considered (see Table 3.1). QSR NUD*IST (NVivo) (2001) was used for the data analysis.

EMPIRICAL FINDINGS: CONSUMERS OF TECHNOLOGY

The context for our study is the everyday life patterns of the young consumers (see Figure 3.1). The complex dimensionality of everyday life is quite overwhelming as shown in the figure. Obviously, not all activities shown in the figure are pursued on an everyday basis (e.g., movies), and some activities have age restrictions (e.g., driving a car). Nevertheless, the plate seems to be quite full for young consumers in our postmodern culture. Although all of the daily activities do not involve interaction with technology, we

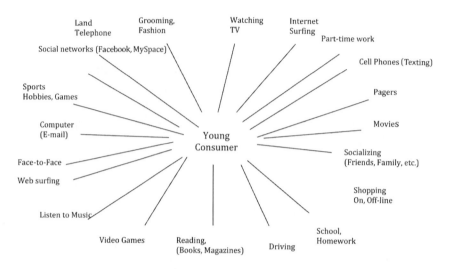

Figure 3.1   Everyday life activities of young consumers.

Table 3.2   Consumption Strategies and Themes

Contexts	Consumption Activities— Uses/Experiences	Applications	Thematic Considerations
Technological	Communication and social engagement (networking)	E-mail IM/texting Telephone Social networks	Physical proximity Nature of relationship Level of involvement Response turnaround Real-virtual world reach
	Leisure and Techno-Entertainment	Games -Video -Internet -computer TV	Quality of graphics Control capabilities Degree of stimulation Social exchange
	Online shopping -Online -Traditional	Internet	Shopping experience Instant gratification Convenience Word-of-mouth
Social	Family arena -Instruction	Computers Internet	Direct commitment Indirect communication
	Peer arena -Influence -Instruction -Sharing knowledge	Internet Computers Videogames	Familiarizing others Knowledge exchange
	Gender	Internet Computer On/off-line communication	Interest Attitudes Aptitudes Sociability

asked respondents to describe their use of technology in order to capture their level of involvement.

We now present findings that address primary research questions stated earlier.

From interviews, we find that young consumers negotiate a wide variety of technological artifacts to facilitate and shape their social and personal environments. Use of technologies can be described in terms of two key contexts: (1) technological experiences/practices (communication and social engagement, leisure and techno-entertainment, online shopping), and (2) social contexts (family arena, peer arena, gender issues) (Table 3.2).

Analyses reveal that throughout their consumption experiences (Table 3.2), young consumers are relentlessly assessing their technological environment based on a number of personal/social considerations (Table 3.2). We continue with a discussion of the two key themes: technological experiences/practices and social contexts. Implications of age or gender will be addressed as applicable.

Theme 1: Technological Experiences and Practices

Communication and Social Engagement

Focusing on four main methods of communication—telephone (including mobile phone), electronic mail, instant messaging (including texting), and social network sites, interviews confirm that respondents classify communication methods based on the features inherent to them. E-mail, for example, is viewed as informative in nature because response is not immediate. As Christine (18) explains, "If I'm having a party or something I would e-mail, like, oh, I'm having a party." In contrast, instant messaging evokes a sense of online cyber community with respondents because it allows a real-time, two-way communication venue. On a different level, social network sites provide respondents with a virtual engagement of a different kind. Julie (18) stresses the benefits that social network sites provide: "*Facebook* helps me catch up with people that I don't always have the time to do face-to-face. I get a sense of what their life is like now."

From interviews, respondents identify several pertinent factors that influence their choice of communication methods used:

i. *physical proximity.* It appears that anyone outside the respondent's immediate daily domain is considered "far." From interviews we find that friends and relatives who are "far" fall in the e-mail category rather than instant messaging. Respondents like Hunter (13) indicate that they did not have much to "chat" about, for example, with cousins who lived far away, so keeping in touch by sending a quick message seemed appropriate.

Social networks, conversely, allow respondents to preserve ties over the long term. For respondents, the consensus is that social networks provide a medium for staying updated and therefore being "present" in each other's lives without necessarily going beyond cursory exchanges. Jeevitha (18) explains why leaving a comment on her friends' social network pages is important: "Leaving a comment for them is my way of saying, 'Just because I don't *call* you doesn't mean I've forgotten you'—it's just kinda letting them know that."

ii. Nature of the relationship. This refers to the type of relationship respondents have with the communicating party. This distinction referenced intimate relationships, "close friends," "relatives," and "parents" and non-intimate relationships, "people I wouldn't talk on the phone to," "people I don't know well," or "people I'm embarrassed to talk to." Consequently, the telephone is reserved for close friends and relatives, whereas e-mail and I-mail are used with "distant" relationships. Christine (18) is typical: "I talk on the phone a lot, but when I'm online chatting it's with people that I don't know as well or wouldn't necessarily call. I have over 50 people on my buddy list that I wouldn't call on the phone." Jennifer (16) believes that texting allows her to appear more casual when she wants to communicate with a "guy" because "it's less embarrassing and it doesn't look like you're going out of your way as much." Likewise, respondents find that social networks allow them a way to maintain a "bird's-eye" connection with more removed or distant relationships. For Devina (19), social networks allow her to "get the scoop, without having to actually barge in."

iii. Level of involvement. The level of involvement required for a particular communiqué dictates to a great extent the mode of communication that respondents use. Hailey (14) makes the point about computer exchanges: "Computers are not meant for a long conversation, like, 'oh, man, somebody did something really bad' and we want to talk about it. It's just takes too long so I'll phone her up and talk to her. But if it's just something short to say you just use I-mail."

The reference to a "long conversation" and "something short" refers to the nature of the topic rather than the duration of the communiqué. The telephone allows for a fluid conversation unhindered by typing. Conversely, e-mail and social networks allow respondents to feel less guilty about not staying in touch. Typical is what Ken (13) says: "I just send off a one liner and feel that we're still in touch."

iv. Response turnaround. Respondents differentiate between the necessity of a "prompt response" and the acceptability of a "delayed response." For Tyler (12), this distinction determines the method used: "If I have a question on homework I call a friend on the phone. It's faster to just ask right away instead of waiting until someone's on the computer." In contrast, respondents have no expectations in receiving an immediate response when using social networks. Kenneth (18) emphasizes this: "If I want to just say 'Hey what's up?' you know, or get someone's attention or give them a reminder then, I'll use *Facebook*. It's like leaving a note in someone's locker."

v. Real-virtual world reach. We find that respondents extend their real-world interactions online. For Samantha (13), this means socializing online, with her friends, and "talking about things you don't hear at school. It's a lot of fun." Christine (18) notes, "If I need help with my homework I just go online at about 10:00." This is because she and her peer group have an unofficial time when they all congregate online. Social networks play a similar role in providing a platform for bringing real-world friends together online. As Vincent (19) points out, "I have kept in contact with many of my friends who I would not have been able to without social networks. I guess it is a big part of our lives right now. I have friends all around the country. So we started a private *Facebook* group."

Leisure and Techno-Environment

For some participants, gaming represents an important leisure activity that has captivated young consumers of all ages. Results show no age effect for males and only limited effect for females (groups in early adolescence showed more interest than those in late adolescence). Analyses reveal that, although female respondents (late childhood and early adolescence groups) play games, they are not as consumed by the experience as males. A distinction is made between computer games and videogames. Respondents reveal that partiality for a particular platform is determined by:

i. Quality of the graphics. Interviews highlight the value that respondents like Chelsea (11) place on accuracy and realism: "The people look like real people and for sports themes if you have to do a trick they have the real tricks and like the realistic surroundings." Respondents will actually switch between gaming platforms to achieve the level of graphic quality they desire. Ross (13), for example, will "play games on the computer and on Nintendo, just depends which game I'm playing 'cause there's usually a difference in the graphics—some games just don't look real on the computer."

ii. Control capabilities. The maneuverability of controls is an important feature. According to Sean (10), "On the computer controls can stall." Consequently, respondents choose the mode of gaming that will provide them with the superior control needed to command a game. Interviews reveal that videogames are favored because they provide players with controllers that are superior to the arrow keys or mouse used in computer games.

iii. Degree of stimulation. Games are stimulating for some because they are "thrilling," "challenging," or simply "fun." They lose interest when it is "not as exciting anymore." Tyler (12) prefers to be challenged: "I like challenging games where you have to develop a strategy and then use that strategy to try to beat the game." For others, complexity is not critical. Ken (13) makes the case for the game he plays: "It's actually pretty simple . . . but it's really fun."

iv. Social exchange. Interviews reveal that respondents share their enthusiasm and experiences of games with peers. Sean (10) notes, "We talk about how fun a game is, and when we're at each others' house we'll play that game." Similarly, Tyler (12) makes the argument that a game can be a unique experience through which friends play, interact, and bond: "My friend and

I are trying to build up this clan online for Iberian Sun. See this game has its own league and if you're in a clan then you can play certain games and you can get maps and stuff and you get to develop better strategies for the game and then you get to play all these other players so it improves your game too. It takes up a lot of time, but it's great."

Online Shopping

Many respondents have had numerous online shopping experiences with books, CDs, clothes, and games, either directly or with the aid of a parent. In their discussions, respondents outline three main properties that delineate online and traditional shopping. Underlying gender issues are indicated.

i. Shopping experience. Respondents were keen to contrast the "feeling" or *experience* of making an online purchase to that of making a store purchase. For them online shopping "just doesn't feel the same as looking for something at the mall." Although respondents were quite content making online purchases for stock items like books, CDs, and computer games, they were more skeptical and less excited when it came to clothes or items that were suspect of visual misrepresentation—especially with female respondents. Part of this had to do with the "touch-and-try" factor as Christine (18) explains: "The only thing that works for me are books not really clothes. On the Internet you have to flip pages to see different pieces. It's harder and also, like, trying stuff on is part of the fun. So I've probably shopped off the Internet for, um, clothes, like, twice and they've both been kind of not good. I've always had to return something."

ii. Instant gratification. Respondents emphasized the aspect of taking delivery when making a purchase. For online items, this translates to delivery turnaround as opposed to walking out of a store with the purchased item. Jordon's (16) remark is typical: "The bad thing with ordering online is that I have to wait seven to ten days to get something. I'd rather pay the extra money and just go to the store and get it that same day. I just want that instant gratification you know, it's worth going to the store." Jordon is assigning an undefined monetary value to his desire for instant gratification. Respondents argue that if possession is not immediate, then gratification is considered postponed regardless of whether delivery happens in "a day," "in seven to ten days," or in "four weeks." It raises the point that respondents may place a higher significance on gratification than on price. Ken (13) highlights this fact when he says, "Online it would probably be a little cheaper but it would take a lot longer to get to you."

iii. Convenience. For respondents online shopping provides the convenience of comparing prices and making purchases without leaving home. Here is what Gunner (12) says: "Like airline tickets, if we're going to go on vacation. You could compare them right there. You don't have to call a lot of people. So it's a lot more convenient." Online convenience allows respondents to decide on the optimal venue from which to make their purchases. They are able to save time, money, and energy because they do not need to physically go from store to store or make numerous calls in search of their product. As Hunter (13) says, "The Internet is cool because you don't have to drive to the store to buy things if you don't want to. You can find out what stores sell certain things too. Like I need some stickers for my bike and they're kinda hard to find, so I went online and tracked down the name of the store that would have them. Now I can either order online or make a phone order." Steve (18) follows on this: "I was looking at something online and it looks like about ten dollars cheaper than going to the store, but once I paid shipping and handling, it's almost the same thing. So, you know, basically, all I'm losing is a few dollars and the gas money if I went to the store."

iv. Word-of-mouth. This is found to influence our respondents' online shopping experiences. Rachel (11) emphasizes the weight of peer recommendations over traditional advertising: "I learn about new sites mainly from my friends. Sometimes I'll see a Web site, like, advertised in magazines or on billboards, but I won't really go there unless I heard about it from a friend as well." Through "telling" and "social-networking," respondents across different age categories (with the exception of late-childhood respondents who are limited in their online interactions) are motivated to check out recommended websites. The first excerpt gives proof that the peer "word-of-mouth" can be much more influential than advertising a site. In fact respondents have such confidence in their peer groups that they encourage and welcome their guidance and assurances when exploring new online sites. For example, Christine (17) knows about *eBay* but is not willing to browse the site unless she is "introduced" by her friends.

Theme 2: Social Context: Family Arena, Peer Arena, and Gender Issues

From interviews we find that young consumers do not negotiate technology within a vacuum. In keeping with the social construction perspective of childhood, we see that in constructing their social and technological environments, they indeed instigate support from family and peers. In addition, we find that gender influences the technological and social environments that children construct. We continue with a look at each of the elements that comprise the social context.

Family Arena

This category refers to the commitment that respondents are shown at home, primarily by parents as well as other family members, with regard to technology. There were no effects for age or gender.

i. Direct commitment. The commitment shown at home can be direct. For example, as one of the respondents stated, "My dad will show me how to do things" or "I'll ask my dad for help." As Hailey (14) puts it, "Sometimes my dad will be, like, really excited, like, really stoked and he'll be, like, Hailey, Hailey, you have to come see what I'm doing and he'll show me how to do things." Conversely, respondents acquire computer knowledge through observation or trial and error: "I just sit and watch that's how I learn." For example, Rachel (11) says, "From when I was younger, my dad sort of taught me all about the computer, like the components of the computer and like, how to load and how to click and stuff."

ii. Indirect commitment. Aspect of instruction depends more on the independence and self-reliance of the respondents because it requires taking initiative to acquire and expand computer knowledge through observation and trial-and-error. Chelsea (11) says, "What happens normally is my cousin, Mr. Technology, will be on the computer and I'll come and sit with him and I'll just watch, you know. So I just learn by watching him do his thing really." Jennifer (16) adds, "I really taught myself everything I know. Just, basically watching my parents and just trying and just looking and playing computer games." Further evidence of self-initiative includes phrases like, "I come and sit . . . I'll just watch," "I've learned just by watching," and "I taught myself . . . just watching and just trying."

Peer Arena

The influence of peers becomes most apparent with Internet sites and games and entertainment, where such influence becomes a source of knowledge. There are no effects for age or gender.

i. Familiarizing others. One aspect within the peer arena relates to familiarizing others with different websites to visit or games to purchase. Chloe (17) says, "My friends are always, like—you know, oh, my gosh, I have this really cool site." Likewise, Rachel (11) enjoys informing her friends: "When I learn a new thing, like a new online game or something fun like a Web site or something, I'll tell them so they'll want to go too." Rachel's phrase, "so they'll want to go too," emphasizes the importance of sharing in common activities, which adds to the sense of camaraderie.

ii. Knowledge exchange. Another aspect within the peer arena has to do with passing on knowledge and experiences. There is a teaching and learning that takes place when friends pass on this knowledge and experience to one another. Teaching can range from "solicited" to "unsolicited." "Solicited" teaching is the transfer of knowledge that occurs on the request of the recipient. "Unsolicited" teaching refers to knowledge that is volunteered. Gunner (12) comments, "When I felt I needed to learn a little bit more about computers, I sat my friend Cody down and I'm like, okay, how do you get to this? He was like, 'Here let me show you.' So he brought me up to speed."

Gender Issues

In analyzing the data for gender differences, we find that it is not a matter of which gender uses the technology more, but rather that gender disparity is a reflection of the varying activities based on gender dispositions. From the discussions, it was apparent that there were five properties that clearly distinguished males from females in their technology use.

i. Interest. The difference in interests refers to differences in the type of computer activities engaged in by the genders. The following quote from Andrew (14) highlights this: "The difference is not how guys and girls use the computer but, I guess, the different things they look up, like whatever they're interested in. Like, my friend Gina was looking up, like, women's soccer results and I'm more into looking up surf stuff. So we both go online and we both do searches. So it just varies by what our interests are. It even varies between, like, guys."

Andrew's point is that both he and his female friend search the Internet for sports. In attempting to further his point, he goes on to say that there is even a difference among males. Here, while stressing the differences in interests that exist even within the same gender, the respondent continues to use two predominantly "male" hobbies/sports in arguing his case. This further stresses that there is a clear "masculine"/"feminine" delineation at play because even when males have different interests, they are still traditionally "masculine" interests.

ii. Attitudes. We find that there is a difference in the attitude males and females have toward technology, and specifically the Internet. Christine (18) discusses this: "I think also the girls that I know tend to go online to read, like, certain, articles about this or that or, you just kind of browse around, whereas the guys seem to be, like, acquiring things, like, downloads things, they're more active, whereas the girls you know, just kind of like just skim around. Yeah, I think they see it a little bit—or at least the guys I know see it a little bit more as a tool and I know that I feel, kind of, like, oh, it's a little, like, fun."

iii. Aptitudes. There does not appear to be a difference in the level of computer skills between genders in the late childhood and early adolescent stages. This is reflected in phrases such as, "The sex of the child doesn't matter, just the environment they grew up in," "Aptitude has nothing to do with whether you're a guy or a girl," "There's no difference," and "Girls and guys are equally capable." These remarks from respondents emphasize the perception of equality in the aptitudes of both males and females when it comes to computer technology.

iv. Sociability. Females were generally found to be more social than males when it came to online interactions, whether using instant messaging, e-mail, or social networks. Respondents like Joe (16) stressed this view: "I think that, um, girls sort of are more social. It's really important for my sister to have her 65 people on her buddy list, but it isn't important for me or my brother." Devina (19) continues: "Also just e-mailing wise, my girlfriends are usually more responsive than my male friends because, uh, they're e-mails are usually, a couple sentences long and, you know, just kind of like da, da, da, thanks for the e-mail. It's very brief."

Interviews reveal that female respondents are more inclined to speak on the telephone than their male counterparts. All male respondents, regardless of their age, claim to "not talk a lot" and "not like having long conversations" on the telephone. Andrew (14) uses the phrase "not sit and gab on the phone" to stress the brevity of his phone interactions.

Late adolescent and early adult females are found to regard the telephone more as a socializing tool—a way to connect and be connected to friends and family. A call may last a few minutes or more than an hour, and typically this pattern will repeat itself many times a day. An example of this is well illustrated by Chloe (17): "On the phone I could spend like, oh, about four to six hours but not straight because my mom makes me get off. But I call back. Yeah, I can actually spend the whole day on it if I could. We talk about school, boys, music, TV, boys (laughing)."

DISCUSSION

For young consumers, technology is a natural and integrated aspect of their lives. Steve (17) articulates this: "I've had a computer for ten years and in some form or other I don't remember life without a computer. So I haven't had to adjust or adapt to this new way of doing things. This is just the norm for me." Clearly, to negotiate this complex environment, young consumers display significant autonomous tendencies that are learned and executed on their own but at the same time within a relational context. One explanation for the active self-direction demonstrated may be the fact that technology, specifically computer technology, provides young consumers with so many alternatives and options right at their fingertips. There is no indication in all of this that they are being formally trained to acquire technological skills or interests. In other words, computer competence is different from technical competence.

Three principal topics emerge from our study, which sum up young consumers' everyday experiences and practices with technology: communication and social engagement, techno-entertainment, and online shopping—all tempered by the influence of social agents and gender considerations.

Everyday Experiences and Practices

Digital Networking and Social Engagement

Young consumers communicate using both computer and non-computer-based methods. One computer-based method for communicating is by using social networks such as *MySpace*, *Facebook*, and *Friendster*. These networks allow users to post comments or blogs of their lives that "friends" can access. Respondents indicate that social networks have been instrumental for them not only to maintain ties with friends they leave behind, but also to keep abreast of news on people they know in general. Another method, e-mail, permits respondents to make contact any time, regardless of whether the recipient is online. Respondents do regard telephones as the medium that most resembles face-to-face interaction.

Interviews reveal that age has an effect on the modes of communication used. Respondents from the late childhood category, by virtue of age, do not routinely use the Internet to communicate. Instead, they predominantly depend on the telephone for their communication needs. Furthermore, respondents from the late childhood and early adolescent categories consider the telephone as a tool for conducting affairs such as making plans with friends. In contrast, respondents in the late adolescent and early adulthood categories consider the phone as a socializing tool. This attitude, however, is isolated to the female respondents of those categories. As such, we find that there is an effect for gender. Females across the board are found to be much more social than males in their online and off-line communications.

Leisure and Techno-Entertainment

With regard to techno-entertainment—which comprises computer, video, and online games as well as television—we find that respondents are very fluid in their preferences. When it comes to games, preference for a particular platform is not dictated by the game itself, but rather by the quality of graphics the platform provides for the particular game and the level of control the platform permits a player. A game holds attraction to respondents when it is "stimulating," "challenging," and "thrilling."

Interviews reveal that age and gender influence the types of games preferred. Respondents, chiefly males, in the late adolescent and early adult categories report interest in simulation and adventure-type games ("It's more of an older kid thing"), as well as strategy games ("I like games where you have to develop a strategy and implement it"). Their female counterparts were found to have minimal interest in games overall. Male respondents in the late childhood and early adolescent age categories are found to be predominantly interested in "sports games," "battle games," and "killing games." Female respondents in the same age category prefer non-violent games such as Barbie games.

Online Shopping

Searching online for different outlets, tracking down hard-to-find merchandise, comparing prices, and making a purchase from home imply a level of control because "you could compare them all right there; you don't have to call a lot of people." Moreover, in recognizing the drawbacks to online purchasing, such as not taking immediate possession of purchases and not being able to replicate the physical shopping experience, respondents exercise the option of whether to make the online purchase. Online shopping is extremely limited in late childhood. Any online shopping is conducted by a parent on behalf of the respondent. Gender appears to come into play with regard to the types of products purchased online. Male respondents are also more active in online price comparison.

Influence of Social Agents

Analyses indicate that young consumers' digital tendencies are tempered by interactions with different social agents, specifically family and peers. Influence from social agents is found to primarily take shape in the form of computer instruction. Despite the varying degrees of skills gained from different agents, it may be concluded that young consumers independently strive to acquire computer competence, by trial-and-error "clicking" in order to "figure it out," or soliciting aid from a knowledgeable individual within their social groups. As Vygotsky (1978) argued, by interacting with others using cultural tools, children become able to carry out certain thinking independently, thereby transforming the cultural tools of thought to their own purposes (Rogoff, 2003). In this spirit, young consumers are able to acquire the skills and knowledge of technology and use them to operate in a self-directed manner within their technological environment.

Gender Issues

Some earlier studies have claimed that younger males are more likely to use and own computers and to have more experience with them (Schumacher and Morahan-Martin, 2001), and that males receive greater support and encouragement to be computer users (Shashaani, 1997). However, some recent studies have shown that gender differences may exist but not at the level of competence but in use patterns (Meelissen and Drent, 2008), especially the social media where a higher percentage of girls use *Twitter* (Lenhart, 2009). Thus, although our study results reveal some disparities in computer use, they do not necessarily imply male technological dominance as much as differentiated interests at the stage of childhood or adolescence.

STUDY IMPLICATIONS

This study shows that young consumers are quite complex and self-directed in their association with technology, specifically computer technology, which provides several important implications to technology producers and policymakers. Although technology producers have traditionally acknowledged the importance of children as significant agents of change, they are only now beginning to understand the dynamics that result in their influence and early adoption of technology. In understanding the socially oriented and networked nature of young consumers, technologists may be able to better harness such an understanding advantageously.

From a theoretical perspective, we uncovered some key dimensions (Table 3.2), but we need more fundamental research for young consumers' segment cannot be viewed as an after thought but consumers in the making. In other words, some of the recent work reported by the likes of Sherry Turkle and Sonia Livingstone must be augmented with children as decision makers. In addition, the different groups of young consumers can be studied separately—such as childhood, adolescence, and early adulthood with larger samples.

From a policy perspective, we need to examine young consumers' online competencies and social networking activities thoroughly.

From a promotional perspective, knowledge of the similarities and differences across age segments is important because it may allow us to focus efforts on promoting features of their products to the market as a whole, rather than following the traditional route of segmenting their market based on age, to capture differences that may not exist. For example, in addition to promoting computer or videogames differently to different age segments, advertisers may focus on promoting the particular features that young consumers value most (i.e., control and realism). In addition, the influence that peers appear to have with one another should also be regarded as an important marketing tool utilized for optimal effect.

From a retailing perspective, this study reveals that young consumers place a premium on the ability to replicate the physical shopping experience online, particularly for items such as clothes. The study shows that young consumers place great emphasis on accurate color representation of clothes, on the ability to mix-and-match clothing items, and on being able to see how clothes fit. For example, investing in better graphics to ensure accurate depiction of colors, designing websites that are user friendly, and utilizing 3D technology can better address young consumers' online shopping needs.

Finally, the study is limited in the sense it is not a major survey of the population of young consumers but is limited and focused on a smaller group. As is customary in employing grounded theory, the focus here is on generating theoretical ideas rather than testing a theory. However, our study provides a special peek into reality that is not possible in large surveys.

REFERENCES

Boyd D. 2007. None of This Is Real, in Structures of Participation in Digital Culture, Joe Karaganis (ed.). Social Science Research Council: New York; 132–157.

Carlson L, Rossbart S. 1998. Parental Style and Consumer Socialization of Children. Journal of Consumer Research 15(1): 77–94.

Cook DT. 2000. The Other "Child Study": Figuring Children as Consumers in Market Research, 1910s–1990s. The Sociological Quarterly 41(3): 487–507.

Denegri-Knott J, Molesworth M. 2010. Concepts and Practices of Digital Virtual Consumption. *Consumption, Markets & Culture* 13(2): 109–132.

Greenfield P, Yan Z. 2006. Children, Adolescents, and the Internet: A New Field of Inquiry in Developmental Psychology. *Developmental Psychology* 42(3): 391–394.

Hansen F, Hansen MH. 2005. Children as Innovators and Opinion Leaders. *Young Consumers* 6(2): 44–59.

Ito M, Horst H, Bittani M, Boyd D, Herr-Stephenson B, Lange PG, Pearce CJ, and Robinson, L. 2009 *Living and Learning with New Media: Summary of Findings from the Digital Youth Project.* The MIT Press: Cambridge, MA.

Lenhart A. 2009. *Teens and Social Media: An Overview.* PEW Internet and American Life Project: Washington, DC.

Livingstone S. 2006. Drawing Conclusions from New Media Research: Reflections and Puzzles Regarding Children's Experience of the Internet. *The Information Society* 22(4): 219–230.

Mackenzie C, Stoljar N. 2000. Autonomy Refigured, in *Relational Autonomy: Feminist Perspectives on Autonomy, Agency, and the Social Self*, Catriona Mackenzie and Natalie Stoljar (eds.). Oxford University Press: Oxford; 3–12.

McCracken G. 1988. *The Long Interview.* Sage: Thousand Oaks, CA.

McNeal J. 1999. *The Kids Market: Myths and Realities.* Paramount Publishers: Ithaca, NY.

Meelissen MRM, Drent M. 2008. Gender Differences in Computer Attitudes: Does the School Matter? Computers in Human Behavior 24(3): 969–985.

Peracchio LA. 1992. How Do Young Children Learn to Be Consumers? A Script-Processing Approach. *Journal of Consumer Research* 18(4): 425–440.

QSR NUD*IST Vivo (NVivo) software. 2001. SCILARI: SAGE Publications Software.

Roedder-John D. 1999. Consumer Socialization of Children: A Retrospective Look at Twenty-Five Years of Research. *Journal of Consumer Research* 26(December): 183–213.

Rogoff B. 2003.*The Cultural Nature of Human Development.* Oxford University Press: New York

Satofuka F, Kantola I, and Kono Y. 2009. Explaining Media Choice; Theoretical Discussion and Empirical Experiment. *AI & Society* 24: 135–150.

Schumacher P, Morahan-Martin J. 2001. Gender, Internet and Computer Attitudes and Experiences. *Computers in Human Behavior* 17(1): 1–8.

Shashaani L. 1997. Gender Differences in Computer Attitudes and Use Among College Students. *Journal of Educational Computing Research* 16(1): 37–52.

Simakova E, Neyland D. 2008. Marketing Mobile Futures: Assembling Constituencies and Creating Compelling Stories for an Emerging Technology. *Marketing Theory* 8(1): 91–116.

Steinberg L. 2002. *Adolescence.* McGraw Hill: New York.

Strauss A, Corbin J. 2008. *Basics of Qualitative Research: Techniques and Procedures for Developing Grounded Theory* (3rd ed.). Sage: Thousand Oaks, CA.

Subrahmanyam K. 2003. *Evolving Digital Worlds: How Teens Are Influenced by the Digital Environments.* Paper presented at the HOIT Conference. April, University of California, Irvine.

Turkle l S. 1995. *Life on the Screen: Identity in the Age of the Internet.* Simon & Schuster: New York.

Turkle S. 2005. *The Second Self: Computers and the Human Spirit.* The MIT Press: Cambridge, MA.
Vygotsky Lev S. 1978. *Mind in Society: The Development of Higher Psychological Processes* (Michael Cole, trans.). Harvard University Press: Cambridge, MA.

4 True Values of False Objects
Virtual Commodities in Games

David Myers

INTRODUCTION

Virtual commodities in games are now commonplace, and there is a fairly common introduction to articles such as this one, establishing their prevalence and use. Here is an example:

> In recent years … it has become increasingly common for virtual goods circulated in consumption games to be exchangeable for real money. Using a credit card or mobile phone, players are now able to purchase virtual items, clothes and characters like any commodities in an online store, except that the goods are never delivered to the physical doorstep. This "virtual item trade" or "real-money trade of virtual property," as it is variously known, has forced a re-evaluation of the status of fantastical consumption play. Economists (e.g. Castronova 2006; Huhh 2008) have observed that what were previously considered fiction can actually be analysed as goods in the economic sense. Legal scholars (e.g. Fairfield 2005; Lastowka and Hunter 2004) have put forward questions regarding the ownership and legal status of virtual assets. (Lehdonvirta, Wilska, and Johnson, 2009: 1060)

Yet despite this commonness, there remains uncertainty regarding the proper referents of the buying and selling of virtual commodities. For instance, do these activities more closely reference and resemble the activities of a marketplace—or a game? The quote above locates virtual commodities within a potentially uneasy amalgamation of market forces and playful intent: "consumption games" and "fantastical consumption play." Of what ingredients and in what measure is this combination of fantasy and consumption composed?

This question is particularly relevant when addressing natural tensions between consumption and play. For, commonly, to consume is to both use and extinguish; and this latter consequence—extinction—then provides and prepares us for further consumption. To play, in contrast, is to both use and sustain a state of play. This sustenance of play is potentially continuous, without any limit or necessity of an exhaustible fuel for its ongoing fire.

Virtual consumption seems to stand somewhere between these two (cf. Lehdonvirta, 2009). The consumption portion of this activity feels very familiar, yet the extinction portion exists only in virtual, or representational, form. And the peculiar nature of this extinction seems to provide well, under certain circumstances, for the sustenance of play. Here I would like to examine the appeal of virtual commodities within the seemingly incongruous circumstances of games and play.

HUMAN PLAY

Dyer-Witheford and de Peuter (2009) in *Games of Empire* (also de Peuter and Dyer-Witheford, 2005) emphasize the fundamental nature of *virtual labor* as key to understanding the influence of social structures (e.g., post-industrial capitalism) on leisure in general and, more pointedly, on digital games. Much current research on virtual commodities offers similar riffs on macro-level structures and influences: markets and economies, politics and policies. My interests here, however, are more on the biological imperatives of a universal human play and the imaginative qualities of "fantastical consumption" as a human subjective experience.

As a particular sort of cognitive behavior rooted in the use of signs and symbols, human play has important antecedents prior to its adaptation and use by modern technologies and times. Regardless of the context of its application, for instance, play is marked by the voluntary and intrinsically motivated nature of its pleasure.

Further, these pleasures of play can be observed in species beyond our own. Many early theories of play attempt to explain the relationship between animal and human play within what Sutton-Smith (2001) calls "a rhetoric of progress," in which simple physical play among amphibians evolves over time into more contemplative and imaginative play among larger-brained mammals and, eventually, humans. However, animal play research (e.g., Bekoff and Byers, 1998) has found play exhibiting representational and referential qualities regardless of the species observed playing. In all cases, play seems to conform in some part to Bateson's (1972) notion of "meta-communication" or self-reference (e.g., play sends a signal that "this is play; this is not real").

Play *within games* is also characterized by a similar property of self-reference or, as Suits (1978) defines it from the point of view of the game player, a *lusory attitude*. This lusory attitude allows players of games to knowingly and willingly accept the rules and artificial restrictions of games. Without this attitude, there is no guide to play but its own pleasure; with it, play within games becomes guided by some *other* against which the player must contend and, simultaneously, with which the player must collaborate.

This dialectical lusory attitude runs in rough parallel with what in literature has been described (originally by Samuel Taylor Coleridge) as the *willing suspension of disbelief*. In literature, a willing suspension of disbelief is deemed necessary in order to assure an eventual belief in the relevance of literary experiences to real-world objects and events: relevance that T. S. Eliot finds within an "objective correlative" of literature.

The objective correlative of the signs and symbols used in literature is, according to Eliot (1920), located in "external facts . . . terminat[ing] in sensory experience." Or, in other words, while a willing suspension of disbelief denies the common, everyday, and ostensibly "real-world" referents of literary works, Eliot would claim these must nevertheless conform to some pre-existing (e.g., biological and/or cognitive) human mechanism: a "formula of emotion."

It is something of Eliot's formula of emotion I wish to trace here regarding the values and implications of the buying and selling of virtual commodities within digital games (i e., a formula for the *aesthetics* of virtual commodities).[1] And, in fact, there are strong parallels between the appeal of virtual commodities within games and prioritizing consumer "play" (Holbrook, Chestnut, Oliva, and Greenleaf, 1984) and "imagination" (Molesworth and Denegri-Knott, 2007) during "hedonic" consumption:

> This type of consumption seeks fun, amusement, fantasy, arousal, sensory stimulation, and enjoyment. . . . Surely, any meaningful attempt to model such relatively pleasure-oriented consumption must pay attention to its hedonic components. (Holbrook and Hirschman, 1982: 135)

Yet, any comparison between the hedonic and the instrumental properties of game objects is neither simple, clear, nor binary. Obviously, for instance, in-game signs and symbols have both instrumental and non-instrumental values depending on the circumstance of their use. Also, as further noted by Holbrook and Hirschman (1993: 14), personal and idiosyncratic values associated with the aesthetic properties of consumer products must be considered within the larger social context in which consumption takes place (i.e., "as a means to some end such as prestige or success [extrinsic value] rather than as an end in itself [intrinsic value]").

This latter realization is particularly relevant in adjudicating the value of virtual commodities in contexts where games are subverted. Indeed, even in obvious game contexts in which the value of virtual commodities are clearly determined by game rules and/or objective physics (as in certain types of simulations), the value of these objects can be, through player choice and during free play, denied.

VALUE DETERMINATIONS

Virtual commodities exist in all sorts. Yet, within games, there are clear categories into which these might fall depending on their relationship to game goals.

In one category are items that aid in accomplishing game goals; in another category are items that are superfluous to those goals. Because of the nature of games, most (although not all) virtual commodities within games have traditionally occupied the latter category. For instance, in traditional board games such as chess and *Monopoly*, there are special pieces—ornate pawns and gold-plated tokens—that can be purchased to enhance the game experience, but these do not affect how pawns or tokens move or function within the game. These are neither necessary nor instrumental to game play.

Early commercial videogames—typified by the arcade and console designs of the 1970s—established now familiar patterns of repetitive and level-based, progressive game play within *a single formal context shared by all players*. The uniformity of early digital game experiences was at least partially dictated by their mass production, which allowed little customization of the game's interface and code. However, equally critical was the common design principle of inequity aversion—often couched as "fair play" (Sheridan, 2007 Simon, 1991).

Ensuring equitable access to game rules and play remains an important—although often idealized—feature of contemporary competitive, skill-based games and sports. And, a similar sort of idealization can be found within a set of related assumptions used by free-market economists (cf. Fehr and Schmidt, 1999) to explain and predict consumer behavior. Within this complex of assumptions is Adam Smith's "invisible hand" notion that consensually determined values of commodities—as revealed in a free and open marketplace—determine "true value." Kohn (2004: 308) calls this a "value paradigm" assuming eventual " 'trading equilibrium'—a situation in which all opportunities for mutually advantageous exchange are being realized."

If so, then non-consensual individual and social preferences—or any similar extraneous variables—can be ignored.

> There is a folk wisdom in behavioral economics that social preferences do not matter in competitive markets. . . . Hundreds of market experiments, starting with Smith (1962, 1964), have shown that the standard neoclassical model predicts the actual market outcomes quite well. (Schmidt, 2010: 1)

From this perspective, the designed game and the open marketplace each serve as formal, rule-based mechanisms inside which the vagaries of external social values are trumped—either by the rules of the game or by the collective wisdom of the marketplace.

In opposition to these sorts of authoritative value-determination models, however, are more subjective and less restrictive models. Kohn (2004: 321), for instance, contrasts his value paradigm with an "exchange paradigm," which sets "no absolute standards" and "possesses no generally agreed-upon normative criteria."

Likewise, in contrast to the top-down designs of rule-based games, there are virtual *worlds*—such as *Second Life* and *Habbo Hotel*—wherein virtual commodities are clearly used to express a diversity of social preferences and values. These values are then integral to the appeal of the virtual world.

If, in the absence of an objective and common, rule-based semiotic system, virtual commodities in virtual worlds are valued through a more personally meaningful semiotic process, what is the nature of this process?

INSTRUMENTAL AND NON-INSTRUMENTAL VALUES

The different aesthetics of the two classes of virtual commodities in games—instrumental and non-instrumental (or hedonic)—can be usefully marked according to their origins in different semiotic systems.

In a game of chess, for instance, the "Queen" is clearly a stand-in for (or reference to) this referent: *move any number of vacant squares diagonally, horizontally, or vertically.* Therefore, *any* symbol can be used to indicate this value, without regard to the value (or meaning, or "sense") of that symbol outside the game. It is the signified, not the signifier, that is most critical to game play, and it is the relationship among the signifieds, not the signifiers, that ultimately points to (if the game is successfully designed and implemented) Eliot's "formula of emotion."

In contrast, the referents of signs and symbols within virtual worlds such as *Second Life* are not confined by the algorithmic aesthetics of a game (cf. also the game's "procedural rhetoric") (Bogost, 2008). *Second Life* "players" are allowed—even encouraged—to import (or create) referents through the manipulation and interpretation of virtual world signs and symbols appealing to their own idiosyncratic aesthetics. While the referents of symbols transformed in this way may be conventionally familiar, their newly created "senses"—and associated values—function only within a player's private and protected semiotic system.

As a result, the aesthetics of these two semiotic systems—digital game and virtual world—diverge.

For the most part and in their traditional form, the semiotic systems of games can be understood in the context of Ferdinand de Saussure's simple binary model of signifier and signified. Within objective, rule-based games, the signifier–signified relationship within this model is *fixed* (even if not completely understood or predictable) by game design and rules. Likewise, in traditional market models, some important portion of a commodity's value—the value of oil, for instance—is fixed by an assumedly incontrovertible law of supply and demand: the supply of oil available and the rate at which that supply is depleted by demand.

Without a signified fixed by outside reference, the semiotic systems of virtual worlds are better represented within a slightly more complex model (see Figure 4.1).

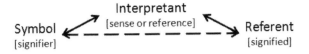

Figure 4.1 A three-part semiotic model (based on Peirce).

This latter semiotic model (closer to that of Peirce than Saussure) inserts an intermediate component between signifier and signified: an "interpretant." In Peirce's model (see Hoopes, 1991), this interpretant indicates the individual thought or "sense" linking symbol (Saussure's signifier) and referent (Saussure's signified). And this latter model is more appropriate for explaining values of signs and symbols in virtual worlds than values in games.

Likewise, this model is more appropriate for explaining the significance of diamonds rather than oil because diamonds (aside from their industrial application) appeal to a particular human aesthetic—assumedly as common among humans as is a preference for shiny baubles among crows. This distinctively human aesthetic "sense" attached to diamonds is then vital to their ultimate value determination. Indeed, distinctive aesthetic (and/or visceral) "senses" of this sort lie at the root of all hedonic consumption.

However, hedonic consumption alone cannot entirely explain valuations within virtual worlds. Virtual world items, by the very nature of their existence within that virtual world, must always have some basic level of instrumentality within that world. That is, the value of virtual world items must always include some minimum reference to [*this item functions within a virtual world*]. Thus, the distinctive value of virtual world items is not that they can be valued without reference to an instrumentality of any sort, but rather that they can be valued (should those that possess them chose to do so) *outside pre-existing semiotic systems*. This includes valuing these items outside the context of embedded game rules, but it also includes valuing these items *outside the trading equilibrium of a free and open marketplace*.

The appeal of such a valuation appears in some part located in the symbolic form itself: the formal, aesthetic pleasure of a signifier divorced of its signified. In related theories of aesthetics (i.e., formalist literary theory) (Erlich, 1981), *habitualization* refers to the replacement, over time, of a signified with its signifier. But, therein, habitualization is considered an impediment to art and associated aesthetic pleasures.

> Habitualization devours works, clothes, furniture, one's wife, and the fear of war. . . . And art exists that one may recover the sensation of life; it exists to make one feel things, to make the stone stony. (Shklovsky, 1925)

Shklovsky and other early formalists thought of the signifiers of natural language as barriers to more direct access of human experience (i.e., the "sense" of a signifier, such as the word "stone," becomes more often determined by the semiotic system of natural language than by its experiential origin). Poetic language—"art"—then reveals the artificiality of this sense and reminds us of the real-world signified that originally motivated its assignation.

Although the term has since been appropriated for other uses,[2] the original meaning of habitualization also includes some part of the meaning of a related term: *habituation*, or a decrease in response to repetitive stimuli. That is, while the original association between "stone" and [*the sensation of stoniness*] was quite fixed and vivid, that visceral association has become diminished and devalued over time through its repetitive use within natural language. Thus, our response to that association has become "habituated"— similar to how our response to clichés, once rich in comparative meanings, diminishes as a result of repeated use.

In interactive digital environments, most particularly digital games, both habitualization (the prioritization of symbolic form) and habituation (a decrease in response to signified–signifier relationships based on real-world experiences) occur: Associations between game objects and their real-world referents are diminished and devalued. This is, in fact, the primary function of an in-game lusory attitude: not to value game objects so much as to devalue their real-world referents, so that the game's semiotic system can function as a default set of values and beliefs on which a unique and novel aesthetic experience can be built. In the early formalist view, such a symbolic or "false" aesthetic experience was necessarily inferior to pre-linguistic sensations, unmediated and raw. In interactive digital environments, however, there are further components of human experience to consider.

The combination of interactive digital experiences and lusory attitude promotes something beyond literature's willing suspension of disbelief: an active reinforcement of false belief. For, while language cannot directly access human experience and therefore must reference that experience indirectly, virtual games (and worlds) can and do access human experience directly through the manipulation of a mechanical interface in the service of game design and code. This physical component of digital game play establishes a novel semiotic system—a new "sense" mediating the relationship between the signifier and signified—based on the embodiment of human experience within a virtual world.

CONSUMER VERSUS AESTHETE

In all forms of art, we commonly hold our personal values and beliefs in abeyance and allow the design of art (e.g., the painting or the novel) to expose us to values of novelty. During this process, we allow our personal, social, and cultural values, at least in part, to be put at risk.

We may subsequently, on reflection, evaluate the strange and novel values of our aesthetic experience more critically and consensually, but this evaluation occurs only after we emerge from that experience. This initial acceptance of aesthetic design—largely on faith—is also the locus and cause of the so-called "magic circle" (Huizinga, 1955) of play and games. It is this magic circle that separates the aesthetic of games from the habitual, the conventional, and the mundane: the real world.

Nevertheless, because of the peculiar liminal status of signs and symbols within games, the real world may be invited within—either by game player or by variations in game design. For instance, in the rough simulations of sport inside popular fantasy games (fantasy football, fantasy golf, and such), certain game objects—virtual sports players—are *fixed* in value by their real-world referents. In contrast, the virtual objects created during *free* play can be valued more idiosyncratically.

The referents within *games*, as an intermediary semiotic form between simulations and free play, are fixed by game rules—unlike those in free play. Nevertheless, the authority of these referents depends wholly on the player's lusory attitude—unlike those in simulations.

The most interesting and informative cases regarding the use of virtual commodities within games are then those that occupy the conceptual space between traditional, rules-based games and more free-play, sandbox-like virtual worlds. Massively multiplayer online role-playing games (MMORPGs), for instance, are ostensibly games, but they are games often and widely trumped by the semiotic systems of the virtual worlds in which they reside.

Lord of the Rings Online

The MMORPG *Lord of the Rings Online* (LOTR)—as an example of a virtual world with game-like qualities—offers a long list of virtual goods for sale in its online "LOTR Store." Within this list are "cosmetic" (i.e., hedonistic) items, which do not directly influence game play, and also "premium" (i.e., instrumental) items, which can increase the ability, either directly or indirectly, of players to achieve in-game goals. Even within MMORPGs that do not, within the virtual world itself, offer these sorts of "premium" items for sale, similar sorts of virtual commodities—those aiding the achievement of in-game goals—are in demand by players and are made available to players from third-party sources.

If the MMORPG designers seek to prohibit out-of-game marketplaces from negatively influencing in-game experiences—as they often do (e.g., Meunier, 2008)—then why do players seek to purchase game objects outside the normal constraints of the game design and subvert that game design?

When in-game goals and achievements are commoditized, as they are in LOTR and elsewhere, these become valued by a different set of aesthetic criteria than that established by game rules. For instance, players often justify the purchase and use of these items of a means of accessing game experiences otherwise inaccessible (e.g., as trading money for time); however, it is not at all clear why this same justification does not lead to a similar level of demand for easier-to-access game-playing experiences in traditional games. There is no similar level of demand, for instance, for "premium" chess pieces that combine the function of queen and knight or "premium" *Monopoly* tokens that allow players extra die rolls.

More reasonably, characteristics of the virtual worlds in which MMORPGs are set, rather than characteristics of the games inside those worlds, spur player demand for both cosmetic and premium, instrumental and non-instrumental, virtual commodities. These characteristics are those that, simultaneously, undermine the authority of the game rules and assert in their stead a relatively unrestricted freedom of play.

Prominent among these characteristics is the level of anonymity within massively multiplayer virtual worlds. This anonymity blurs the traditional relationship between and among in-game competitors, who can no longer be easily identified and evaluated within the same shared space and time. Likewise, the obfuscation of game rules through the implementation of multiple and often ambiguous goals inside MMORPGs, forces (rather than simply allows) Peirce's interpretant to play a more influential role in assigning values and meaning to game objects.

Even then, however, the anonymity of massively multiplayer games is no greater than the anonymity of the solitary player in any solitaire game, where there is seemingly less desire for "premium" virtual commodities of the sort popular in MMORPGs. And the increased role of the interpretant in a virtual world's semiotic system is also not in itself sufficient to explain differences in player demand for cosmetic and premium items. The "premium" label, after all, assumes some added value accrues to items more relevant to game goals and achievements, regardless of any idiosyncratic "sense" attached to these items. And, in fact, within the virtual marketplaces of virtual worlds, with little intervention by game designers, players clearly attach greater value to instrumental than non-instrumental offerings.

The most critical and distinguishing characteristic of virtual worlds shaping demand for virtual commodities must then become their *society*. For, in the absence of game rules with clearly fixed signifieds, yet still in the presence of what is generally regarded as a *game*, social pressures and powers value game achievements and goals according to in-game performances (i.e, instrumentality), yet, simultaneously, outside the constraints of the semiotic system imposed by game rules and design.

City of Heroes

City of Heroes (CoH) is another MMORPG situated inside a virtual world, with many of the same game-related characteristics as LOTR. Both games were initially offered through a conventional subscription model—although as of September 2010, LOTR became free-to-play, with revenue generated solely through the sale of virtual items.³ CoH, threatened like most mature MMORPGs by its waning novelty, has also increased the number and variety of virtual items for sale within the game over time, although these currently remain, in LOTR's scheme, largely cosmetic.

However, CoH—like LOTR and similar games—also offers numerous "veteran benefits" to long-time players. Many of these veteran benefits (special weapons and abilities) can be considered "premium" items in that they offer game-play advantages.

If the representations of virtual marketplaces within massively multiplayer online games were fixed simulations of real-world marketplaces, then veteran benefits might not be considered virtual commodities. After all, such benefits are incapable of being bartered, bought, or sold inside the game's virtual marketplace. However, both veteran benefits and the virtual commodities within an MMORPG must function within the same semiotic system of the virtual world in which they originate. Accordingly, the presence of veteran benefits—and similar perks—within MMORPGs undermines the game's unique semiotic system and therein influences the valuation of all objects within that game. Indeed, the culminate example of this sort (which prioritizes and promotes hedonic consumption over lusory attitude) is the commoditization of entire MMORPG accounts.

In CoH and elsewhere, the most complete representation of a player's play is her avatar and its "gear"—or, in CoH, its "build." The basic characteristics of this build are acquired during game play, although some of these characteristics can also be purchased, directly or indirectly, through in-game currencies. By far the simplest way to obtain this representation of in-game play, in its entirety, as a whole account, is to purchase it outside the virtual world, through a third-party vendor, using real-world currencies.

Insofar as MMORPG currencies—and all representations of MMORPG play—are available for purchase in this way, there is then the inescapable valuation of virtual world commodities in real-world marketplaces and, correspondingly, the devaluation of any sense peculiar to or bound within the semiotic system of a *game*.

Nevertheless, this sort of cross-world valuation is always dependent on and ultimately fixed, not by the current exchange rate or the value of any individual MMORPG account, but rather by value attached *to the game mechanics*. For, regardless of any subsequent transformations, it is only through and because of the semiotic system established by the game that the instrumental items within MMORPGs—like CoH and LOTR—attain their initial value.

Further, if the semiotic system of the game is always in conflict and tension with real-world values and beliefs—as required by Suit's lusory attitude and the notion of the game as a set of intentionally "false" beliefs—then its values are always, by nature of their origin, impermanent.

That is, the instrumental properties of game objects exist and must exist in a *temporary* bubble of demand, regardless of their subsequent appropriation within alternative markets. It is this fundamental characteristic of impermanence, *based on the peculiar nature of games as aesthetic forms*, that ensures the eventual extinction of the instrumental class of virtual commodities within MMORPGs. And, once these items are extinguished—that is, consumed—their aesthetic appeal cannot be replaced by items from the same game, but only by items from some *new and more novel game.*

Ultima Online or *Everquest* I accounts, for instance, may certainly retain cosmetic and hedonic value over time—as does the Ford Model T and the *Atari* 2600—but their instrumental values are fated to expire. For this reason, the consumption of virtual commodities, insofar as these originate and are valued as instrumental items within a game, does not occur in the same manner, nor according to the same schedule, nor with the same consequence, as does the consumption of real-world commodities. Virtual commodities in a game are inescapably a part of the liminality, novelty, and impermanence of the peculiar semiotic context in which they originate: a game.

CONCLUSIONS

Commonly, analyses of virtual commodities have sought to use various contexts—particularly legal (Fairfield, 2005; Lastowka, 2010) and economic (Castronova, 2005) contexts—to demonstrate similarities between virtual commodities and their real-world referents. These contexts can equally be considered semiotic systems wherein values are assigned according to a particular set of assumptions—often idealized as universal and consensual.

However, games, by their very nature (and perhaps, at least in some part, virtual worlds as well) purposefully assign "false" values to signs and symbols. That is, the "true" values of game objects are somehow anathematic to the unique aesthetic properties of games.

We began this discussion by noting some interesting features of virtual consumption: that, within play, we might consume without extinguishing the object of our consumption. From this point of view, objects of play are rather the opposite of consumables: These objects are durables of seemingly infinite duration. A single episode of play does not in any way diminish our capacity to play further; in most cases, it enhances that capacity.

However, unlike the objects of play within it, *games* can be consumed. Upon repeated play, the novelty of a game's semiotic system, depending on its design, wears increasingly thin, until it no longer evokes a lusory attitude among players. In such cases, when the "false" values of game objects have been extinguished, the commoditization of that game—and the objects within it—becomes increasingly possible and, within current social, economic, and legal contexts, increasingly likely.

The question then is this: If there are significant differences between the semiotic systems of games and markets, are these differences worth preserving? Do we in any way recognize and value games as distinct aesthetic forms with unique aesthetic consequences?

Focusing on generic "experiential consumption," Addis and Holbrook (2001: 52) noted this relationship between a functional (or an instrumental) product and its symbolic form:

> the function of the product as a good or service decreases in relevance, while its role as an embodiment of symbolic meaning increases.

More currently, perhaps the inverse of this relationship is more telling: As the embodiment of the symbolic meaning of virtual commodities within games decreases in relevance, the function of those commodities as goods and services correspondingly increases. If so, then in order to commodify the unique aesthetics of game-objects—in particular, in order to commodify that part of their meaning that is [*I am not commodifiable*]—the semiotic system of the game must be devalued and transformed to that of the marketplace.

Many MMORPGs seem to accomplish this by blurring the distinction between the subjective "sense" of game objects and their more objective, rules-based referents: that is, by undermining and devaluing game rules. Game designers also aid this, at least in part, by basing the appeal of their games on visceral, experiential, and/or addictive objects of human desire—common, for instance, as regards the game objects within some so-called "casual" games, such as Zynga's *Farmville*. Free markets may also be biased toward this devaluation and subsequent transformation in their assumption of a trading equilibrium valuing all objects according to a common and consensual semiotic system, regardless of the origin of those objects.

In such circumstances, the game's magic circle becomes increasingly permeable and incapable of isolating any dissonant semiotic system operating within it. And, while this loss of the magic circle of gaming seems to have little effect on free play, it may well have more serious and prohibitive effects on what de Peuter and Dyer-Witheford (2005) and, subsequently, Apperley and Dieter (2010) have labeled "counterplay"—or, elsewhere, "anti-play" (Myers, 2010).

This counterplay results in "the disruptive creation of the new through the reiterations of gaming" (Apperley and Dieter, 2010). In-game objects motivating these reiterations of gaming have little to offer in either aesthetics or novelty if they are, at both the beginning and end of their in-game appeal, already referenced and valued according to their subsequent function as commodities in free-market contexts.

NOTES

1. See also Vankatesha and Meamberb (2008) for further analysis and catego-
   rization of the aesthetics of consumption.
2. The term "habitualization" seems now used (if it all) more often and more
   generically in social constructivist contexts to indicate the acquisition of something like what Peirce calls "habits" (or related complexes of beliefs and values). These habits or "schemas" (cf. Ferri and Fusaroli, 2009) then drive our
   interactions with other objects of value, particularly new and novel objects, in
   socially situated ways that tend to confirm pre-existing semiotic systems.
3. During the summer of 2011, CoH is scheduled to become free-to-play as well.

REFERENCES

Addis M, Holbrook MB. 2001. On the Conceptual Link Between Mass Customi-
   zation and Experiential Consumption: An Explosion of Subjectivity. *Journal of
   Consumer Behaviour* 1(1): 50–66.
Apperley T, Dieter M. (eds.). 2010. Editorial. *Fibreculture* 16. Available at http://
   sixteen.fibreculturejournal.org/ [accessed on 12 September 2011].
Bateson G. 1972. *Steps to an Ecology of Mind*. Ballantine Books: New York.
Bekoff M, Byers JA. (eds.). 1998. *Animal play: Evolutionary, Comparative, and
   Ecological Perspectives*. Cambridge University Press: Cambridge.
Bogost I. 2008. The Rhetoric of Video Games, in *The Ecology of Games: Connect-
   ing Youth, Games, and Learning*, Katie Salen, (ed.). The MIT Press: Cambridge,
   MA; 117–140.
Castronova E. 2005. *Synthetic Worlds: The Business and Culture of Online
   Games*. University of Chicago Press: Chicago, IL.
de Peuter G, Dyer-Witheford N. 2005. A Playful Multitude? Mobilising and Coun-
   ter-Mobilising Immaterial Game Labour. *Fibreculture* 5. Available at http://
   journal.fibreculture.org/issue5/depeuter_dyerwitheford.html [accessed on 12
   September 2011].
Dyer-Witheford N, de Peuter G. 2009. *Games of Empire: Global Capitalism and
   Video Games*. University of Minnesota Press: Minneapolis.
Eliot TS. 1920. *The Sacred Wood*. Methune: London. Available at http://www.
   bartleby.com/200/ [assessed on 12 September 2011].
Erlich V. 1981. *Russian Formalism*. Yale University Press: New Haven, CT.
Fairfield J. 2005. Virtual Property. *Boston University Law Review* 85(4):
   1047–1102.
Fehr E, Schmidt KM. 1999. A Theory of Fairness, Competition and Co-operation.
   Quarterly Journal of Economics 114: 817–868.
Ferri G, Fusaroli R. 2009. Which Narrations for Persuasive Technologies? Hab-
   its and Procedures in *Ayiti: The Cost of Life*. Paper presented at the 2009
   AAAI Spring Symposium. Available at http://www.aaai.org/Papers/Symposia/
   Spring/2009/SS-09–06/SS09–06–007.pdf [accessed on 12 September 2011].
Holbrook MB, Chestnut RW, Oliva TA, and Greenleaf EA. 1984. Play as a Con-
   sumption Experience: The Roles of Emotions, Performance, and Personality in
   the Enjoyment of Games. *Journal of Consumer Research* 11(2): 728–740.
Holbrook MB, Hirschman EC. 1982. The Experiential Aspects of Consump-
   tion: Consumer Fantasies, Feeling, and Fun. *Journal of Consumer Research* 9:
   132–140.
Holbrook MB, Hirschman EC. 1993. *The Semiotics of Consumption: Interpreting
   Symbolic Consumer Behavior in Popular Culture and Works of Art*. Mouton
   de Gruyter: Berlin.

Hoopes J. (ed.). 1991. *Peirce on Signs: Writings on Semiotics*. University of North Carolina Press: Chapel Hill.

Huizinga J. 1955. *Homo ludens: A Study of the Play-Element in Culture*. Beacon: Boston.

Kohn M. 2004. Value and Exchange. *Cato Journal* 24: 303–339.

Lastowka G. 2010. *Virtual Justice: The New Laws of Online Worlds*. Yale University Press: New Haven, CT.

Lehdonvirta V. 2009. *Virtual Consumption*. Publications of the Turku School of Economics, A-11:2009, Turku. Available at http://info.tse.fi/julkaisut/vk/Ae11_2009.pdf [accessed on 12 September 2011].

Lehdonvirta V, Wilska, T-A, and Johnson M. 2009. Virtual Consumerism: Case Habbo Hotel. *Information, Communication and Society* 12(7): 1059–1079.

Linden Research, Inc. 2003. *Second Life*. Available at http://secondlife.com/ [accessed on 12 September 2011].

Meunier N. 2008. Blizzard Cracks Down with Battle.net Ban. *The Escapist*, 12 November. Available at http://www.escapistmagazine.com/news/view/87392-Blizzard-Cracks-Down-With-Battle-net-Ban [accessed on 12 September 2011].

Molesworth M, Denegri-Knott J. 2007. Digital Play and the Actualisation of the Consumer Imagination. *Games and Culture* 2(2): 114–133.

Myers D. 2010. *Play Redux: The Form of Digital Games*. University of Michigan Press: Minneapolis.

Sheridan H. 2007. Evaluating Technical and Technological Innovations in Sport: Why Fair Play Isn't Enough. *Journal of Sport and Social Issues* 31(2): 179–194.

Shklovsky V.1925. *Theory of Prose*. Dalkey Achrive Press: Normal, IL

Simon RL. 1991. *Fair Play: Sports, Values, and Society*. Westview Press: Boulder, CO.

Suits B. 1978. *The Grasshopper: Games, Life, and Utopia*. University of Toronto Press: Toronto.

Sutton-Smith B. 2001. *The Ambiguity of Play*. Harvard University Press: Cambridge, MA.

Venkatesha A, Meamberb LA. 2008. The Aesthetics of Consumption and the Consumer as an Aesthetic Subject. *Consumption Markets and Culture* 11(1): 45–70.

5 First Person Shoppers

Consumer Ways of Seeing in Videogames

Mike Molesworth

INTRODUCTION

In this chapter I want to consider videogames as a practice informed by consumer "ways of seeing." This produces a possible critique of videogames that far from being "interactive," they are a form of pleasurable but pacifying consumer leisure. Although I'm not suggesting that this is all they are or can be, this complaint may stand in contrast to both criticisms that games produce violence or isolation and celebrations of new freedoms found through Digital Virtual Consumption (DVC). I'm going to argue that videogame players may enact the performance of familiar consumer scripts but do so in spectacular virtual environments that "re-enchant" the consumption experience. However, in reproducing consumer acts, videogames are open to criticism that just like other consumer spectacles may depoliticize and alienate the consumer.

Criticisms of videogames may be dominated by concerns over their violence (see Anderson and Bushman, 2001), such that other aspects of their social impact may be overshadowed. I want to briefly consider George Romero's (1978) film *Dawn of the Dead* to illustrate the problem that violent imagery may overshadow other analysis of media. Romero's film contains scenes of graphic violence: stomachs ripped open, decapitated heads, flesh bitten from limbs. Not surprisingly it was caught up in the video nasty witch-hunt in the UK in the 1980s (Wright, 2005), such that the violence in the film masked Romero's commentary on the nature of shopping (most of the film is set in a mall). His apparent purpose with this film was not to incite violence in viewers, but to critique by parody a growing consumer society that produced alienation and commodity fetishism. The punch line to *Dawn of the Dead* is that the zombies are consumers. In making the zombies consumers—an unknown mass—Romero also gives permission for the viewer to enjoy their destruction, but in doing so also draws attention to that very aspect of our consumer society. In the mall we are surrounded not by people, but objects. We are thus dehumanized by a consumer way of seeing others. However, the reception of Romero's film suggests another possibility that complicates things. Ironically, Loudermilk (2003) acknowledges that far from getting viewers to question their consuming lives (or inviting copy-cat crimes), *Dawn of the Dead* may induce a pleasurable daydream of what a viewer might do should they find themselves free-range in their local mall. *Dawn of the Dead* re-enchants the shopping experience by making ordinary shopping extraordinary. Harper (2002) also notes how a mall may become exciting again as shoppers imagine their local mall as zombie-infested. And the film was a commercial success, inspiring numerous remakes and a number of videogames (Wright, 2005). Romero used graphic violence to argue against the mundane, one-dimensional "false security" of consumption; however, the film's popularity as a commodity that drives consumers' imaginations and that invigorates the marketplace hints that far from undermining consumption as a way of life, Romero offered a cultural product capable of stimulating the consumer imagination. *Dawn of the Dead*, then, may be misread as merely gratuitously violent, and in doing so its critique of consumer culture, or its value as resource for consumers' imaginations, may be missed.

Much the same may be said of videogames. In focusing on their violence, we may ignore what they say about our consumer society. If we look beyond the violence in games, we might also ask whether videogames re-enchant the jaded consumer through new spectacle, but risk dehumanizing them by reproducing the consumer gaze and shopping script.

I therefore want to consider aspects of shopping culture as a way to understand videogames as a form of DVC. Here I am not interested in consumption as the rational acquisition of goods, but as an experience based on the gaze and the imagination: A story of shopping that has roots in Benjamin's flâneur (e.g., see Urry, 2002) but is now informed by a body of work on the consumer imagination and desire. Unlike Simon (2006), who sees the "cyber spatial" flâneur/game-player as remote and elite, I will argue that the flâneur-like experience of game-playing might be familiar to any Western shopper. I hope to demonstrate a relationship between recreational shopping and playing videogames based on the "scopic regimes" of the shopper that opens up new arguments for both celebrating and criticizing games based on similar approaches used to attack and defend shopping.

CONSUMER AESTHETICS AND THE GAZE

Recreational shopping may be seen as an aesthetic experience that uses the resources of the environment to provide stimulation for the imagination in order to create a pleasurable dream-space (Falk and Campbell, 1997; Featherstone, 1991; Gottdiener, 2000; Urry, 2002). This view of consumption includes a consideration of what Falk (1997) has referred to as the "scopic regimes of shopping," similar to what Urry (1992) has termed "the tourist gaze" in relation to the consumption of tourist sites. Such approaches foreground the way in which consumers look at things, rather than the objects that are looked at, emphasizing the experience rather than the image.

One basis for the debate about the shopper's gaze is Benjamin's review of the flâneur. In this context Featherstone (1998:13) suggests that "the flâneur seeks an immersion in the sensations of the city, he seeks to 'bathe in the crowd,' to become lost in feelings, to succumb to the pull of random desires and the pleasures of scopophila." So shopping is a visual experience that stimulates the imagination of an individual as he or she moves through space. Contemporary flâneur-shoppers or consuming tourists (and for Urry these have become much the same) move through urban spaces absorbing images in a dream-like state, but occasionally they stop as something literally captures their imagination. They then gaze on this intriguing commodity producing a shift in their way of looking. They ask themselves about its future purpose and consider what such an item might "mean." This may or may not result in purchase. In any case, the shoppers will likely continue on their way. There is always more to see as they fluctuate between two modes of looking and associated types of engagement and gain pleasure from doing so. I will argue that such pleasure may also apply to many digital games. Videogames are experienced as moving through a dream-space, occasionally or frequently settling on specific objects to contemplate their meaning. In this respect I'm suggesting that playing many (but obviously not all) videogames may be experienced rather like an exciting form of recreational shopping.

Urry (1995) refers to these consumer ways of looking as the "romantic" gaze and the "spectorial" gaze (which is more like a glance). Or to put it another way, we might make a distinction between temporal looking (a glance) and spatial looking (a gaze) (Shields, 2003). Scenery is ideal for gazing on (Falk, 1997), and this constitutes the main way of seeing for the sightseeing tourist. The temporal glance, in contrast, better captures the experience of moving through urban spaces, soaking up the atmosphere. However, this turns out to be a far more "dangerous" pursuit because it is not just the shop displays that provide resources for a glancing shopper. Much of the attraction is other people, and the implication is that the flâneur-shopper is observed by others. An unwritten rule is that these exchanges must be no more than a glimpse. For example, Shields (2003) refers to the "street gaze" (from Lacan's analysis of Benjamin), where a gaze is bounced back and forth like a projectile propelled from one subject to another and then defected back again. A consequence of this activity is that shoppers become self-consciously aware that they too are on display. They are also increasingly under the gaze of imagined mall security and their cameras. As Falk (1997) points out, the shopper should not hang around too long because loitering is strongly discouraged. This results in a third sort of gaze—a "panoptic" gaze—consistent with Foucault's explanation of self-surveillance, which results in self-regulated behavior based on an imagined gaze of another.

We may understand the experience of modern consumer-leisure as the pleasurable combination of the glance and the gaze, managed through the use of self-surveillance. The designers of shopping and tourist environments exploit these scopic regimes of shopping. They design and construct shopping spaces to encourage shoppers to remain lost in a consumption-related dream world of endless novelty and expectation. They provide the right temperature and lighting, the right spaces to move in, food to eat, and even themes to help the individual lose a sense of reality and to allow his or her imagination to take over (Gottdiener, 2000; Sherry et al., 2001). The result is that the behavior of the individual is influenced by an imagined gaze of others that prevents complacency and lethargy; the promise of novelty that motivates him or her forward, and occasional spectacles that require detailed reflection and thought. Could it be that because this experience is culturally desirable, the designers of digital games have learned the same tricks when constructing digital virtual spaces? It might make sense if playing games somehow "tapped into" a familiar leisure performance.

THE PLEASURES AND PROBLEMS OF SHOPPING

Before I consider videogames specifically, I also want to reflect on some implications of this conceptualization of shopping by further considering the sorts of experiences that these ways of looking may produce. Firstly, we may note that they encourage consumers to inwardly direct emotion toward their imagination where the play proper takes place (Lehtonen and Maenpaa, 1997). The mall creates a crowd of strangers where recreational shoppers look and then occasionally imagine things about what they have seen but seldom interact beyond "projectile-like" temporal glances. It is therefore a place of imagining individuals.

It isn't just sociability that is lost in the mall; the present is suspended too. The temporal glance produces an experience of anticipation. For example, Shields explains that the glance "might serve to remind us of the strange quality of visualicity which always attempts to surmount the present and empirically visible to see forward into the future" (Shields, 2003:7). It brings recognition and imagination into the current moment so that what comes next is as important as what is seen now. This interaction between novel visual stimulus and the imagination is a key aspect of the recreational shopping experience. As Lehtonen and Maenpaa (1997:143) put it, "Shopping is about moving in the city, in malls, in shops . . . where the plurality of possibilities are fundamental." Novelty is always sought, but in a controlled way, so that shopping allows for "predictable" chance, offering "a controlled degree of novelty and controlled adventures of taste with a predictably happy ending" (Lehtonen and Maenpaa, 1997).

Consumers have leaned to crave this "safe" adventure as a contrast to the predictability and routine of work, for example. For recreational shoppers, it's what makes shopping "fun". For Featherstone (1998) the flâneur-shopper is also actively seeking to make the strange familiar and the familiar strange. This removal of the individual from the ordinary is a key aspect of entering this play-space, and so we might note similarities between this shopping aesthetic and Huizinga's (1938) magic circle or play itself, and this is well captured by the idea of experiential consumption (e.g., see Pine and Gilmore, 1999). Featherstone confirms that the experience of shopping has become "carnival-like" involving a controlled de-controlling of the emotions, and he suggests that this process becomes more important the more everyday life itself is controlled, made safe, and made predictable. That which is increasingly excluded from culture escapes through carnival because it becomes an object of desire. In effect, controlled decontrolling allows the ever more regulated adult to become child-like again, to see the world afresh and enchanted, even if this is temporary and even if they are simply regulated in other ways. The "risk" of shopping is enjoyed as a game of chance, the pleasure based on the idea that something unexpected and special might happen (Lehtonen and Maenpaa, 1997).

However, even experiential marketing has its limits as consumers increasingly find that they have "done everything" that the material world has to offer (Scitovsky, 1976) or, worse, that the marketplace has become both too complex to know with any certainty, yet offers little novelty and thrill. The result is a desperate unknowable sameness (Schwartz, 2004) where high street diversity has perhaps given way to "clone towns" (Simms, Kjell, and Potts, 2005). One potential remedy for individuals socialized to prefer the novel and spectacular is the digitally virtual. Games may be comforting as a form of consumer spectacle because they are in some ways safe and predictable and in other ways new and exciting: a sort of knowable difference and therefore a perfect consumer adventure. If we accept this narrative of the shopper, then the step to digital virtual worlds is a small one. Consumers enjoy videogames because they combine familiar ways of seeing with spectacular new things to see and think about, and this experience may be pleasurable when contrasted with daily routines.

Such an enjoyable experience of shopping needs to be learned (Lehtonen and Maenpaa, 1997). It is cultivated from youth and reinforced by life's experiences. As we grow up as consumers, we learn to privilege the visible, to seek endless novelty, and to imagine and desire what that novelty might bring. For example, Mary Douglas (1997: 23) presents shopping as agonistic, claiming that "far from being mindless, shopping demands infinite attention. Pressed hard by enemy forces, it calls for constant vigilance, subtlety and resource." A skillful pursuit is emphasized. Alternatively, for Featherstone (1998) the flâneur is described as a detective, trying to "read" the city and to understand it. He may take notes that everything may be significant. The result is that the shopper develops an ongoing aesthetic sensibility that swings between involvement and detachment, between decontrolled pleasure and moments of careful recording and analysis. This is a socialized, cultivated pleasure, a product of a commercial landscape, and something that requires consumers' ongoing attention to maintain their skill. As consumers we expect the shopping environment to be a space of adventure that is always spectacular, but it requires practice to get the most from it because over-familiarity and boredom are always a threat to pleasure. Again, we may ask whether this combination of skillful agon and calculated alea against a spectacular backdrop is something found in videogames and sought out by players.

If it is, we might be tempted to celebrate games' ability to provide this enjoyment for otherwise jaded consumers, but there may be consequences to this retreat to fantasy. Featherstone highlights a danger that a focus on leisure-shopping produces individuals who are mere "gapers," so intoxicated by the urban scene that they lose themselves. Narrative becomes lost, and the *badaud* merely gawps zombie-like at an incomprehensible volume of spectacle. This hints that all might not be well with the aesthetic shopping gaze, and such a sentiment was of course the thrust of Romero's parody. As a commercial space, the mall's purpose is quite different from simply creating free pleasure—"experiential freeware" as Falk and Campbell (1997) call it. These spaces seek to seduce the consumer into ways of seeing that perpetuate a life-focus on consumption. Shopping socializes people to want to shop further (see Friedberg, 1993), to seek pleasure in the mall, and so ignore the inadequacies of work or the rest of their lives. For consumers, the pleasures of consumption may block out other social concerns, and this retreat from social responsibility in favor of spectacular commodity forms presents us with possible grounds for criticism. If videogame play and shopping produce similar pleasurable experiences, but with the possibility of similar "side-effects," then these criticisms might also be applied to videogames.

SHOPPING AND VIDEOGAME AESTHETICS

Those who have played videogames might already note similarities between the playing experience and these descriptions of shopping—at least for some games. Indeed, Atkins (2006) pre-empts the argument here by suggesting that when we analyze a videogame we might be tempted to focus on the violence on the screen as a still image and ignore that images in a game do not always try to capture us in a gaze in the same way as a fixed image does (i.e., in a spatial gaze). In a game the player is actively and endlessly working to dismiss the image in favor of the next stimulus. The play, as Atkins points out, has a future orientation based on imagining what is yet to happen and acting on the basis of this speculation. I don't want to deny the violence in games or deal directly with the merits and limitations of the various "effects" debates, but for most videogame players, I suspect the emotions experienced are possibly not murderous anger and hate, but rather a desire to endlessly experience thrilling new visual stimulus: the same aesthetic that produces recreational shopping.

I now want to explore the similarities between shopping and videogames in more detail. Consumer ways of seeing could be applied to a wide range of games, and it might be possible to map games according to their emphasis on each scopic regime (temporal, spatial, and panoptic). For example, does the ever changing but endlessly repetitive Tetris typify a game dominated by the temporal gaze, whereas *The Sims*, with its emphasis on gazing on one neighborhood, suggests a spatial gaze? Do survival horror games rely primarily on the panoptic gaze? A number of games are actually set in a mall, for example, State of Emergency or the *Dawn of the Dead*-inspired *Dead Rising*. Others have a large shopping element, such as *The Sims*, and some have shopping as a "side-game," such as the stroll through car showrooms in *Gran Turismo*, or even the initial character generation and avatar "upgrade" sections of many role playing games. So some games contain obvious "shopping simulations," but without many of the space, time, and financial restrictions found in the mall (e.g., *The Sims* or *Gran Turismo*); others "re-enchant" via "deviant" consumer behavior (e.g., *Dead Rising* or *Grand Theft Auto*), or stretch the imagination with exotic goods and services not normally found in physical malls (e.g., *World of Warcraft*). However, I want to specifically focus on experiences that, although at first seem nothing like shopping, may be readily understood by consumers as an exciting stroll with the possibility of acquiring desirable "stuff." The point here is that although many videogames offer shopping experiences as exotic simulation, the scopic regimes of shopping may be seen much more widely, including in games that at first seem to have little to do with the consumer experience.

The design of many games encourages a constant, steady movement through the environment, and therefore the primary mode of looking seems to be a temporal glance. As Grieb (2002) observes of *Tombraider*, "Exploring the simulated places staged in a video game is initially likely to take the shape of an aimless 'stroll,' . . . not unlike the Dadaist excursions through the urban landscape of Paris." Such is the acceptance of this aspect of games that it is also frequently discussed in consumer reviews, for example, Accardo's (2004) review of *Doom 3* declared: "It's simultaneously innovative and derivative. . . . After you land, you're given some time to wander around and soak in the surroundings. . . . There's an amazing amount of detail in these opening areas, and it's worth taking your time to explore." Accardo also refers to the idea that videogames are both familiar and strange (innovative and derivative). Each new game works to make the familiar strange again, just like each new visit to the mall where a consumer expects new storefronts and offers but doesn't expect to have to re-learn the act of shopping.

Accardo notes a "pre-action stroll," but when the action starts in a game, there is a heightened focus on moving through a virtual space while reacting to the stimulus in the environment. Fielder (2001), reviewing *Halo*, states, "One of the best things about *Halo* is that it manages to attain that perfect level of difficulty that provides you with plenty of challenge but little or no frustration . . . , its levels are huge and your goals shift from moment to moment as events happen around you." In this sense, frustration is expressed as an inability to "move forward," and the "shifting goals" are again an indication of mechanisms to ensure novelty of experience. Like the shopper exploring unfamiliar shops in a new mall, an individual is drawn through space by desire for novelty: the next room, the next weapon, and the next foe. Usually players need to get to some as yet unvisited place or acquire some desired artefact, but often this is just an "excuse" for the thrilling journey, just as the recreational shopper seeks the *experience* of shopping rather than a quick purchase.

Adams (2004) review for *Doom 3* includes: "the art actually kept getting better than it was at the beginning and the pacing was very good. The action was fairly repetitive and AI was not the most impressive . . . , but by the end of the game, I just didn't care. I was having a great time being in that environment while mindlessly blasting mindless creatures." The focus is on visual novelty and a known set of behaviors, but Adams also notes a characteristic of the creatures that is similar to Romero's consumer-zombies. Foes in FPSs might be seen as resource for the imagination in a similar way that the shopper views other people. Like other shoppers, they are objectified, merely part of the dreamscape. They are thought about (when is the next one, what will it do, what will it look like), but they are not thought of as subjects; they are "mindless" and may therefore be eliminated. Like the shopper, a player generally makes no attempt to interact with them other than instrumentally. Once their visual novelty is experienced, they are "dismissed." Of course the mere eye contact of the shopper is not enough to dismiss a glance in the virtual world of a videogame, so rather than "metaphorical projectiles" described by Shields (2003), games use simulated weapon-fire. The result is similar, however. A player moves through space, "glancing" at foes, but quickly dismissing them for fear that they themselves might be caught by a damaging projectile gaze. My suggestion here is that players don't see "violence," but rather they see something novel and then look past it for the next thing. Zombies, monsters, and aliens are attractive to players because they are something new and unusual. They therefore make a familiar movement through space unfamiliar.

These descriptions and Atkin's 'future orientation' of the image articulate the importance of the temporal glance during game-play. Where there are negative comments about a game in a review, these are often based on a lack of novelty or a failure of the temporal glance to stimulate the imagination in this way—a feeling that the player has "done it all before." For example, Adams (2004) writes of *Doom 3*: "I still had fun running from room to room killing these monsters, I just wish there was more variety to it—like the escort mission halfway through. Small puzzle solving instances, of which there weren't many, would have been nice as well. Getting past areas by finding PDAs with a new security code got old quick." We might think of such games as similar to walking through the same shopping center week after week or the same supermarket, looking to buy the same things. It gets boring. Alternatively, games that don't provide something to do other than move around, or especially those that have rigid environments where there is little to be interacted with, are like walking through a mall were all the stores are closed. Game designers, like store or mall designers, need to give the consumer more than just an attractive space to move around.

This notion suggests an additional need for something that invites a more considered imagination by capturing the player's spatial gaze. Like the shopper, specific objects or commodities may serve this role. In a game these are occasionally gazed on special items PDAs, weapons, power-ups, armour, health icons, and puzzles taken to the extreme in games like *Dead Rising*, where almost anything in the mall may be used to eliminate zombies and where much of the fun is "shopping" for lethal weapons. Each new item may arrest attention and ask a player to consider its benefits. If collected, some may become markers of the experience—souvenirs of the trip into another world and "physical" evidence of accomplishment and skill. Fielder's (2001) review of *Halo* again illustrates the desire for such consumer-like choice in a game but with more exotic goods: "There are also many choices available to you in the parts of the game where vehicles appear. At some points you even have the opportunity to pick from multiple vehicles, such as the Warthog jeep, the Ghost hovercraft, the Scorpion tank, or the Banshee attack craft."

In the mall shoppers may seek the refuge of a café, from where they may gaze at other shoppers "safely." Without such a mechanism in games, a player may easily become fatigued and reduced to a mere "gawper," lost without the narrative. Too much temporal glancing in a videogame and sooner rather than later the pointlessness of the activity presents itself. There may be several in-game mechanisms to overcome this. Firstly, the between-level cut scene presents an opportunity for reflection and a change to imagine a new goal, for example, Accardo's (2004) review includes: "Occasional cut scenes (rendered within the game's engine) help round out the story, and are presented at a perfect pace. When all is said and done, it's still a pretty basic sci-fi story, but in *Doom 3*, presentation is everything." The cut scene allows the player to "sit back" and simply gaze. There may also be times during a game where the player is still in control but invited to take in a spatial gaze without fear of enemy engagement. In these circumstances, dramatic, even tourist-like scenery is often employed, as Fielder (2001) notes in his review of *Halo*: "*Halo*'s a stunning-looking game, full of huge environments that are packed with eye candy." Gameplay in *Halo* ensures that a player is given a chance to take in the spectacle of a level before the action starts, such that they may understand what they are aiming for. Another technique used in *Halo* to produce a café-like spatial gaze is the sniper rifle. With this weapon, a player may observe from a safe distance without the risk of being seen and may therefore gaze on the enemy at length before engaging them.

All this means that players come to crave new games for new things to see. As King (2002) points out, new spectacle is a key aspect of the attraction of games with each new game required to offer something new (a new vista, or at the very least new detail or effects). However, new games also offer new objectives to meet, just as Campbell (1987) sees in the consumer an endless desire for new commodities that may form the objective of desire and that drive recreational shopping behavior. So new weapons and artefacts such as armour or vehicles when collected in a game serve as consumer goodies—players expect to have lots when they finish a game—and new games must offer new artefacts as objects of potential desire.

The spaces for reflective, spatial looking are carefully managed and for the most part, just like the shopper (who is encouraged to shop and not just look), loitering is not an option in videogames where there is always the possibly of an enemy appearing and the knowledge that the computer that controls the monsters knows exactly what you are doing too. In *Doom 3* for example a player soon learns that 'inappropriate' inaction may trigger a monster attack. Avoiding street loitering because of the panoptic gaze of security forces or shop staff is akin to avoiding loitering in a game to avoid the imagined gaze of the computer controlled foes. As in the modern city, there is little escape from disciplinary gazes in a game. As King (2002:57) puts it: "Too much idle enjoyment of spectacular environments can be bad for the health of the avatar who is liable to be shot, eaten or to face some other unpleasant fate in many games if attention is directed solely to the quality of surroundings." Of course a game must also drive a player to finish in order that they should buy the next game.

These excerpts from consumer and scholarly reviews don't just illustrate the scopic regimes I have articulated, but also highlight that players want to know about these aspects of a game before investing time and money. They represent the ways in which we think about games as pleasurable in ways similar to recreational shopping. FPSs are designed to take the player out of the ordinary: to a future, a past, or another world. They are inherently imaginative but never entirely new—not even in terms of the game worlds they create. As Kasvin (2004) highlights in his review of *Doom 3*, part of the pleasure for players of the original game will be in seeing familiar foes recreated in higher resolution. The same is true of *Halo 3*—a "return" to Master Chief's world, but this time with the enhanced graphics of the Xbox 360 and new spectacle. For example Goldstein's (2007) review states: "The levels in *Halo 3* lend to spectacular pacing that weaves from close-quarters, intense battles with Chief and a few soldiers, to more epic arenas." Throughout Goldsteien's review references are made to what is "new," "better," and improved over the previous games. This is a familiar narrative for the consumer and one that supports the scopic regimes I have discussed. So when we play a game we tend to know it already, but better graphics, new weapons, and new scenery mean that the ordinary or familiar become something worth seeing because they are seen anew, just as when we enter a mall that we have never previously visited our sense is of somewhere we know but that also promises novelty. Like shopping in its ideal form, games are both reassuringly familiar and yet hold a promise of novelty, surprise, and thrill. In contrast we might consider that a "truly" novel game—one that did not exploit familiar ways of seeing—may be confusing and inaccessible to the majority.

A CRITIQUE OF VIDEOGAMES AS VIRTUAL FLÂNERIE

In this final section I want to consider some broader implications of the popularity of virtual environments that seem to reproduce consumer ways of seeing. The construction of temporal, spatial, and panoptic gazes may be seen as an art of game design just as it has become an art in the design of retail environments. The spaces and the objects games contain must invite exploration, offering novelty and visual stimulus; must contain mechanisms that courage reflection on and desire for specific outcomes; and must also discourage loitering in one place so that the game is ultimately consumed. Game designers and retail planners may usefully learn from teach other here, and we may note the development of retail play spaces as one trajectory of the experience economy. What we see then is the potential for individuals to spend more of their leisure time in more spectacular manufactured spaces both in home and on the screen, and in shopping centers, which produce similar experiences based on the gaze and on the consumer-imagination (one that desires to posses novel objects). Videogames may be seen as technologically enhanced developments of an older set of practices and as alternative solutions for "jaded" individuals who desire to be removed from the mundane and the ordinary.

However, with this technological trend, there is a persistent move to commodification where any cultivated, pleasurable experience is captured by and subject to a market. So Urry (2002) highlights that tourist gazes are now constructed by professionals and through a market and media system become "authorized." Kline, Dyer-Witheford, and De Peuter (2003) similarly see videogames as part of a market system that must constantly stimulate the consumer imagination in new ways. In such a market system, resistance may easily be exploited to reinvigorate market offerings (e.g., see Fiske, 1989). For example, Romero's attempt to "reveal" the pointlessness of consumption as a way of life ended up re-enchanting the mall and formed the basis of various videogames and film re-makes, therefore feeding a consumer imagination it tries to critique. What we see then is that attempts to escape the work-to-consume routine of our consumer society—for example, the dull and repetitive routine at work and now even the predictability of much consumption—through the use of tourism, experiential shopping, or new videogames fails because the escapes are all within the very system that caused the trouble (see Firat and Dholakia, 1998). They encourage the same ways of seeing and subsequent experiences that ensure the maintenance of consumer lifestyles.

This may cause problems for any attempt to celebrate games as a form of consumption that re-enchants life. Social realities are hidden by "a dream world of mass culture that hides the failure of political progress in the image of progress as material abundance" (Miller, 1997: 34) or in this case the image of progress as endlessly more spectacular videogames that provide for consumers a sense in which "things are getting better." Videogames are experienced as "improvements"; they suggest technological progress through consumption, but in doing so they hide aspects of society that are not so easily seen as "getting better." Far from presenting us with a violence-fueled cultural crisis, games may actually serve a conservative function, just as Benjamin argued that by presenting the stimulus for an imagined future the arcades were an important political tool of the present.

From these perspectives both shopping and videogames suffer from not having the productive purpose of the work, but being a poor form of its opposite (artistic play) because of their commercial focus. For example, Best and Kellner (1999) argue that the concept of the spectacle has become normalized or expected and that interactive media (the Web in their case) provides just one more commercial stage for spectacle that individuals are socialized into preferring. Drawing from Debord, they highlight that the society of the spectacle is a commodity society. The point of consumer scopic regimes is that they represent uncritical ways of seeing the world. Novel spectacle is sought through newer games and consoles that are bought in the market, and this is assumed to be a naturally "good thing, and more than this *the* thing that an individual might strive for in their free time. Like Benjamin, Debord (1994) also saw the spectacle as a tool of pacification, depoliticization, and therefore control. The passive consumption of spectacle prevents the individual from actively producing one's own life in ways capable of challenging existing political structures. Instead the videogame players merely reproduce the consumption act in their activities.

A focus here is on the ability of the individual to create, beyond what a market offers. Creative praxis has been reduced to having a thing—the fetishism of commodities—and later for Debord (and for experiential marketing) the appearance of things. Debord's situationalist call that individuals create their own existential events is lost in the re-enactment of someone else's commercial spectacle. As Debord (1994: 30) puts it, "His own gestures are no longer his but those of another who represents them to him." So the player escapes from the frustrations and inequalities of the routines of work only through new routines of leisure consumption, designed, packaged, and handed to him or her in the form of the latest spectacular videogame.

However, this line of criticism seems to suggest a superficiality to both recreational shopping and videogame play as a form of consumption that hides some other mode of being that is more meaningful. It is worth thinking about this further. For example, for Miller (1997), the surface of shopping might be reality. Campbell (2005) has made a similar point about shopping as a meaningful experience of "who we are." He sees consumption as an opportunity for the development of skills that have meaning to the "craft consumer" who gains achievement through the creative act of consumption. We might see such creative and meaningful achievement in game-play, too, and if shopping "matters" to people because it has meaning to them (Miller, 1997), so might digital, playful experience. So is the "meaningless consumption" line of criticism just nostalgia for an imagined less commercial age, or an elitist call for more worthy activities?

The final claim that Best and Kellner (1999) make for the Web is that there is at least a potential balance between further alienation and an opportunity for transformation. This might also be claimed for videogames, yet most players are excluded even from participation in the creation of games, let alone access to political power that might challenge the structures of the global game industry. Featherstone (1998) has also questioned whether the commercialization of spaces (now including digital virtual spaces) leaves room for the original spirit of the flâneur as they become mere consumers in everything. Flâneur shoppers are distanced from their "real" lives and reduced to "mere consumers" or now to "mere videogame players" He asks that we might imagine that the contemporary city contains considerable diversity (more so than the Paris that Benjamin described) and that this might be a good thing. The result could be an extension of the material and imaginary resources, "for a new more complicated game of experiencing, reading and representation" (Featherstone, 1998: 912), where diversity results in an experience of the exotic. But he also compares such models of the city that actively represent shared values with a more recent model of "Babylon," "where diversity is such that individuals tolerate each other but do not interact" (Featherstone, 1998: 911), and such is the case with the alienated experience of crowds in modern malls, and in videogames where "interaction" might be restricted to a quick twitch kill. This highlights ethical and not just aesthetic issues. Individual, privatized pleasure of the new through videogame play might be compared with a need to engage with others, to build trust and consensus, and to take responsibility for actions. When leisure consumption moved to the commercial interior of the mall, it de-emphasized the experience of others and placed more emphasis on the commodity object as the source of consideration and pleasure. A broader trajectory seems to have been from wilderness, to street exterior, to mall interior, and finally to digital game interior in a commercialized home full of hi-tech audio-visual equipment. According to Featherstone, the mall resulted in more control of the individual. For example, only those with economic means are permitted to experience its well-scripted pleasures, and rowdy, dangerous behavior is not permitted. Control may extend further still when politicized action is reduced to in-home, in-game play. For example, the game State of Emergency makes a superficial spectacle out of anti-corporate demonstrations while being played on the latest console and widescreen TV and branded with the cool logos of big videogame business. The result is that far from examples of new producerly "theatres of consumption" where Firat and Dholakia (1998) hope consumers will find new freedoms and new identities, videogames may represent further low participation, passive, individualized, alienated consumption that reinforces consumption as the primary way of experiencing the world.

CONCLUSIONS

Some or even much videogame play may be seen as re-enchanted "shopping" and may be understood in terms of the construction of familiar scopic regimes: the disciplinary, panoptic gaze of the machine; the flâneur's glance as a player moves through virtual space; and a romantic gaze as the player takes in a cut scene, scenery, or considers which virtual artefacts to collect. As an enchanting and thrilling experience with a level of potential novelty and diversity that a mall may never achieve, they may be celebrated. But there is also room for criticism in such a development of consumer culture. Although there is no denying that videogames are pleasurable, the label "interactive" as a term that suggests a high level of control and involvement hides games as a largely passive consumption experience. Consumer players remain seduced by a fantastic and spectacular form of commercialized flânerie where the virtual is fetishized at the expense of actual social experience. I wonder whether an attempt to critique consumption through a game would be more successful than *Dawn of the Dead*? But then I remember that *The Sims* and *Grand Theft Auto* (both which may be seen as including criticisms of consumer lifestyles) are best selling franchises in a $20 billion industry.

REFERENCES

Accardo S. 2004. Doom 3. *Gamespy*, 6 August. Available at http://uk.pc.gamespy.com/pc/doom-3/536705p1.html [accessed on 8 November 2010].

Adams D. 2004. We Take Part in an Immaculately Presented Trip to Hell and Back. *IGN.com*, 5 August. Available at http://uk.pc.ign.com/articles/536/536387p1.html [accessed on 8 November 2010].

Anderson CA, Bushman BJ. 2001. Effects of Violent Video Games on Aggressive Behaviour, Aggressive Cognition, Aggressive Affect, Physiological Arousal, and Prosocial Behaviour: A Meta-Analytic Review of the Scientific Literature. *American Psychological Society* 12(5): 353–359.

Atkins B. 2006. What Are We Really Looking at?: The Future-Orientation of Video Game Play. *Games and Culture* 1(2): 127–140.

Best S, Kellner D. 1999. Debord and the Postmodern Turn: New Stages of the Spectacle. *Illuminations*. Available at http://www.uta.edu/huma/illuminations/kell17.htm [accessed on 12 October 2010].

Campbell C. 1987. *The Romantic Ethic and the Spirit of Modern Consumerism*. Blackwell: Oxford.

Campbell C. 2005. The Craft Consumer: Culture, Craft and Consumption in a Postmodern Society. *Journal of Consumer Culture* 5(1): 23–42.

Debord G. 1994[1967]. *The Society of the Spectacle.* Zone Books: New York.

Douglas M. 1997. In Defence of Shopping, in *The Shopping Experience*, P. Falk and C. Campbell (eds.). Sage: London; 15–30.

Falk P. 1997. The Scopic Regimes of Shopping, in *The Shopping Experience*, P. Falk and C. Campbell (eds.). Sage: London; 177–185.

Falk P, Campbell. 1997 C. Introduction, in *The Shopping Experience*, P. Falk and C. Campbell (eds.). Sage: London; 1–14.

Featherstone, M. 1991. *Consumer Culture and Postmodernism.* Sage: London.

Featherstone M. 1998. The Flâneur, the City and Virtual Public Life. *Urban Studies* 35(2): 909–925.

Fielder J. 2001. Halo Review. *Gamespot.* Available at http://uk.gamespot.com/xbox/action/halo/review.html [accessed on 8 November 2010].

Firat AF, Dholakia N. 1998. *Consuming People: From Political Economy to Theaters of Consumption.* Routledge: London.

Friedberg A. 1993. *Window Shopping: Cinema and the Postmodern.* University of California Press: Berkeley and Los Angeles.

Goldstein H. 2007. Halo 3 Review: The Fight Is Finished, Anyone Got a Cigarette? *IGN.com*, 23 September. Available at http://uk.xbox360.ign.com/articles/821/821911p5.html [accessed on 10 November 2010].

Gottdiener M. 2000. The Consumption of Space and Spaces of Consumption, in, *New Forms of Consumption*, M. Gottdiener (ed.). Rowman and Littlefield: Lanham, MD.

Grieb M. 2002. Run Lara Run, in *Screenplay: Cinema/Videogames/Interfaces*, G. King and T. Krzywinska (eds.). Wallflower: London.

Harper S. 2002. Zombies, Malls, and the Consumerism Debate: George Romero's Dawn of the Dead. *Americana: The Journal of American Popular Culture* 1(2). Available at http://www.americanpopularculture.com/journal/articles/fall_2002/harper.htm [accessed on 18 October 2010].

Huizinga J. 1938. *Homo Ludens.* The Beacon Press: Boston, MA.

Kasavin G. 2004. Doom 3. *Gamespot*, 4 August. Available at http://uk.gamespot.com/pc/action/doom3/review.html [accessed on 10 November 2010].

King G. 2002. Die Hard/Try Harder: Narrative, Spectacle and Beyond, from Hollywood to Videogame, in *Screenplay: Cinema/Videogames/Interfaces*, G. King and T. Krzywinska (eds.). Wallflower, London; 50–65.

King G, Krzywinska T (eds.). 2002. Screenplay: Cinema/Videogames/Interfaces, in *Screenplay: Cinema/Videogames/Interfaces*. Wallflower: London.

Kline S, Dyer-Witheford, N, and De Peuter G. 2003. *Digital Play: The Interaction of Technology, Culture, and Marketing.* McGill-Queen's University Press: Canada.

Lehtonen T-K, Maenpaa P. 1997. Shopping in the East Centre Mall, in *The Shopping Experience*, P. Falk and C. Campbell (eds.). Sage: London; 136–165.

Loudermilk A. 2003. Eating "Dawn" in the Dark: Zombie Desire and Commodified Identity in George A. Romero's "Dawn of the Dead." *Journal of Consumer Culture* 3(1): 83–108.

Miller D. 1997. Could Shopping Ever Really Matter?, in *The Shopping Experience*, P. Falk and C. Campbell (eds.). Sage: London.

Pine J. Gilmore J. 1999. *The Experience Economy.* Harvard Business School Press: Boston, MA.

Romero G. dir. 1978. *Dawn of the Dead. Extended version.* The MKR Group. DVD. Anchor Bay Entertainment, 2004.

Schwartz B. 2004. *The Paradox of Choice: Why Less Is More.* HarperCollins: New York.

Scitovsky T. 1976. *The Joyless Economy.* Oxford University Press: New York.

Sherry JF Jr, Kozinets RV, Storm D, Duhachek A, Nuttavuthisit K, and DeBerry-Spence B. 2001. Being in the Zone: Staging Retail Theater at ESPN Zone Chicago. *Journal of Contemporary Ethnography* 30(4): 465–510.

Shields R. 2003. *Visualicity—On Urban Visibility and Invisibility.* Available at http://www.carleton.ca/~rshields/index.htm [accessed on 18 October 2010].

Simms A, Kjell P, and Potts R. 2005. *Clone Town Britain: The Survey Results on the Bland State of the Nation.* New Economics Foundation: London.

Simon B. 2006. Beyond Cyberspatial Flâneur ie: On the Analytic Potential of Living With Digital Games. *Games and Culture* 1(2): 62–67.

Urry J. 1992. The Tourist Gaze "Revisited." *The American Behavioural Scientist* 36(2): 172–186.

Urry J. 1995. *Consuming Places.* Routledge: London.

Urry J. 2002. *The Tourist Gaze* (2nd ed.). Sage: London.

Wright E. 2005. The Church of George. *The Virginia Quarterly Review*, Winter. Available at http://www.vronline.org/viewmedia.php/prmMID/9011 [accessed on 18 October 2010].

6   Transforming Digital Virtual Goods into Meaningful Possessions

Janice Denegri-Knott, Rebecca Watkins, and Joseph Wood

INTRODUCTION

Consumer appetite for digital virtual goods is voracious. Sales of e-books on *Amazon* are now greater than paperback and hardback books combined (New York Times, 2011), music is preferably consumed 'light' in a compressed Mp3 format, and videogame commodities are slavishly customized and gifted to friends and avatars alike (Couldry, 2008; Denegri-Knott and Molesworth, 2010; Gillespie, 2007; Hand, 2008, Lehdonvirta, Wilska, and Johnson, 2009; Magaudda, 2010; Siddiqui and Turley, 2006). Even our most intimate photograph collections are now scattered across clouds, with only 11 percent of consumers choosing to print their digital photos (Mintel, 2009). The impressive rate of adoption of smart phones extends digitized consumables such as apps even further, with all sorts of digitized content now readily available to be accessed and stored. In the UK alone, demand for smart phones has increased by 80 percent year on year (Mediatel, 2010), and the global market for Apple and Android applications is today worth £1.63 billion and expected to grow to £4.8 billion in the next three years (HIS Screen Digest, 2011).

At a theoretical level, our eager consumption of digital virtual goods tests what we have come to understand as the strategies through which we stamp our ownership on goods. Existing analyses are appropriately anchored on the materiality of things and the physical processes that are required to singularize them. We know how we transform ordinary, homogenous commodities into meaningful possessions through a range of ritualized and habitual practices (e.g., how we ceremoniously use, clean, customize, repair, collect, display, and memorialize special possessions in a bid to protect their precious symbolic meanings). Such efforts are energized by our need to make visible boundaries between what is ordinary and what is sacred and impose order to the ecology of goods found in our homes (Belk, Wallendorf, and Sherry, 1989; Douglas, 1966, 2001; Douglas and Isherwood, 1979; McCracken, 1986).

Our efforts to singularize and de-commodify seem to be challenged by the vaporous nature of digital virtual goods (Kirk and Banks, 2008, Kirk and Sellen, 2008; 2010). They deny owners the simple markings that would have magically moved an object from a commodity state to that of a cherished possession. For example, the kind of contamination that is produced more forcefully when items are worn close to our bodies or are associated with sacred events or places (Belk et al., 1989; McCracken, 1986; Richins, 1994) is difficult to achieve. This, too, seems to rob them, according to Siddiqui and Turley (2006), of the emotional quality that characterizes a physically tangible equivalent. However, research on digital heirlooms has also hinted at the emotionally charged nature of attachments formed with desktop backgrounds, online spaces, and other digital instantiations, like digital music collections that remind us of loved ones (Kirk and Banks, 2008; Kirk and Sellen, 2008; 2010). For example, the most recent and comprehensive study into archival practices in the home carried out by Kirk and Sellen (2010) concluded that digital objects served similar functions to those dispensed by material possessions—they extend our sense of self, they speak of our friends and family, they connect us to our past, and they fulfill our sense of duty. Although research to date is limited, findings so far if anything highlight the inherent ambiguity of digital virtual goods, meaningful sometimes, too transiently owned at others.

These challenges prompt us to ask: Can digital virtual goods be possessed and made meaningful by their owners? If so, what are the strategies through which appropriation takes place? Whereas existing research has tended to focus solely on how archived digital content may aid memory (Bell and Gemmel, 2009; Rodden and Wood, 2003) or document the various practices involved in storing and preserving all sorts of digital content (Kirk and Sellen, 2010), here we are more interested in unpacking the processes through which consumers transform homogenous digital goods into cherished possessions. It seems opportune to account for, as Belk, Wallendorf, and Sherry (1989) did in their work on the sacralization of everyday goods, the ways in which certain goods attain a preferential stature within owned possessions. To begin with, we frame our exploratory work within a broader understanding of digital virtual consumption (DVC) as a space that combines aspects of both the ideally real and the actually real and supports new experiences and practices not always possible through material consumption (Denegri-Knott and Molesworth, 2010). Notably, DVC expands what may be actually owned, beyond the mundane, to include a plethora of whimsical and fantasy items like spaceships or magic swords that are bought or gained through game play.

In this chapter we share preliminary findings of an ongoing project aiming to understand how consumers experience ownership of digital virtual goods. To begin with, we position our work within the context of consumer culture research by way of offering a synopsis of literature that may help us understand how digital virtual goods are made into meaningful possessions. We then describe the nature of the research undertaken. Based on the insights gleaned from our conversations with 26 participants living in

England and Wales, we argue that digital virtual goods are transformed through the process of cultivating digital virtual energies in manipulating, archiving, reproducing, and materializing digital virtual possessions.

Transforming Goods into Meaningful Possessions

Not all goods are personally meaningful possessions. There are categorical differences between commodities and cherished possessions. Commodities are defined by their relation to monetary exchange value, whereas possessions are goods that in essence have been removed from a commodity sphere and incorporated, subjectified (Miller, 1987), or singularized (Kopytoff, 1986) by people according to personal meanings, relationships, or rituals. What Miller (1987: 215) suggests transforms the object is not simply the process of taking possession of it, but its incorporation into a total stylistic array, such as a ritual gift or memorabilia. He refers to this process as the recontextualization of the commodity in such a way that goods are transmuted into "potentially inalienable culture" (Miller, 1987: 215). Meaningful or cherished possessions are a particular type of possession, which are classified as such because over time their owners have invested time, resources, and attention into cultivating their use or maintaining their special stature through various curatorial practices—cleaning, storing, grooming, and displaying (Belk et al., 1989; Csikszentmihalyi and Rochberg-Halton 1981; Fournier, 1998; McCracken 1986; Richins, 1994).

This drive to singularize is best explained by the need to attain some kind of cognitive order that equips individuals with the necessary meaning frameworks to differentiate what is valuable and what is not (Appadurai, 1986; Douglas, 2001; Kopytoff, 1986). So here culture works by providing a "shared cognitive order" (Appadurai 1986: 70) through which what is inherently singular can be portioned through discrimination and classification and areas of similarity or homogeneity differentiated from the overall heterogeneity. Put simply, cultural narratives or meaning frameworks are in place to provide ways of differentiating the homogenous commodity from the singular personal possession. Doing this requires a degree of self-investment. Consumers have to make the homogenous commodity their own by charging it with personal significance and incorporating it into their everyday lives. In doing so, consumers invest tremendous amounts of psychic resources, and it is such investment that imbues objects with all sorts of meanings, deepening the degree of incorporation. Csikszentmihalyi and Rochberg-Halton (1981) referred to these labor intensive processes as cultivation. In their study of cherished possessions found in the Chicago homes of 82 families, they found it wasn't anything inherent in the objects themselves that made them cherished but rather the effort invested in harnessing such objects in order to achieve a given goal. As desired intentions are realized, like controlling a ball proficiently or doing tricks with a bike, this provides feedback that produces a moment of reflection, where we realize that we are good at controlling a particular object.

It follows that when psychic resources are invested in goods they take on a personal significance of their own because they have been cultivated and have absorbed part of the subject's ability to channel their attention and pursue other objectives. The fact that there are infinite objects to cultivate but finite psychic resources to do so intimates that there is a reflective prowess required to invest some objects and not others. Not only do objects absorb our own psychic resources, but they substantiate others' too. So a jumper lovingly knitted by a mother and gifted to a son, captures attention invested, and this charges the item with emotional values. Hence, there is an inherent reflective requirement in choosing what one spends time on, and self-awareness in realizing that a given object's latent intentionality has been actualized through its use or that they capture a loved one's psychic energies.

More recently, Colin Campbell (2005) has invited us to think about crafting as a means through which consumers engage in a creative, productive activity re-assembling commodities in ways that suit idiosyncratic preferences and tastes. So here appropriation not only involves 'small' transformations produced by grooming rituals or removing price tags, but much more involved processes that require the skilful process of constructing recognisable assemblages that are more than the sum of their parts (e.g., cooking, creating outfits and entire wardrobes of clothing, woodworking, and DIY).

In summary, personal significance derives from the reflective potential that goods may incite in us as means of self-discovery over time, but also as means of capturing traces of others and our relationships with them.

METHODS

In-depth interviews with 26 owners of digital virtual goods were carried out between September 2010 and February 2011 in England and Wales. Our sample was made up of ten females and sixteen males between the ages of 20 and 54 years who reported having digital virtual goods either stored in their computer, external memory drives, videogame consoles, or smart phones. The sample was small as the aim was not to produce generalizable theory or a statistically representative account of digital virtual ownership and possession, but rather variation in experiences (Creswell, 2007; McCracken, 1988; Thompson, Locander, and Pollio, 1989, 1990).

The interviews adopted a phenomenological perspective that privileged the lived experiences of our participants and situated their accounts in the larger socio-cultural context in which they occurred so that we could come to understand the phenomenon of ownership and possession from the individual's point of view (Burawoy, 1991; Creswell, 2007; Strauss and Corbin,

1998; Thompson et al., 1989, 1990). Most of the interviews were held at participants' homes. Additional interviews took place in coffee shops and on a university campus. On average interviews lasted approximately one and a half hours, with individual interviews ranging from one to two hours in length.

To begin with, grand tour questions (McCracken, 1988) such as, "Can you tell me a bit about yourself?" and "How you spend your free time?" were asked to obtain biographical annotations on participants' life worlds and immediate context. From there, a general conversation ensued on their past and present engagement with digital virtual goods. The conversation was continued until a saturation point was reached where participants had *exhausted* the stock of stories they remembered or were willing to share with us (Cresswell, 2007; Thompson et al., 1989).

In total, approximately 30 hours of data were recorded. Verbatim transcripts and detailed notes of interviews were made and read carefully and in an iterative fashion. Data interpretation took place hermeneutically, involving a part-to-whole reading, made up of individual interpretation of interviews at an ideographic level and cross-case analysis. From this exercise thematic descriptions of experience were derived (Thompson et al., 1989, 1990). Syntheses then followed to identify common structures or the global themes in the experience, which were then built on for theoretical elaboration.

FINDINGS

In this section, we discuss themes emerging from our interviews that deal with the experience of owning digital virtual goods, in particular the ways in which participants practiced ownership of their meaningful possessions. To begin with, we identify a particular type of psychic energy investment, a form of digital virtual cultivation that accounts for a whole range of technologically mediated practices through which digital virtual goods are appropriated and made meaningful over time. Building on Csikszentmihalyi and Rochberg-Halton's (1981) notion of cultivation, we see digital virtual cultivation as a particular type of psychic investment that is solely focused on the handling of technological artefacts needed to animate objects and characters in the digital virtual and in their preservation.

Where special meanings associated with cherished possessions are wired into the materiality of a good itself (Wallendorf and Arnould, 1988), which make it inalienable (Miller, 1987) and only amenable to a symbolic transfer of meaning via ritualistic behaviors (Belk et al., 1989; Denegri-Knott and Molesworth, 2009; Lastovicka and Fernandez, 2005; McCracken, 1986), with digital virtual goods, the meaning itself can be literally transferred onto other devices. This we found was a key form of material and symbolic work undertaken to attain a kind of "closure" regarding what was deemed personally meaningful.

Digital virtual goods are perceived as highly ambiguous things; this we see as resulting from their lack of visibility and corporeality. The lack of corporeality means that they are perceived as being fragile and ephemeral but at the same time more likely to be preserved, via copying and storing. It follows that transforming digital virtual goods into meaningful possessions is more obviously centered on the purposeful contemplation of what has been invested in the process of adapting, changing, storing, and re-materializing them. This ambiguity means that the preservation of digital virtual goods themselves, the copying and storing, or its re-materializing become a form of curatorial practice through which meaning is cultivated. We now discuss our themes in more detail.

Domesticating as Possession

The transformation of digital virtual goods starts via an iterative process or trials through which owners understand the object's limits and possibilities, as well as their own. For the majority of participants, this process tended to be about developing a sufficient level of know-how (Lehtonen, 2003; Reckwitz, 2002) in acquiring digital virtual goods or in the handling of handsets, keyboards, controllers, and software required to access, use, and store them. For example, Joe, a 23-year-old design engineer working for a hydro-electricity firm, described his actions when he first got his latest phone—an HTC Desire. Joe recalled that he had learned to use the phone quickly. He explained that when he bought the phone, he tried to "explore everything within an hour" of getting the phone. Joe described this as an exciting experience, as it was his first smart phone—this excitement lasted for days as Joe became more accustomed to the phone and "played" around with his favorite features. Joe's use of the term "explore" portrays a perception of his new phone as an undiscovered space that he was free to roam and make his own.

Similarly, when playing videogames, our participants often accounted for how both emotional and psychological energies had been invested in harnessing the skills necessary to mark distinctions and attachment among goods they amassed in their videogame play. Rhiannon, a 20-year-old forensics student from Reading who enjoyed playing *The Sims*, expressed a certain detachment to her pre-created characters, explaining that it is only upsetting to lose a game when you play with a character you have invested effort in creating.

Other participants cherished less object-like things like scorecards. Score-cards gained totem-like qualities for our participants. Daniel, a 21-year-old student and veteran videogame player, passionately retold his videogame experience in terms of achievement and goal reaching. He had spent years fostering his skills in cracking games like Mass Effect, Earth Defence Force 2017, *The Sims*, and Crackdown. For him, achievement was memorialized within the game itself, through the graphic representation that he had reached a particular level, and to him these records needed to be preserved. He told us the following incident involving his iPhone:

> I recently had to get my phone sent away to a repair center and lost all my angry birds process, progress even. And, that's kind of a bummer, I haven't opened it since, because I can't bear to look at the screen that says no levels unlocked, after I've done them all. And, I guess it's more about investment, if I feel like I've invested in something then, it matters, if I haven't then it doesn't.

In this narrative, the digital virtual, or the sheer possession of a digital virtual possession, is sacralized as a trophy of achievement, as Daniel told us later on: "It mattered because it just seemed like [he] couldn't believe [he] had wasted all those hours and nothing to show for it." He recalled feeling like he had wasted time, having invested "a lot of time into the game, at various points over a period of months, having nothing to show for it."

Crafting as Possession

In transforming digital virtual goods into meaningful possessions, often participants expressed a desire to "make it theirs" through skilled manipulation of available technological resources. The behavior that participants described to claim ownership of digital virtual goods exhibits clear parallels with possession rituals described by McCracken (1986) and Belk et al's (1989) discussion of sacrilization through ritual. Many participants achieved this by "putting their own stamp" on digital virtual goods, altering them in some way to make them highly personal and "unique." One example is the case of Anne, a 47-year-old housewife from Cardiff. Originally buying *The Sims* for her daughters, Anne started playing the game herself and her same Sim family for over a year, using a cheat to prevent her Sims from aging. Within the game, Anne had created a replication of her "real" family to which she feels very attached. Whereas in "real life" Anne is a housewife, her Sim version of herself is the breadwinner while her Sim husband stays at home to look after the house and children. Anne recounts her experience of "moving house" within *The Sims* and her desire to make the new house "hers."

> I was in the politics career, pretty near the top, and my Sim was going to work in a suit. I remember thinking, "She looks so out of place in that suit in our tiny house." So I moved the family into this mansion. . . . Don't get me wrong, it was lovely. The attention to detail was amazing! But it just felt like someone else had made it . . . like I was living in someone else's house. It's like when I moved into my first flat, in the real world mind, and there were marks on the door where they [the previous owners] had marked their children's heights in biro. As long as those marks were there it just felt like it wasn't my house, so I painted

over them. So, on *The Sims* I thought, right, I need to make it the way I like it. All wooden floors and nice pale walls, modern furniture, got rid of those horrible candelabras. My Sim did some paintings and I hung them on the wall. When I finished it was like . . . it really felt like it was my house. I've made it my own.

It was clear from the interview that Anne was strongly attached to this house, and that through this act of "making it her own," Anne developed a sense of ownership over the house. Upon purchasing a new house within *The Sims*, Anne instantly modified it to suit her own tastes and preferences, making the house "hers." Through this process, the house was de-commodified, becoming not merely a purchased, mass-produced commodity but a possession with personal significance.

James, a professional videogame journalist we spoke to, provides an illustrative example of this type of digital virtual cultivation as crafting. James had played an impressive number of games, many of which he had forgotten the detail of. Yet, there were a handful of games he had programmed himself and "he would go mental if he lost." He enthusiastically told us about a particular collection of games that he created with his girlfriend on a holiday a few years ago. They had decided that rather than buying "tat souvenirs and postcards," they were going to chronicle the holiday through games they would create. He described the process as follows:

It was just about like, 'cause we went to the Peggy Guggenheim collection which is sort of an impressionist art collection and we just decided to make a game where this impressionist art attacks the player, and you've gotta like break them by prodding them with the stylus, and it took us literally the whole 4 hours to put this game together and I think again it's the time invested. It's just a memory of us putting our creativity together and the time we put in and the place we were at, you know, all of those things can tie into it. But I think that's a very unique type of virtual possession. 'Cause the other kind of possession I guess is where you buy something off someone else, like *World of Warcraft* or whatever, where you'd buy like a sword or whatever I guess that was really powerful that somebody happened to have found or made. So then, you know, I personally wouldn't feel as close to something someone else had made.

This sense of "feeling not too close to something some else had made" is so because the level of perceived self-involvement is what produces appropriation itself. As a form of crafting our participants find themselves applying skill, knowledge, judgment, and passion in producing creations that "consist of several items that are themselves mass-produced retail commodities" (Campbell 2005: 27). Subject to level of skill, we found participants purposefully creating their own digital virtual possessions, engaging in what

Campbell (2005) has termed craft consumption. It follows that the more involved the process of crafting was, the more meaningful and cherished the possession. Differently put, levels of attachment escalated with the perceived sense of one's investment in not only adapting content but engaging in more complex and demanding processes of craft consumption. We can extend that to mean that higher degrees of crafting require higher levels of skill, passion, and knowledge, and this, via a process of digital virtual cultivation, creates moments of self-awareness and reflection.

Often it was the case that digital virtual goods that we knew had been transformed or changed by a loved one by proxi became meaningful too. Dafydd is a 29-year-old minibus driver from Cardiff and lives with his girlfriend, Rachel. He plays Xbox360 games such as *Call of Duty, Fifa*, and *Forza* most days to relax and unwind after a busy day. Dafydd describes letting Rachel create a car on his *Forza* racing game. Dafydd describes how he became strongly attached to a virtual car within racing game *Forza*.

> That's a car Rachel's made, a purple Chevrolet and she's put like flowers, grass, butterflies, she's even written her name on it, look. It's weird, it's on my Xbox but it feels kind of like it's hers as well because she sat down and made it with me. We sat down and I customized it to make it as fast as it can be and she made it look pretty. When I see it, it does make smile 'cause it reminds me of her. I think I'd be most upset to lose that one, because I can't replace it. I could try, but I would know that it was me that made it so I wouldn't be the same. It wouldn't be ours it would be mine, and it wouldn't have, like, all the memories. That's what would upset me.

It became clear that this virtual car was important to Dafydd because he associated it with Rachel and with memories of time spent customizing the car together. Other participants also described possessions that were strongly associated with other people as "irreplaceable"; they felt that although these possessions could be replaced, they would not have the same history and associations. These experiences seem to indicate that digital virtual goods are transformed into meaningful possessions because they are extensions of the creator's self (Belk, 1988) who has saturated the digital virtual with meaning by investing his or her own psychic energy.

Possession as Archiving

Instead of grooming rituals, our participants spoke about the need to organize owned virtual possessions, in part, because limits to excessive accumulation were sought or because a manageable collection was sought. Belk, Wallendorf, Sherry, and Holbrook (1991) write that collecting legitimises acquisitiveness. However, given the nature of the digital virtual, what we see here is legitimized acquisitiveness facilitating collection. To elaborate, whereas

McCracken (1986) associates collection with scarcity and rarity, collection as digital virtual cultivation is prompted by abundance. Given the speed with which stuff can be accumulated, an associated practice through which digital virtual goods were cultivated resided in the investment necessary to organize owned goods. That is, personal significance is continually negotiated through boundary defining frameworks of meaning where an internal hierarchy of valuation can be used to determine what is meaningful. For example, Sam, a 22-year-old student and iPhone4 owner, recalled how he immediately and indiscriminately "filled up [his smart phone]" and boasted with glee the "hundreds" of apps he had downloaded. The actions that Sam continued to depict resemble what might best be described as stockpiling. He described the relationship between his phone and his computer, explaining how he moved digital virtual artefacts from his phone to various other spaces, such as his Dropbox app, *Facebook*, and his MacBook (the "hub"). Sam's movement and storage of things in the digital virtual seemed sporadic, and the things moved were seldom talked about in the context of their location away from the phone. It appeared that once fleetingly appropriated digital virtual artefacts became neglected—photos uploaded to a social network provide a stellar example of this phenomenon. Here, the meaning cultivated in a stockpile appears ambiguous, yet it was clear that meaning existed as participants exhibited motivation to stockpile and an intention to continue. Belk et al. (1989) describe a similar behavior, namely, hoarding, whereby things are accumulated selectively with some form of future utilitarian value envisioned for the things hoarded. Our account of stockpiling differs from hoarding inasmuch as consumers are not so much selective or under the impression that there is a future utilitarian value for their stockpile—the stockpile merely presents itself as a default in digital virtual cultivation. There is merit to an argument suggesting that the nature of this stockpiling compromises one's ability to attach meaning to things due to a lack of direction for psychic energy.

However, not all participants described a tendency to stockpile. Others were more careful and selective in their accumulation. This behavior might be best described as curatory consumption. Some participants described experiences of taking on the role of curator. For example, Jon described being selective and organised with the apps that he downloaded and kept:

> I use the multi-tasking just for that purpose—just to keep applications grouped together. So, for instance, I've got a multi-task zone called travel, and if I go into travel there's a compass, maps, London tube, erm, SatNav, Trainline, what's going on on the weather, Every Trail—which is a cycling application, so you can plot routes and it will tell you how many miles you've covered and people can share their routes—and then the National Trust app.

Here, we see Jon demonstrate discernment and skill as a curator of his applications. Jon also explained that he tended only to keep applications he used (i.e., if psychic energy was not being invested in an application, the app was deemed void of meaning and was disposed of accordingly). When digital virtual goods had been earned in videogame play, collections were experienced as having an internal coherence and additional significance for their owners. Daffyd, for instance, retells with pride how he earned the final Pokémon, his excitement in completing the game before his two brothers and his friends, and showing off his collection.

Re-Materializing and Reproducing as Possession

In making sense of their digital virtual possessions, our participants often found themselves referring to the materiality of other treasured possessions and the intangibility of memories they were so keen to preserve. This virtual–material binary meant, on the one side, that digital virtual goods were valued because they provided a more tangible and permanent memory for past events located in the virtual (the mind), but problematized as needing themselves a more material substantiation, somewhere in the materially real (Denegri-Knott and Molesworth, 2010). In any case, we can see re-materializing practices as vehicles through which our participants sought to substantiate memories located in the virtual, first onto the digital virtual and from there to the materially real (print outs, saved screen shots, saved games in memory drives).

Often during our interviews, our participants found themselves framing their attachments to their avatars and digital virtual goods on the basis that they reminded them of time spent with others, achieving goals individually or collectively. Catrin, when talking about one of her WoW characters, told us:

> She's my baby. I made her back in March 2007, a couple of months after I started playing WoW. She was my first level 70, back in the day, and for a very long time she was my only high level character. . . . She's special. I'd be devastated if I ever lost her. It is, kind of . . . she has a lot of memories, you know? There are a lot of memories in the character. Sort of, good times, relationships, friendships, and things that I've done with her. And I guess it is partly because she was my little gay character. I came out online through Bikido before I came out in real life, so I'll always remember that . . . I have a really close friend who also plays a troll priest, and one night we both got exceptionally drunk and we were both dressed up as pirates. That's probably my most fond memory, I've got all the screen shots of it and everything . . . I do worry about accidentally vending Bikido. Sometimes I worry that if I split up with Jodie she might hack her *and* delete her. . . . It is stupid because I know I could go and I could make another priest, I could make it look exactly the same and I could level it. But it just wouldn't feel like the same character. . . . It just wouldn't be her. . . . It's to do with the memories and the stuff that I've done with her.

Thus, in the four years since her creation, Bikido has become associated with memories of personal achievement (reaching level 70), personal experiences ("coming out" online), and times spent with others. As a result, Catrin worries more about losing Bikido than any other virtual possession within a videogame. She feels that this avatar is irreplaceable because she feels that the memories associated with the character would be lost. It follows that, although lacking material substance, Catrin and other participants felt that these digital virtual possessions were more tangible than the memories themselves and worried that by losing these possessions they may lose the memories attached to them.

In order to preserve these memories, our participants engaged in heroic efforts to reproduce their digital virtual possession through serial copying and seeking multiple storage points. In this sense, technologically mediated processes seemed to stand in for the more ritualistic and symbolic transfers of meaning documented in the preservation of sacred goods (Belk et al., 1989). For example, Taylor, a 22-year-old computing student at Bournemouth University, told us about the lengths he went to protect his cherished digital virtual possessions:

> If it was due to hacking I have the option to "roll back" my account, an option that was introduced in 2009 after a spate of hacking. I'm not worried about that though, because I have a . . . you know how with some banks they give you little tokens and they generate one-time codes? Well, I have something very similar for the game so that when I log in I have to have a one-time code to log in. So it's very difficult for anyone but me to get into my account. So fortunately I don't have to worry about that. I don't worry because it won't happen. I'm more likely to win the lottery.

Taylor had paid "real" money for this token to protect his virtual possessions, but felt it was worth this extra expense for the peace of mind it offered.

Other participants engaged in a literal transfer of meaningful possessions from a host device, considered inadequate, to other more reliable and accessible storage points. Jon, a 28-year-old IT technician who worked for the RNLI, described how he had upgraded from an iPhone2 to his current iPhone4. For Jon this involved saving the contents of his iPhone2 to his computer before connecting his iPhone4 and transferring all the contents to the new phone. Jon explained how, beyond a handful of slightly upgraded features, he wanted the new phone to be as similar to his old phone as possible—he even transferred the settings and interface from his old phone:

> Because it was just like some upgraded techy bits from the one that I already had, I was very familiar with it. . . . So a lot of the settings just so they were in the same place, 'cause after a while, psychologically, I was just going with the left of your thumb or the right of your thumb

for messaging or for phone—and it's just stuff like that, that you don't want to have to move stuff around to get it how you wanted again . . . it was seamless, it was nice.

Jon's account raises interesting questions about the possession or divestment rituals that people use to imbue or extract meaning (Lastovicka and Fernandez, 2005; McCracken, 1988). Jon did not recall any carefully planned routinized act (Douglas, 1966) when he discussed the change in phone—meaning transfer occurred, literally, at the touch of a button and was, as Jon put it, "seamless." These accounts clearly position the mobile phone as a vessel where meaning can be created but is easily transferable to other digital virtual goods and is therefore not bound to the original mobile phone.

Existing literature on the subject suggests that meaning and physical objects are to a reasonable extent bound together (McCracken, 1988). However, accounts provided by participants describe how meaning (data) can be electronically transferred from one digital good to another, allowing significant amounts of meaning independence from any given digital good. While freeing the meaning from a physical good, electronic processes introduce an element of risk—physical transfer may fail, and data may be lost or corrupted. This element of risk means that while meaning becomes independent it also becomes more vulnerable and potentially more reliant on the performance of a physical vessel. Digital virtual meaning may not be bound to a particular good, but it is still bound to materiality.

Conclusions

The overall aim of this chapter was to begin to make sense of the strategies through which consumers seek to transform digital virtual goods into more meaningful, personal possessions. Despite some concerns over consumers' ability to fully singularize digital virtual commodities because of their incorporeity or because they are wrapped up with intellectual property provisions (Harwood and Garry, 2010), our data suggests that emergent forms of appropriation are being undertaken. There is discrimination of the like covered in existing research, but it is enacted in different ways. Instead of ritualistic transfers of meaning, where special meaning is only transferred symbolically through processes of contamination, for instance, we have more practical, technologically mediated processes that allow for a literal removal and transfer of the meaning itself. It follows then that the meticulous processes involved in overcoming the challenges of owning digital virtual goods is an emergent and important way through which the category of meaningful digital virtual possession is arrived at. In order to make sense of this, we found it useful to build on Csikszentmihalyi and Rochberg-Halton's (1981) concept of cultivation adapting it to include a specific type of psychic energy invested in the handling of technological artefacts to animate and preserve objects and characters in the digital virtual. That is, what is deemed special or meaningful is so by virtue of how much time and energy was spent in securing and safekeeping an item; this also applied to digital virtual objects that were deemed special because they were either made or gifted by significant others.

This transformation is a fractious affair in part because digital virtual goods are experienced as highly ambiguous, never here or there, inviting posterity through endless reproduction and copying, but demanding a more material, secure instantiation. On the one side, they shift the virtual (memories in our mind) into the more palpable domain of the digital virtual but are still not actually real enough. Yet they themselves are taken as fragile things one shouldn't get attached to because there are inherently prone to get lost—accounts can be hacked, phones stolen, or computers broken.

DVC practices depend on a whole range of very embodied and materially mediated processes. Like Magaudda (2010; Chapter 8, this volume), who writes about digital music consumption practices, we find that DVC is always materially prefigured and mediated. Our participants' stories of the digital virtual were tangled up with very tangible, material artefacts, mobile phones, hard drives, cartridges, consoles, and disks. So rather than seeing a de-materialization of consumption because we are dealing with a digital virtual good, we find that what makes the digital virtual good special or meaningful is that it has been re-materialized.

In conclusion, the experience of ownership is fraught with worries over their fragility, the potential of losing them, the impossibility of gaining time invested back, and their ability to link them back to a particular golden past involving significant others. However, they are highly mobile and transferrable things, which prompts the development of a new vocabulary for appropriation practices, where consumers must find ways of preserving and to an extent re-materializing meaning.

REFERENCES

Appadurai A. 1986. *The Social Life of Things: Commodities in Cultural Perspective*. Cambridge University Press: Cambridge.

Belk RW. 1988. Possessions and the Extended Self. *The Journal of Consumer Research* 15(2): 139–168.

Belk RW, Wallendorf M, and Sherry JF. 1989. The Sacred and the Profane in Consumer Behaviour, Theodicy and Odyssey. *Journal of Consumer Research* 16(1): 1–38.

Belk RW, Wallendorf M, Sherry JF, and Holbrook MB. 1991. Collecting in a Consumer Culture, in *Highways and Buyways, Naturalists Research for the Consumer Behaviour Odyssey*, R. W. Belk (ed.). Association for Consumer Research: New York; 178–215.

Bell G, Gemmell J. 2009. *Total Recall, How the E-Memory Revolution Will Change Every-thing*. Dutton Books: New York.

Burawoy M. 1991. The Extended Case Method, in *Ethnography Unbound, Power and Resistance in the Modern Metropolis*, M. Burroway (ed.). University of California Press: Berkeley; 271–287.

Campbell C. 2004. I Shop Therefore I Know I Am, the Metaphysical Basis of Modern Consumerism, in *Elusive Consumption*, Karin M Ekström and Helene Brembeck (eds.). Berg Publishers: Oxford; 27–44.

Campbell C. 2005. The Craft Consumer, Culture, Craft and Consumption in a Postmodern Society. *Journal of Consumer Culture* 5(1): 23–42.

Couldry N. 2008. Mediatization or Mediation? Alternative Understandings of the Emergent Space of Digital Storytelling. *New Media & Society* 10(3): 373–391.

Creswell JW. 2007. *Qualitative Inquiry and Research Design, Choosing Among Five Approaches* (2nd ed.). Sage Publications: Thousand Oaks.

Csikszentmihalyi M, Rochberg-Halton, E. 1981. *The Meaning of Things, Domestic Symbols and the Self.* Cambridge University Press: Cambridge.

Denegri-Knott J, Molesworth M. 2009. "I'll Sell This and I'll Buy Them That": Ebay and the Management of Possessions as Stock. *Journal of Consumer Behaviour* 8(6): 305–315.

Denegri-Knott J, Molesworth M. 2010. Digital Virtual Consumption, Concepts and Practices. *Consumption, Markets & Culture* 13(2): 109–132.

Douglas M. 1966. *Purity and Danger.* Routledge Classics: London.

Douglas M. 2001. Why Do People Want Goods?, in *Consumption, Critical Concepts in the Social Sciences*, D. Miller (ed.). Routledge: London; 262–271.

Douglas M, Isherwood B. 1979. *The World of Goods.* Routledge: London.

Fournier S. 1998. Consumers and Their Brands, Developing Relationship Theory in Consumer Research. *Journal of Consumer Research* 24(4): 343–373.

Gillespie T. 2007. *Wired Shut, Copyright and the Shape of Digital Culture.* MIT Press: Cambridge.

Hand M. 2008. *Making Digital Cultures, Access, Interactivity, and Authenticity.* Ashgate: Aldershot.

Harwood T, Garry T. 2010. It's Mine! Participation and Ownership within Virtual Value Co-creation Environments. *Journal of Marketing Management* 26(3–4): 290–301.

HIS Screen Digest. 2011. *Android Market Summary*, 14 April 2001. Available at http://www.screendigest.com/intelligence/mobile/world/mob_intel_world_125/view.html [accessed on 14 September 2011].

Kirk D, Sellen A. 2008. On Human Remains, Excavating the Home Archive. *Microsoft Technical Report.* MSR-TR-2008-8.

Kirk D, Sellen A. 2010. On Human Remains, Values and Practice in the Home Archiving of Cherished Objects. *Transactions on Computer-Human Interaction* 17(3): 1–43.

Kirk D, Banks R. 2008. On the Design of Technology Heirlooms. In *Proceedings of the International Workshop on Social Interaction and Mundane Technologies* (SIMTech'08).

Kopytoff I. 1986. The Cultural Biography of Things, Commoditization as a Process, in *The Social Life of Things Commodities in a Cultural Perspective*, A. Appadurai (ed.). Cambridge University Press: Cambridge; 64–94.

Lastovicka JL, Fernandez KV. 2005. Paths to Disposition Divestment: The Movement of Meaningful Possessions to Strangers. *Journal of Consumer Research* 31: 813–895.

Lehdonvirta V, Wilska T-A, and Johnson M. 2009. Virtual Consumerism, Case Habbo Hotel. *Information, Communication & Society* 12(7): 1059–1079.

Lehtonen T. 2003. Domestication of New Technologies as a Set of Trials. *Journal of Consumer Culture* 3(3): 363–385.

Magaudda P. 2010. When Materiality "Bites Back": Digital Music Consumption Practices in the Age of Dematerialization. *Journal of Consumer Culture* 11(15): 15–36.

McCracken G. 1986. *Culture and Consumption, New Approaches to the Symbolic Character of Consumer Goods and Activities.* Indiana University Press: Bloomington, IN.

McCracken G. 1988. *The Long Interview, Qualitative Research Methods.* Sage: Newbury Park.

Mediatel. 2010. *Mobile, Executive Report.* Available at http://mediatel.co.uk/ mobile [accessed on 8 February 2011].

Miller D. 1987. *Material Culture and Mass Consumption.* Blackwell: Oxford.

Mintel. 2009. *Digital Cameras and Camcorders.* Available at http://academic.mintel.com/sinatra/oxygen_academic/search_results/show&/display/id=393890/ display/id=449341#hit1 [accessed on 2 March 2011].

New York Times. 2011. *E-books Outsell Printbooks at Amazon.* Available at http://www.nytimes.com/2011/05/20/technology/20amazon.html [accessed 3 July 2011]

Pabillano J. 2006. *Bad Pharma.* Available at http://adbusters.org/the_ magazine/62/ Bad_Pharma.html [accessed on 31 August 2006].

Reckwitz A. 2002. Toward a Theory of Social Practices: A Development in Culturalist Theorizing. *European Journal of Social Theory* 5(2): 243–263.

Richins M. 1994. Valuing Things, the Public and Private Meanings of Possessions. *Journal of Consumer Research* 21(December): 504–521.

Rodden K, Wood, KR. 2003.   How Do People Manage Their Digital Photographs? In *Proceedings of the SIGCHI Conference on Human Factors in Computing Systems (CHI'03).* ACM: New York; 409–416.

Siddiqui S, Turley D. 2006. Extending the Self in a Virtual World. *Advances in Consumer Research* 33: 647–648.

Strauss A, Corbin J. 1998. *Basics of Qualitative Research.* Sage: Thousand Oaks, CA.

Thompson CJ, Locander WB, and Pollio HR. 1989. Putting Consumer Experience Back into Consumer Research, the Philosophy and Method of Existential-Phenomenology. *Journal of Consume Research* 16(2):133–146.

Thompson, CJ, Locander WB, and Pollio HR. 1990. The Lived Meaning of Free Choice, an Existential-Phenomenological Description of Everyday Consumer Experiences of Contemporary Married Women. *The Journal of Consumer Research* 17(3): 346–361.

Wallendorf M, Arnould E. 1988. "My Favorite Things": A Cross-Cultural Inquiry into Object Attachment, Possessiveness, and Social Linkage. *Journal of Consumer Research* 14: 531–547.

7 Reflections in Spacetime
Reconsidering Kozinets (1999)
Twelve Years Later

Robert V. Kozinets

{Spacetime Tanks. High doses of caffeine, taurine, ginseng, wheat grass juice, and Nootropil. Transmissions. Beyond the Infinite.}

I lower my body into the warm, highly concentrated saline solution kept at a constant temperature of 93 degrees Fahrenheit. Within moments, I lose the sense of where my skin ends and where the warm water begins. Complete darkness surrounds me. The dark chamber is soundproof. For a few moments I am in complete silence, hearing my own heartbeat, the fluids slushing through my arteries and echoing dimly against the metal walls. "Spirits of Virtuality," the She-God intones, as the loud techno beats of Juno Reactor begin. They shock me, then ease up. Then smash again.

I will log seven hours in the tank this day. Seven hours to collect my thoughts about online communities and marketing. Seven hours of Juno Reactor alternating with a HemiSynch hemispheric synchronizing brain tape. There is a lightning flash—filled with images—behind my closed eyes. The high doses of neural stimulants began to kick in. Picture and images sprint across the screen of my opening mind. The tank seems to light up with a brilliant network of images, with shapes, diagrams, worlds.

> First, there is the chaos of the online world,
> expanding out like a universe. Then, I see it as
> Unity. The vast online world of marketing and
> consumption split into two dimensions. Each of
> them split again. Movement, constant vitality.
> Virtuality. Community. Life itself.

During a cold and snowy Christmas break season in 1998, by the corner of Fullerton and Halsted in downtown Chicago, I had devoted myself to a small experiment. It is inspired by visionary neuroscientist John Lilly's (1972) amazing book, *Programming and Metaprogramming in the Human Biocomputer.* I had decided to subject my body and mind to over half a day in a dark, quiet, warm isolation tank just a few blocks from the Lincoln Park Zoo.[1]

Following Lilly's conventions (but substituting espresso for illegal stimulants), I had set myself a single task. Over the past few days I had been reviewing all of my notes on online community and marketing. I had been meditating on my findings and using hypnagogic and hypnopompic suggestions to find patterns within them. Now, in the tank, in a heightened state of consciousness, I was going to concentrate firmly on what I had learned over the past two years of observation. I was going to model my insights into what was happening online in these consumption-oriented communities. I was going to organize and make sense of it. I was going to explain its significance to marketers. And I was going to attempt to prognosticate on where it was all headed in the future.

After the sessions, I emerge from the tank soaking, sweating, and lit up with new ideas. Heart pounding, breathless with excitement, eager to capture it before it slipped away, with my wet hands shaking with excitement, I scribble almost constantly in my notepad for almost two hours afterward, capturing the many ideas and insights that flooded my restless brain, until I am too tired to hold a pen anymore, too emptied even to stand.

The tank experiment was my preparation for my first theoretical article setting out what I had learned about the emerging interface among the worlds of online communities, marketing, and business. Professor Paul Stonham of the European School of Management at Oxford had read something written by me and subsequently asked me to write about online communities for the *European Management Journal*, the journal he was editing. As a new author and a very junior academic, I was flattered by the interest and happy for the opportunity to get some of my ideas into print.

With the insights from my Spacetime Tanks experiences, writing the article was not difficult. In fact, the words and diagrams had practically poured from my fingertips in those dripping few hours after that tank. After years of studying it, days of meditating on it, and hours of letting it all come together in the tank, I had tons to say about the topic. Working from my smeared notes, the article, start to finish, took me three days of devoted writing. Putting the words into the computer, printing it on my dot matrix, and then submitting the paper copy via snail mail, because that was the only way we did it back then, was a joy.[2] It was accepted almost exactly as I sent it, with just a few small, helpful changes based on Paul's suggestions.

Janice and Mike, the editors of this book, have provided me with another exciting opportunity in this chapter for the *Digital Virtual Consumption* volume. They suggested that I engage in a reflection on the original article. So, with this chapter, I may be giving them a little bit extra. Returning you to the scene of the original crime, I re-examine and re-envision the original, now twelve-year-old, article. Reviewing my excited and waterlogged intuitions and re-newing my commitments to the conceptual space and time, I write both around and through the original text, treating it now as a set of predictions to be samples and assessed, now as a set of memories and awakenings, now as a list of theoretical positions, and always hermeneutically as a still-very-much-alive historical document. The result is a type of merged conversation between a past and present self co-reflecting on futuristic topics of marketing, social media, consumption, and where they are still headed, an auto-ethnographic, semi-deflective, and quasi-poetic inflection on an extant document previously entered into the academic register.

So are you ready to lower yourself into the tank? Can you feel that warm water, hear the techno beat, sense that expansion of consciousness? Are you ready to squeeze through a time tunnel and hear the ringing of the past tinnily beating in your ears?

AND HERE WE GO AGAIN

In 1970, only one single year after the few tentative, initial nodes of the DOD-driven ARPANET Internet were set in place and electrified into life, Marshall McLuhan (1970) expounded that "cool" and inclusive "electric media" would "retribalize" human society into clusters of affiliation. Marshall knew his stuff. After almost two decades of the Web and twice that of the Net, networked computers and the communications they enable are driving enormous social changes that have led to many new types of social clustering and consciousness.

"By the year 2000," I wrote, "it is estimated that over 40 million people worldwide will participate in 'virtual communities' of one type or another." Holding the passive voice writing critique aside for the moment and stifling your chuckles about that antique bygone term "virtual" from the days when the word cyberspace-was-said-with-serious-face, consider that number.

Forty million. As in the population of Mexico City and New York City areas combined.

That 40 million figure seems ridiculously minute, does it not? As of May 2011, as I am writing this chapter, Internet users number two billion people worldwide, and *Facebook* membership already sits at over 550 million. Ponder that. Two billion Internet users and over half a billion of them members of *Facebook*.

It is critical to put your skeptical view into context at the very outset of this chapter. What you need to realize in this minor opening of a mini academic time capsule is that, when I began my research in 1995, there were only approximately 40 million people in total estimated to be *on the Internet*. In the article, I was predicting, in other words, that within a couple of years, as many people would be participating in online communities *as there were currently people on the Internet*.

The reason this is worth noting is that 1998 and 1999 were still very much the era of the read-write Web, what has been called Web 1.0. The Internet was for information, for reading, like a text. It might be hard to imagine or remember that time, but this article and this chapter are your time portal, oh Gentle Reader.

TIME TRAVEL 1.0

In an age filled with skepticism, I took a stand on the future of the Internet. Yes, these were Dark Times. Several of my academic advisors told me not to stake my career on Internet studies because it was quite clearly just "a fad." And, although irrational technological utopian exuberance was more the order of the day from the press and in particular the business press in which I was invested, one did see articles such as the one Clifford Stool (1995) infamously wrote in *Newsweek*: "What's missing from this electronic wonderland? Human contact. Discount the fawning techno-burble about virtual communities. Computers and networks isolate us from one another."

As the first person in most of my social groups with an Internet connection, with a Web page, a blog, a *Twitter* account, and e-mail, I can tell you that, although people were excited about technology in the 1990s and early 2000s, this discounting opinion was still rather widely held. Yet I predicted that, with the increasing growth rates of the Internet, "prodigious growth in the quantity, interests, and influence of virtual communities is guaranteed." I also saw that, rather than replacing physical encounters or traditional media, online would, at least in the foreseeable suture, "supplement" them. Not either/or, but both/and.

At that time the idea of participating in a virtual community, in an online social network of one kind or another, was considered to be very rare. I was widely considered by many to be studying and writing about exceptions—marginal folk, like Star Trek fans or Burning Man participants.[3] Communicate *anonymously* with *strangers* through your *computer*? *Who would want to do that*?[4]

But I saw a straight path between the Web 1.0 and Web 2.0 worlds—a sort of suspension bridge, if you will. Once a person entered on it and kept putting foot in front of foot, she moved almost inexorably from the Web 1.0 world of information to the Web 2.0 world of sociality.

Giving credit and standing on the broad pioneering shoulders of thinkers such as McLuhan (1970), Armstrong and Hagel (1996), and visionary writer Howard Rheingold (1993), I postulated that "the longer an Internet user spends online, the more likely it is that they will gravitate to an online group of one sort or another." It was a prediction of a mass trend based on an aggregation of individual behaviors. It stated that the future of the Internet was not only as an informational medium but a social gathering place, a digital hangout: "Once a consumer connects and interacts with others online, it is likely that they will become a recurrent member of one or more of these gatherings, and increasingly turn to them as a source of information and social interaction."

How could I capture this idea in a quick meme? How might I package the thought that the Internet is a cultural phenomenon, that this Age of the Net is an anthropological moment? McLuhan's insight was that technology would "re-tribalize," and I loved that. In work that I loved, Bernard Cova

(1997; Cova and Cova, 2001) had recently been writing about the tribalizing of marketing. The tribe was the answer. And not a "re" tribe, but an "e" tribe, an electronic, electric, electrified tribe.[5]

This idea of e-tribes was the whole. It made sense of the behaviors online. It was the One Single Concept from which all the other concepts flowed.

THE SECOND DIMENSION

From unity came the split into duality.

In the tank, I saw it as clear as an ocean sunrise shimmering like red foil on the horizon. The one, reflected, into two. And suddenly, it was there, in every piece, through every slice of the article I was to write.

Consider first the definition, the central definition. Yes, yes, it is unwieldy, clunky, and anachronistic: "virtual community of consumption" (VCC). In my later writing I adopted the term "online community of consumption" or "online consumption community." But it all means the same.

The novel contribution of the VCC designation was that it sought to distinguish from among all online or virtual communities, those that had "explicit consumption-related interests." The reason this was a contribution was that online communities had not yet been conceptualized in a way that had been relevant to marketers and consumer researchers. They are "affiliative groups whose online interactions are based upon shared enthusiasm for, and knowledge of, a specific consumption activity or related group of activities."[6]

Looking back, the examples I gave sound rather crude and basic. The "members of an e-mail mailing list sent out to collectors of Barbie dolls" and "the regular posters to a bulletin board devoted to connoisseurship of fine wine." But what about political bloggers—was that consumption? Non-profit and social movement related groups? What about greenhouse effect debaters? Those who read the news online? People who shopped for iPad3s but never ended up buying them? Were these forms of consumption, too? If so, then what was not consumption? Was consumption everything?

It might be of interest that, at the time, I was already conducting my own netnography of the coffee connoisseurs of the alt.coffee newsgroup (published in Kozinets, 2002a). That probably contributed to my thinly veiled reference to oenophiles. It would have probably been much better to talk about muscle car bloggers, Coca Cola fan group members on *Facebook*, or technology enthusiasts on *Twitter*. Mundane, easy examples, right? But the article, of course, predated all these forms of social media, not to mention more recent manifestations like FourSquare and the smart phone-powered mobile Internet explosion. At the time, there was not all that much available to draw on.

Where was the duality in the Unity that I grasped from within the Spacetime Tank? Within this short definition. That is where the article actually stakes its first new theoretical claim, a proposition that sets the central theme for the article: that consumption leads to community. My basic contention proposed that members of VCCs proceed from an informational search about consumption to a social one about community.

This is the fundamental duality, the repeat theme throughout the article: the counterpositioning and linking of socializing and belongingness with marketplace consumption interests.[7] Their inextricable intrication in online communities of consumption.

THE MORPH

Consider next the first figure, the first process. The dynamic transition and mutation. The reflection, the liquid transmuting of one psychic substance into another.

If you can find the original article, please have a look at Figure 1. Do you see how curiosity or circumstance leads a consumer to go online seeking "consumption knowledge"? That knowledge could be brand information. It could be an online contest, an offer of product or even lifestyle information such as one would find on a weight loss or body building site. However, because the online environment is a "social web" as well as a "consumption web" (see Kozinets, 2002a: 68), this search for information about consumption is very often presented to the lone consumer in a very social fashion:

> Consumption knowledge is learned alongside knowledge of the online group's cultural norms, specialized language and concepts, and the identities of experts and other group members. . . . Cultural cohesion ripens through shared stories and empathy. A group structure of power and status relationships is shared. What began primarily as a search for information transforms into a source of community and understanding. (Kozinets, 2002a: 254)

This is the process theory. This is the Fundamental Evolution. Because consumption-related information in online communities is often presented in not only a cultural (as with advertising) but also within a social (as with multi-level marketing) setting, searches that begin with one type of information become intricated in the online community context with the other.[8] The informational/consumption-related becomes the social/communal. Consumers become communities. The duality merges into one.[9]

THE TYPO

Can you see the basic and revealed duality as it manifests within the next round of theorizing?

The first typology cleaves the e-tribe reality, the basic duality of the online consumption community into its basic two parts: consumption and community. It turns them into two descriptive factors. It views them both as types of relationships.

One is the relationship that the person has with the consumption activity. This could certainly be a relationship with a brand, but it could also be a relationship with a hobby, a lifestyle category, or an interest. Drawing on my Star Trek-related theorizing (see the Larry Grossberg-inspired work on "mattering maps" in Kozinets, 2001: 78), I conceptualized a continuum of personal centrality that looks at how central to an individual's identity project this particular form of consumption was. If, for example, you were a hardcore comic book collector who loved *The Avengers*, then it was a lot more likely that you would be involved with online (and off-line as well) communities dedicated to comic books, comic book collecting, and *The Avengers* than someone who was not so inclined. What drew a person to favor online communal participation rather than off-line is an interesting question that I left out of the article. However, it is well worth postulating that personal characteristics such as social aversion/attraction, self-confidence, depth of devotion, or the need for a "daily fix," as well as simple convenience, all likely play their part. Social psychologists, there is certainly a lot of material to work with, validate, and hypothesis test here.

The second factor is the social relationships one has with other members of the online community. The former theory and figure suggested that the more time the individual spends looking for information about his or her consumption interest, the more he or she becomes knowledgeable about the social and cultural contexts surrounding these online communities where that information was presented.

In this theoretical exposition, the level of centrality of those consumption interests to an individual's identity project was seen as a strong motivating force drawing them toward online (and off-line) community participation. If we sum the two contentions, we find that it is probable that people with identity-central consumption interests will go online seeking consumption-related information and be drawn into a web of social, cultural, and communal relationships as well.

AND THEN THERE WERE FOUR

These two factors—the person's relationship with the consumption activity, and his or her relationship with the online community—are conceptually distinct. Each was in fact a continuum, but the ends could be split into high or low relationship intensity.[10]

As I saw it, the two dimensions split again. Crossing the two dimensions provides four distinct and ideal online community types. Those who have a low connection both with the particular consumption activity and with the particular online community I called "tourists." Later, following much practice, I renamed this member role, relationship style, or type the "newbie" (Kozinets, 2010: 33). The next type, the minglers, was there mainly for the party. They were more connected to the people in the online community than the consumption interests. The third type was the devotees, who inverted the relationship priority. They were more into the consumption interest than the community members. Finally, in the ever-valorized top right quadrant were the insiders, those who were highly connected to both the community and the consumption interest.

In the article, I treat the typology as a segmentation scheme and offer up a bit of marketing advice: "From a marketing strategy perspective, it is the devotees and the insiders who tend to represent the most important targets for marketing." There is some speculation behind my contention (i.e., that a Pareto rule will be operative in online communities whereby a small percentage of people will be influential content creators and providers of sought-after recommendations). This group, I reasoned, would likely come from the ranks of the insiders and devotees.

In their dissertation research at Lund University in 2008, Hjalti Hjaltason and Marie Vernersson tested this model to see whether it was an effective way to segment an online community. Although their study is limited by its use of only one rather unusual online community—a poker-playing site—they found general support for the notion that these four categories captured meaningful differences in online community membership. The researchers offered two other valuable insights: (1) a finding that the percentages of members in the various quadrants were unevenly distributed and did not seem to follow a Pareto rule, and (2) evidence that questions the idea that insiders may be the only ideal targets for social media marketing (Hjaltason and Vernesson, 2008).

At the time, I was attempting to convey a sense of the fluidity between these categories. Minglers start out social, then learn more about the community's consumption interests and become insiders. Tourists dip into some of the community's collective consumption knowledge and become devotees. There is dynamism and movement in the process as people shift roles over time and even within the same community. I illustrate the process of online community consumption socialization much more thoroughly in the netnographic illustration in Kozinets (2002a), but the initial germ of the idea was present in this article: "The virtual community itself may propagate the development of loyalty and heavy usage by culturally and socially reinforcing consumption. In this way, tourists and minglers can be socialized and 'upgraded' to insiders and devotees" (Kozinets, 2002a: 255). Like a subculture of consumption or microculture, the online community socializes consumption tastes, language, styles, patterns, and practices.

STICKY WIDGETS: FIVE NEW FORMS

Looking back, much has changed, but much has also stayed the same.

"The race is on for contemporary marketers to understand and build connections with [social media consumers] before more net-savvy competitors can discover how to bond with them. Internet [social network and mobile] information access and interactivity are behind a fundamental shift occurring right now in the way people think about their purchasing and consumption activities . . . massive market instabilities [are] currently underway among information technology-savvy industries and companies" (Kozinets, 1999: 261). Those statements, which open the article's close, would be at home in almost any current article about the impact of social media marketing.

Based on its alliance with the prior, much shorter *Financial Times* article (Kozinets ,1999 [1997]), the article provides a cartographic type of orientation. This "lay of the online land" offers a very broad, cursory overview of online community types: dungeons (from multi-user dungeons, which were some of the original play spaces, the original predecessors of virtual worlds like *Second Life* or videogame worlds like *Farmville*), rooms (such as chat rooms), rings (Web rings are defunct, but related to the blogroll blogs), lists (such as mailing lists; like e-mail itself, the listserv format is still alive and well), and boards (groups and forums are popular manifestations of the bulletin board format). That article did, in fact, already update some of these terms. Dungeons were linked to networked videogames, current called MMOs (for massively-multiplayer online games, which would include such formats as *World of Warcraft*). The article mentioned "graphically-intense virtual meeting places" such as Palace software, which was an early format for virtual worlds. Overall, the article expressed my then-preference for boards, but it also noted that each medium type provided interesting marketing and consumer research opportunities.

In the twelve years since the article's publication, we have seen a virtual explosion of online formats, something that I wrote about with a Big Bang metaphor as an "ever-expanding netnographic universe" in Kozinets (2005). In Kozinets (2010: 84–87), I redefined some of the "original five" and then, like a sports expansion draft, added five of the most important new formats to this early list. The expansion media for online community interaction were as follows:

- *Blogs*: a special type of webpage, consisting of dated entries arranged in reverse chronological order, so that what appears first is the most recent entry.
  - o *Microblogs* (e.g., Twitter): a recent extension of the blog using small amounts of frequently updated text, distributed selectively and often across multiple platforms, including mobile.

- *Wikis:* (e.g., Wikipedia) a specialized, collaborative online format in which the webpage is designed to be completely open to communal contributions or modifications of its content.
- *Audio/visual sites:* online locations where consumer share and comment on one another's graphical, photographical, audio, or audiovisual productions.
- *Social content aggregators:* sites and services where consumers communally discover and share Internet content, vote on it, and comment on it. Three popular social content aggregators are Digg, del.icio.us, and StumbleUpon.
- *Social networking sites* (or services; both abbreviated to SNS; a key example is *Facebook*): a hybrid communication medium that offers devoted individual pages alongside a myriad of interaction-based media, groups, and communities.

As with the original article, our understanding of how these social media can be used (and abused) in marketing practice and consumer research grows by leaps and bounds every year. Although marketers are currently fascinated with *Facebook* and *Twitter*, it is useful to remember that the only constant in this online space is that of dynamic and constant transformation. The media and the messages continue to rapidly evolve.

RECALCULATING THE GRAND INTERACTION

As I originally understood the space of the online communal interaction, there was such movement, such mobility, and such amazingly electric activity. Like an astronomer, I tried to understand some of the gravitational kinds of forces that were bringing people together into collectivities and driving them apart into separate clusters.

The final major new diagram in the article tries to combine static description with some sense of this movement and fluidity. It offers four different modes of social interaction that take place in online consumption communities: informational, relational, recreational, and transformational. Again, I use two axes to arrive at the two-by-two typology, but these are new dimensions.

The first new dimension looks at the underlying motivation for engaging with the online consumption community. Is it a more purposeful (which I merge and confound with an informational) motivation? Or is it a more playful (which I confound with being social) motivation? The next new dimension is the orientation of the communication, the type of communication that the member offers to the community. Is the communication short-term and self-interested or self-absorbed? Or is it longer-term, outward-looking, helpful, and communally focused? This dimension seems to have considerable overlap with the first dimension, and the strong informational to relational diagonal echoes Figure 1's contention that engagement in these communities proceeds from an informational to a social orientation.

However, with over a decade of near-continuous social media theorizing and observing under my belt, I feel good about attempting a small revival of that third, and perhaps weakest, theoretical model.[11] I believe that this typology may be more valuable today when reconsidered as a typology of online consumption communities. I believe that I was aware at the time I wrote this article, as I am currently, that a single online community could serve different purposes for its members and even different purposes for the same members at different times.

TRANSFORMING ACTIVISM, RIGHTS, AND PROFITS

Looking back, one of the more interesting aspects of the third typology is its emphasis on "transformation." This topic has gained more attention in recent years with the publications of various popular business books about the potential of social media to be used to engage social change (see e.g., Aaker and Smith, 2010). Along with Frank-Martin Belz and Pierre McDonagh, I recently completed a chapter on this topic for the *Transformational Consumer Research* volume (see Kozinets, Belz, and McDonagh, 2011).

In the 1999 article, I discuss the "transformational mode" of social media interaction. In this mode, "consumers communicate in order to attain some other objective that is focused on longer-term social gain" (Kozinets, 1999: 256). The example I used was online "consumer activists" such as the boycotters that Jay Handelman and I had studied (Kozinets and Handelman, 1998).

In the section of the paper termed "Activism," a term I intended to bridge both "activity" and "resistant" connotations, I predicted defiant and rebellious outcomes from the growth and spread of online consumer communities. "Empowered by information exchange and emboldened by relational interactions, consumers will use their online activities to actively judge consumption offerings, and increasingly resist what they see as misdirected" (Kozinets, 1999: 258). The article positions this as a power shift of Tofflerian dimensions: "The existence of united groups of online consumers implies that power is shifting away from marketers and flowing to consumers. For while consumers are increasingly saying yes to the Internet, to electronic commerce and to online marketing efforts of many kinds, they are also using the medium to say "no" to forms of marketing they find invasive or unethical" (ibid). In this section, which we cite at some length in the beginnings of the Kozinets, Belz, and McDonagh (2011) chapter, the article portrays social media as "an arena for organizing consumer resistance," a site for engaging in transformational interactions aimed at social, communal, and individual betterment, a place where corporate efforts can be challenged and undermined, and a medium with "inherent political possibilities."

During a time before Napster, the Millennium Digital Rights Act, iTunes, and DRM, the article broaches the boundaries among marketing, legal studies, and political science by submitting a perspective on the emerging debates around intellectual property and ownership rights. I discussed News Corp's Fox Broadcasting crackdown of fan webpages devoted to popular television shows such as the (still-running!) *The Simpsons*. These legal crackdowns inspired activism, resistance, and eventual consumer victories, setting the stage for a very familiar pattern that has been studied by many inside and outside of consumer research.[12]

The article envisioned the continuing contentiousness of rights in a digital age. Music (the article mentions the "new compression standard" of "Mp3"), motion pictures, television, newspapers, magazines, and books: No informational or entertainment format is immune to the spread of "illicit informational goods." However, the article warns against exclusive reliance on digital rights management strategies for two simple reasons. First, these locks have proven very easy to break. Second, there is an economy built on giving things away: "Networks are what build value, and networks are often created by giving things away" (Kozinets, 1999: 263; cf. Anderson, 2009).

The rather simple, and perhaps overly simplistic, advice I had to offer to marketers navigating those dangerous shoals was to perform a complex cost-benefit on the changing value of information, protection, and consumer community presence and devotion. "Marketers must try to weight the moral and social benefits with the very difficult costs of this strategy. With limits and within reason, giving things away that can be easily copied is perhaps the wisest marketing alternative. Giving things away allows marketers to build loyalty and trust and allows the company to make their margins on what is difficult for others to copy." On other things—the new, the flashy, the live, the extra-featured, the full-serviced, the privacy-enhanced—marketers can and most definitely should charge a reasonable and profit-making premium.

THE THREE PRINCIPLES: ACTIVITY, MULTIMODALITY, AND MULTIDIMENSIONALITY

The article needed to make an offering on the altar of marketing and marketers, and as it moved beyond typologies and definitions, it aimed more increasingly practical and grounded advice. Offering yet another name—virtual communal marketing (VCM)—the article offers three general guiding principles that attempt to build on, extend, and add required nuance to the prior assumptions of relationship marketing.

The first of these principles is familiar and derived from the above-mentioned precepts: Online consumers are active. After taking a few easy potshots at database marketing, which evolved into customer relationship management and/or marketing, the article makes its central points about consumer activity: "Consumers are active, deeply involved in articulating and re-articulating their consumption activities. Insiders and devotees are especially involved in setting standards, negotiating them with other members, redrawing group boundaries in terms of consumption, and constantly assessing the corporations whose products are important to them." Online consumers are active in standard setting, negotiating and discussing, managing and organizing the groups and its members, and evaluating companies and products. Their interactions are nuanced, they differentiate, they debate, they defend, they deconstruct, and they involve relationships of power and dominance. These particular types of consumer activity are still ripe for further exploration and development (for an example, see Schau, Muñiz, and Arnould, 2009).

The second principle is subtler and draws from Hoffman and Novak (1996), but it extends the conceptual work to the community sphere. It thus prefigures the exemplary work on communities and brand communities by scholars such as McAlexander et al. (2002: 39). The idea is that "customer relationships with marketing companies manifest not simply as binodal relationships but as multinodal networks." In this case, by first exploding the then-extremely-popular but acultural and overly-micro idea of "one-to-one marketing," the article seeks to make it clear that not only are marketers broadcasting messages to individual consumers, but individual consumers can also broadcast back and have important effects on marketing and marketing. Marketers are broadcasting messages to a community composed of individual consumers. The individual consumer also has a relationship with the community and with the other individual members of that community that is independent of the marketer.

The article explicitly associates the multimodal relationship change to a shift in power: "Interactions based on information shift knowledge and power from marketers to consumers. Organizations of consumers can make successful demands on marketers that individuals can not." What is the result? In this brave new world of social media, "online marketers will need to realize that . . . they are communicating not only with many 'ones,' but also with many 'manys.' 'The customer' increasingly will need to be envisioned and modeled not only as an individual, but as a complex and interrelated global network. This global network is comprised of series of communicating consumers who draw on each others' knowledge and experience to evaluate the quality and worthiness of product offerings and the honesty and integrity of companies and their marketing communications." Although I had not yet read the book, this idea is very similar to the notions of "collective intelligence" proposed by Pierre Lévy (1997) in his book of the same name. However, in this case the collective intelligence was explicitly located in the realm of consumption—"communicating consumers who drawn on each others' knowledge and experience" to evaluate products, brands, companies, and their marketing efforts. What is the outcome?

Again, in terms that have now become quite familiar to the point of being taken-for-granted this necessitates "openness, inclusiveness and forthrightness" in marketing, a transparency and honesty in the social media sphere that is unlike that which has ever before been asked of marketers.

The article suggests some intriguing strategies: "Astute marketers find not only that virtual communities influence online consumers, but that marketers and marketing are, in fact, a part of their communities. Marketing to an entire community becomes a realistic online option." This is the radical shift from marketing as broadcasting to marketing as partaking in an ongoing-and-out-of-your-direct-control conversation that is only now becoming widely accepted through social media marketing. What exactly does it mean to "market to an entire community" rather than to market to individuals, or to individuals situated in a particular community? In 2011, astute, cutting-edge marketers like McDonalds, Zappos, Amazon, Frito-Lay, and Procter & Gamble continue their experimentations and are still struggling mightily to try to figure this out.

The third and final guiding principle deals with online communities as a site for the conduct of qualitative marketing research. At the time, with e-commerce being all the rage online, I was swimming against that particular tide of data. Sales data (from e-commerce transactions) and demographic data (either from consumers filling out various online forms, or from sneaky cookie and ISP-tracking datastream sniffing) were important and useful, I grudgingly admitted. However, they were not the end all and be all of online data collection. Instead, marketers and marketing researchers should pay close attention to the "multidimensional potentialities" of online community interactions: "Virtual communities, in contrast, provide at little or no cost a wealth of much more multidimensional information."

In the article, I cited the old Dejanews community search engine, which was bought by Google in 2000 and has long been incorporated as part of Google Groups. Of the many qualities of qualitative data, the article emphasized several. One was simply to account for where consumers were focusing their chatter attention. What are consumers talking about today? What topics are tending? Are they mentioning your brand? The next thing I discussed was a simple measure of whether those mentions are positive or negative. Finally, it was useful to understand how much depth or passion was included in those conversations. It is worthwhile to note that, although this discussion derived in large part from my own personal experience in pioneering, advocating, and developing netnography, the actual discussion does not talk about netnography but rather seeks to distill some large overall characteristics that might be amenable to semantic search processing (for those who interested in the recent intersection of these related areas, please see my NetBase white paper, available online at netbase.com). By emphasizing the online qualitative measurement of emotional characteristics such as passion, and linking them to notions of loyalty, the discussion anticipates much of the contemporary discussion of qualitative social media marketing measurement and assessment.

ENGAGING REFLECTIONS: SEVEN REFLECTIONS OF ENGAGEMENT

One can learn much about how a particular article is situated in time and in its context through a revisitation exercise such as this one. Much of the middle part of the article was built as a structured response to relationship marketing and loyalty-based segmentation, using the basic frameworks of those approaches as a way to distinguish the beginnings of a new approach, which I variously termed "e-tribalized marketing" or "virtual relationship marketing."

In so doing, I questioned some basic assumptions about the two approaches and offered alternatives. There were, in fact, seven key contentions that we can examine from the argument that help to inform our understanding of digital consumers and digital virtual consumption in general.

1. Assumptions of relationships based on in-person contact need to be revised in light of the addition of online relationships
2. Assumptions of solitary, isolated consumers are contradicted by online consumer communities
3. Assumptions of silent, passive consumers are contradicted by active online community members
4. Assumption of inactive consumers must be adjusted because of the word-of-mouth, evangelical, conversion potential of online community members
5. Assumptions of equal value of consumers online must take into account the greatly enhanced value of some online consumers as influencers, opinion leaders, and influential insiders
6. Assumptions of brand loyalty or community loyalty are contradicted by loyalty to a lifestyle, product class, or form of consumption
7. Assumptions of the economic, switching, or retention bases of loyalty are contradicted by community's emphasis on the experiential depth and emotional devotion, and thus intensity of engagement rather than mere purchase

We can think of these observations as suggesting the following seven general social media marketing principles, many of which have, especially since the social media boom began in earnest in approximately 2007, become *de riguer* and oft-repeated advice:

1. Online/off-line: remember that online relationships are now part of consumers' social lives and cultural sphere

2. Collectivity: remember that online consumers are not isolated but act as collectives and communities
3. Activity: remember that consumers actively co-create online experiences
4. Word-of-mouth spread: remember that the opinion spreading of online consumers creates and destroys value and can add or detract from your marketing
5. Influencers: remember that some word-of-mouth sharing consumers are highly valuable targets
6. Lifestyle-centricity: remember that online consumers may not be in love with your brand, but they are passionate about them as they link to their relationships and their lifestyles
7. Engagement: remember that online consumption is also driven by experience and emotion with your content, not only by economic, informational, or rational decision-making

Some of the closing recommendations offered in the article still contain some potentially useful advice. To close this chapter, which was a cathartic and energizing exercise for me to write, I cull and edit a few that may still be useful and worthy of further reflection and, perhaps, further research and practical development (for sources, please see pp. 263–264).

- Social media is about creating meaningful ways for consumers to socially communicate with other consumers, not about broadcasting how great your brand is to a captive audience.
- "The goal is not to control." Do not try to control a community; dance with it by helping communal insiders in an authentic way.
- Social media is about "the trusting relationship" among community members, companies, brands, and leaders.
- Overall, when using social media, "it is important to use a light touch. Marketers must zealously guard brand identity, but they also must provide community members with the raw materials they need to construct a meaningful community."
- "Remember that community building is a creative activity."

FROM DARKNESS, LIGHT

Looking back into the past of this article and using it as a lens to peer into the present and ever toward the future has been an immensely enjoyable and engaging exercise for me in 2011. I have needed no tank this time, no legal stimulants, and only a bit of techno. Excavating and meditating on that past, the original sense of Unity returns to me, and the realization that an anthropological, cultural, human sense of online world is the firmest foundation for an understanding of the social online phenomenon is every bit as strong today as it was that day back in 1998.

In fact, it may be even stronger. As social media becomes accepted as an important, currently insanely, and exuberantly trendy part of contemporary marketing, we are witnessing an increasing distancing of managers from the cultural activities of online consumers, a major retreat from the front lines of this engagement, and an incredibly vacuous delegation of online contact to third parties such as agencies and public relations specialists.

This is a shame. But I do not believe it will stand. I believe that, eventually, most marketers and much marketing will see the immense value of the cultural view of consumer, online and off. It is worth considering just how much we know about human relationships and sociality, and how many of the fundamental principles about what we have learned continue to apply, and continue to cry out for further development and refinement, in this allegedly "new"—but actually very continuous extension of our communication capabilities—that we currently, and for the moment, term social media.

Looking back into our history as social human beings, as safe-in-our-collective primates and competitive alpha-screeching hairless apes, as what Goisseaux and Moran (2010) call our "Human 1.0" heritage, will teach us much that we need to know about the new-seeming but old-fangled digital consumer. Marshall McLuhan (1970) saw this and knew this. In his brilliant article about word-of-mouth, Ernst Dichter (1966) foretold much of what we know about the principles of social media today.

The online space is a cultural space of collections tribes; this is the Unity. Consumption and community = the duality. There are three guiding principles of activity, multimodality, multidimensionality. And there are basic fundamental rules for marketing in these spaces. This was what I realized, in the darkness, soaking as a bodiless mind in a warm saline sea, shaking to the digital beat of the online universe.

Speaking for twelve years, it speaks to me still.

NOTES

1. The 1980 film *Altered States*, starring William Hurt, was loosely adapted from the story of Dr. Lilly's LSD-fueled revelations in the isolation tank. Fortunately, I did not regress into a monkey. And my cranium only expanded minimally. Man, I love that movie.
2. It is well worth remembering that William Gibson's 1984 book, *Neuromancer*, the prescient science fiction novel that coined the term and concept of cyberspace, was written completely on a manual typewriter.
3. But those are other stories for other days.
4. Honest to God, I heard that sort of thing so many times I cannot even venture a count.
5. For much, much more on the electronic tribes metaphor, see Adams and Smith (2008) for an entire, and very interesting, book on the topic.
6. As an astute reader might notice, the article's definition borrows quite heavily on Schouten and McAlexander's (1995: 43) definition of subcultures of consumption.

7. It is well worth noting that, although the article was written years before I read the original Muniz and O'Guinn (2001) brand community article, we were already on parallel tracks with this unification of the commercial and the communal, a central theme that has followed me through much of my research to the current day (e.g., Kozinets, 2001, 2002a, 2002b; Kozinets, Hemetsberger, and Schau, 2008; Kozinets et al., 2010).
8. The example I chose is consumption-related information, but the reverse is also true.
9. We develop this process theory of online consumption community encultura-tion further in Kozinets, Hemesterberger, and Schau (2008, see Figure 1).
10. For an intriguing book all about the two-by-two matrix as a form for think-ing about business problems, see Lowy and Hood (2004).
11. In fact, I find that Figure 3 and its related theory might be an early version of the theory that Andrea Hemetsberger, Hope Jensen Schau, and I presented in our 2008 article "The Wisdom of Consumer Crowds" (Koziners, Hemets-berger, and Schau 2008: 345).
12. For a very interesting theoretical take, see Giesler's (2008) dramatic model of the Napster wars.

REFERENCES

Aaker J, Smith A. 2010. *The Dragonfly Effect: Quick, Effective, and Powerful Ways to Use Social Media to Drive Social Change*. Jossey-Bass: San Francisco, CA.

Adams TL, Smith SA. (eds.). 2008. *Electronic Tribes: The Virtual Worlds of Geeks, Gamers, Shamans, and Scammers*. University of Texas Press: Austin, TX.

Anderson C. 2009. *Free: The Future of a Radical Price*. Hyperson: New York.

Armstrong A, Hagel J. 1996. The Real Value of On-Line Communities. *Harvard Business Review* (May–June): 134–141.

Cova B. 1997. Community and Consumption: Towards a Definition of the "Link-ing Value" of Product or Services. *European Journal of Marketing* 31(3/4): 297–316.

Cova B, Cova V. 2001. Tribal Aspects of Postmodern Consumption Research: The Case of French In-Line Roller Skates. *Journal of Consumer Behavior* 1(1): 67–76.

Dichter E. 1966. How Word-of-Mouth Advertising Works. *Harvard Business Review* 44 (Nov-Dec): 147–166.

Gibson W.1984. *Neuromancer*. HarperCollins: London

Giesler M. 2008. Conflict and Compromise: Drama in Marketplace Evolution. *Journal of Consumer Research* 34(April): 739–753.

Gossieaux F, Moran E. 2010. *The Hyper-Social Organization: Eclipse Your Com-petition by Leveraging Social Media*. McGraw-Hill: New York.

Hjaltason H, Vernersson M. 2008. *Segmenting Online Communities*. Unpublished Master's Thesis. Lund University: Lund, Sweden.

Hoffman D, Novak T. 1996. Marketing in Hypermedia Computer-Mediated Envi-ronments: Conceptual Foundations. *Journal of Marketing* 60(July): 50–68.

Kozinets RV. 1999. E-Tribalized Marketing?: The Strategic Implications of Vir-tual Communities of Consumption. *European Management Journal* 17(3): 252–264.

Kozinets RV. 1999 [1997]. How Online Communities are Growing, in *Power, in Mastering Marketing: Complete MBA Companion in Marketing*, T. Dickson (ed.). Pearson Education: London; 291–297.

Kozinets, RV. 2001. Utopian Enterprise: Articulating the Meanings of Star Trek's Culture of Consumption. *Journal of Consumer Research*, 28 (June): 67–88.

Kozinets RV. 2002a. The Field Behind the Screen: Using Netnography for Marketing Research in Online Communities. *Journal of Marketing Research* 39(February): 61–72.

Kozinets RV. 2002b. Can Consumers Escape the Market? Emancipatory Illuminations from Burning Man. *Journal of Consumer Research* 29(June): 20–38.

Kozinets RV. 2005. Communal Big Bangs and the Ever-Expanding Netnographic Universe. *Thexis* 3: 38–41.

Kozinets RV. 2010. *Netnography: Doing Ethnographic Research Online*. Sage: London.

Kozinets RV, Belz F-M, and McDonagh P. 2011. Social Media for Social Change, in *Transformative Consumer Research to Benefit Global Welfare*, D. G. Mick, S. Pettigrew, C. Pechmann, and J. L. Ozanne (eds.). Routledge: London and New York; 205–224.

Kozinets RV, de Valck K, Wojnicki A, and Wilner S. 2010. Networked Narratives: Understanding Word-of-Mouth Marketing in Online Communities." *Journal of Marketing* 74(March): 71–89.

Kozinets RV, Handelman JM. 1998. Ensouling Consumption: A Netnographic Exploration of Boycotting Behavior, in *Advances in Consumer Research, Volume 25*, J. Alba and W. Hutchinson (eds.). Association for Consumer Research: Provo, UT; 475–480.

Kozinets RV, Hemetsberger A, and Schau H. 2008. The Wisdom of Consumer Crowds: Collective Innovation in the Age of Networked Marketing. *Journal of Macromarketing* 28(December): 339–354.

Lévy P. 1997. *Collective Intelligence: Mankind's Emerging World in Cyberspace*. Perseus: Cambridge, MA.

Lilly JC. 1972. *Programming and Metaprogramming in the Human Biocomputer*. Julian Press: New York.

Lowy A, Hood P. 2004. *The Power of the 2 X 2 Matrix: Using 2 X 2 Thinking to Solve Business Problems and Make Better Decisions*. Jossey-Bass: San Francisco, CA.

McAlexander JH, Schouten JW, and Koening HF. 2002. Building Brand Community. *Journal of Marketing* 66(1): 38–54.

McLuhan M, 1970. *Culture Is Our Business*. McGraw-Hill: New York.

Muniz, AM, O'Guinn, TC. 2001. Brand Community. *Journal of Consumer Research*, 27 (March): 412–32.

Rheingold H. 1993. *The Virtual Community: Homesteading on the Electronic Frontier*. Addison-Wesley: Reading, MA.

Schau HJ, Muñiz AM Jr, and Arnould EJ. 2009. How Brand Community Practices Create Value. *Journal of Marketing* 73(5): 30–51.

Schouten JW. McAlexander JH. 1995. Subcultures of Consumption: An Ethnography of the New Bikers. *Journal of Consumer Research* 22(1): 43–61

Stoll C. 1995. The Internet? Bah! *Newsweek*, 27 February.

8   What Happens to Materiality in Digital Virtual Consumption?

Paolo Magaudda

THE MATERIALITY OF DIGITAL VIRTUAL CONSUMPTION PRACTICES

The transition toward the digitalization of consumer practices and other forms of digital virtual consumption (DVC) clearly represents a key characteristic of the contemporary age. In the last ten years, not only most of Western society has started to buy goods through the different means available on the Internet, but digitalization has also triggered deeper changes in overall approaches to the consumption of goods and services. With the aim of furthering our understanding of DVC, this chapter proposes a perspective that looks at how materiality still remains a relevant dimension in DVC practices. Although decisively influenced by the emerging role of virtual and de-materialized objects and interactions, DVC practices do not imply that there are no material objects involved or that these objects do not play an important part in shaping consumers' experiences. In short, what I want to make evident is that in DVC materiality still matters. And it matters a lot.

The relationship between DVC and materiality is a relevant and not a simple issue. In conceptualizing DVC, Denegri-Knott and Molesworth have rightly highlighted that the relationship between virtual consumption and materiality is not only important, but it is also complex and variously articulated, pointing out that DVC is related to "a hybridization of the material and the virtual-as-imagination," which implies that "the digital virtual may contain the actualizing potential of the material with the idealizations of the virtual" (Denegri-Knott and Molesworth, 2010: 114–115). In this chapter, I will focus on the relationship between virtuality and materiality in DVC practices by presenting an example of the persistent role of material objects in the digital music consumption. My aim is to show that the analysis of DVC practices also requires taking serious consideration of the status of materiality in shaping and making sense of new emerging digital consumer cultures.

Looking more generally at transformations of contemporary consumption, we can say that digitalization of consumption and the changing role of materiality are intriguing at both the theoretical and empirical levels. On the one hand, one of the main features of the DVC is the massive shift toward the de-materialization and virtualization of products and goods that people consume. This is especially true in relation to the consumption of many kinds of cultural objects, such as music, books, magazines, and movies as well as for other creative and leisure practices, such as amateur photography, home movies recording, and gaming.

On the other hand, anthropologists and sociologists of consumption know that the material dimension of consumption is a fundamental and constitutive element in the consumer's life and culture. Since the works of scholars such as Mary Douglas and Byron Isherwood (1978), Arjun Appadurai (1986), and Daniel Miller (1987), we have come to accept that the materiality of consumption is not just the external form of internal psychological processes or the superficial mirror on which consumers project their socio-cultural desires and dispositions, but also represents the pragmatic interface that actively generates meanings, actions, and social connections. From another perspective, advances in the social study of technology (Bijker et al., 1987; Latour, 1987) have shown that everyday life artefacts and technologies are both outcomes of the society that has created them and active agents influencing the social context where they are used. When we take on these well-established perspectives, the need to research and reflect on the changing role of materiality in the context of the DVC practices appears even more pressing. Illuminating on the complex relationship between the material and DVC provides both anthropologists and sociologists an opportunity to better understand the relationship among cultural meanings, their material substantiations, and the social world where the interaction with material objects occurs (see Vannini, 2009).

DVC, MATERIALITY, AND PRACTICE THEORY

In order to understand the interplay between DVC and materiality, I adopt an approach rooted in the general framework of practice theory (or theories) (Schatzki, 1996; Schatzki et al., 2001). To put it very shortly, practice theory is a theoretical framework based on the idea that social phenomena should be better understood considering "practice" as the main unit of analysis and, consequently, that the sources of change in behaviors and activities should be identified in the evolution of the practices themselves (Sassatelli, 2007; Warde, 2005). In consumer studies, practice theory assumes that consumption activities are the result of individual performances involved and intertwined in a complex socio-material context where meanings, objects, and embodied activities are arranged in specific configurations of "practices." In this framework, the concept of "practice" is regarded as a whole, shared, and stabilized "configuration" consisting "of several elements, interconnected to one another: forms of bodily activities, forms of mental activities, 'things' and their use, a background knowledge in the forms of understanding, know how, states of emotion and motivational knowledge" (Reckwitz, 2002: 249).

In consumer studies, practice theory has been specifically developed by Shove, Pantzar, and other scholars (Shove and Pantzar, 2005; Shove et al., 2007), whose main contribution was to assume that the heterogeneity of elements constituting a "social practice" can be more easily simplified according to three main analytical dimensions intertwined with one another. These three dimensions are: (1) the dimension of meanings and representations; (2) one consisting in objects, technologies, and material culture in general; and (3 and one including embodied competences, activities, and "doing" (see especially Shove and Pantzar, 2005). Thus, practices represent the outcome of the performative linkage of these three elements, a linkage in which materiality evidently plays a crucial role (see Halkier et al., 2011). This articulation of the theory of practice has put specific emphasis on the situated understanding of dynamics of change and transformation of social practices that give us an interesting conceptual vantage point to begin to make sense of emerging DVC practices because it hones in the material dimension of social life, recognizing materiality as a constitutive element in the evolution and change of social practices. In the following sections of this chapter, I am going to adopt a practice theory-based framework to account for the role of materiality in the co-evolution of music consumption practices after the diffusion of digitized music. Specifically, I will focus on listeners' experiences and the iterative relationships unfolding among materiality, cultural representations, and consumers' pragmatic activities. However, before showing and discussing these examples, I will elaborate on some broader considerations on the relationship among materiality, consumption, and the rise of digital music.

THE RISE OF DIGITAL MUSIC AND THE "RE-MATERIALIZATION" OF CONSUMERS' EXPERIENCE

Music consumption is probably one of the most interesting areas to analyze the processes surrounding the relationship between materiality and DVC practices. Music has been the first cultural object among the traditional ones (literature, movies, magazines) to become fully digitized (in 1995 with the technical patent obtained for the creation of the Mp3 codification), to be appropriated by big industries (in 2003 with the launch of the iTunes Store), and, above all, to outclass physical formats in terms of sales (in 2008, iTunes became the largest seller of music, including physical music formats, in the US, prevailing over the Wal-Mart chain; see Apple 2008).

At the same time, we have also note that, in the last decades, music has flourished within a consumer culture where material objects have unquestionably been fundamental. This is not only due to the fact that music listening would not even be conceivable without the material technologies invented since Edison's 1877 phonograph (Sterne, 2003), but also because popular music cultures mainly (see Symes, 2004) grew around the value of, the attachment, and sometimes the addiction to material objects like albums, artists' t-shirts and clothes, personal stereos, and memorabilia of any sort (Eisemberg, 1987). The social history of music after the rock and roll age could not even be imagined without making some sort of reference to non-musical objects that people appropriated, consumed, and loved.

If we consider more closely the field of digital music consumption, we can see that in the last ten years, the music market has undergone a period of deep transformation as a direct consequence of the process of digitaliza-tion of music and the development of Internet-based services such as peer-to-peer networks and online music stores (Hesmondhalgh, 2009; Katz, 2004; Millard, 2005). We have witnessed many changes in the world of music consumption due to the shift from a fixed materiality of music consumed—represented, for example, by audiotapes or compact discs—to the fluidity of intangible digital formats. These changes affecting musical consumption practices have often been analyzed in terms of loss of relevance of music mate-riality, with greater emphasis being placed on the different ways that music consumption has become virtual, free, and boundless, giving space to the metaphor of music circulation as the "water that flows from the sink" (Kuzek and Leonard, 2005; Rodman and Vanderdonckt, 2006). While it is clear that the changes that occurred in music materiality have deeply influenced the ways in which people consume music, we also have to recognize that inter-preting these changes as a loss of relevance in the role of material objects in shaping people's habits and cultures may be somewhat misleading.

The first counterintuitive consideration we can make in this regard is that today we can find many and varied material objects connected with music listening as never before in the history of music consumption. While the first and more evident example we can give is the iPod's successful and widespread diffusion (and we will come back to it later), we can also note that the diffusion of digital music has coincided with the multiplication of several music listening material objects and, consequently, with the prolif-eration of cultures and politics surrounding the use of these objects.

Let's take the example of the musical headphones. The mainstream US online store *Amazon* lists for sale (in July 2011) about 2,000 differ-ent models of headphones and ear-buds, which range from 5$ to $2,749 (the more expensive is a German limited-edition model of luxury head-phones). If interested in knowing more about headphones, we have at our disposal many different websites on this topic like *Head-fi* (www.head-fi.org), which counts (in July 2011) with about 160,000 members and 6.5 million posts, with an average number of more than 3,000 posts per day. Recently, the problem of the high volume emitted through the headphones has also become a social problem directly handled by the European Union (EU). In October 2008, the European Commission officially warned that listening to personal music players at a high volume over a sustained period can lead to permanent hearing damage and that 10 million people in the EU may be at risk (European Union, 2009). In sum, the large diffusion of digital sounds seems to have grown along with a renewed interest in the material accessories needed to interface with these sounds. The growth of headphones and interest surrounding them are indicative of how the diffusion of virtual consumer practices co-evolved with a "re-materialization" of the experience with new and renewed musical material objects.

My point here is to stress the idea that, far from causing a decline in the role of material objects and artefacts within music consumption, the rise of digital music (and generally of DVC) has also triggered a whole process of reconfiguration of the materiality of sound and music, a process that I define as "re-materialization." This re-materialization essentially consists of processes through which a social practice—in this case musical consumption—witnesses a radical reconfiguration of the relationships among cultural meanings, artifacts, and practical activities. At a closer look, the present transition toward digitalized and de-materialized consumption practices—in music as well as in other cultural spheres—is a rich form of re-materialization.

In the next sections of the chapter, I will clarify what I mean by the process of re-materialization in digital music listening consumption by showing three examples of how meanings, artefacts, and ways of doing are intertwined with each other, starting from situated experiences of the consumption of digital music. In order to make clear the process of co-evolution among objects, meanings, and ways of doing involved in digital music consumption, I will illustrate these examples by using a visualization device, which consists of a chain showing the co-evolution of the relationships among objects, representations, and behaviors in consumers' experience and whose structure is theoretically based on a practice-theory framework. The quotes from the interviews I use come from qualitative research on the appropriation of music listening technology carried out in Italy between 2005 and 2007 with young music listeners (for more details on the research, see Magaudda, 2011).

THE IPOD AND THE "RE-MATERIALIZATION" OF DIGITAL MUSIC CONSUMPTION

When we look at the recent history of digital music, we see that the whole reconfiguration (at the same time technical, industrial, cultural, and situational) of music consumption has been reorganized around one specific object: the iPod portable Mp3 music player. It is not a case that the iPod is a beautiful and materially attractive object and that it is also incredibly satisfying to use. A brief look at the iPod as a material object makes evident how materiality played a role in the universal appropriation of this player and in the commercial success it brought to Apple. For instance, one of the key functions that differentiated the iPod from other Mp3 players was the "click wheel," which replaced the conventional play and stop buttons, making possible a new and original experience. The question is not whether the development of digital music consumption in these last few years has been determined by the aesthetic and functional qualities of the iPod, but how its aesthetic and functional qualities had a relevant part in the process.

In this respect, the work of Michael Bull (2007) is one of the best examples of the ways in which the use of portable players has made possible a new relationship between people and the objects that surround them. The iPod has also become a powerful, key cultural and symbolic icon of the new century and, moreover, has opened up the marketplace for the development of further portable personal devices, such as the iPhone and the iPad. In the music consumption context, which is characterized by a shift to intangible music digital flows, the iPod clearly represents a material object around which the digital music realm has been reconfigured culturally, socially, and economically (Dant, 2008).

Elsewhere consumer culture and material culture researchers have considered the various ways in which newly introduced objects are appropriated or domesticated. Drawing from that body of work, we can see digital music consumption as entailing a whole range of materially mediated practices through which artefacts are appropriated or singularized, such as the adoption of other artefacts such as headphones. Often people feel the need to carry their iPod around in a case (to protect it from damage), and they generally tend to choose a case that makes this beautiful, but anonymous, musical object more personal. An example from my research illustrates this point. A 32-year-old man told me that he found one of his mother's old jewelry cases and used it for safeguarding his iPod so that he could emphasize the symbolic distance that he wished to create between himself and the mainstream trend of having the iPod on show:

> I don't care so much about the idea of the iPod as a status symbol, I don't give a damn about that. [. . .] That's why I don't buy accessories. . . . I carry it around in a small velvet bag from a jeweler's that I found in a drawer in amongst my mum's old stuff . . . , that way it's not so visible and I can hide it so that strangers can't see it. (Marco, M, 32 years old)

This personal way to appropriate the iPod is a good example of what Grant McCracken (1988: 83–87) defined as a "ritual of consumption" and also highlights the fact that new devices need to be articulated at a material as well as a cultural and symbolic level, according to personal dispositions, feelings, and participation in trends and cultures. Moreover, this example helps introduce the fact that the adoption of new digital music devices has not only affected the ways people use music in social context—as it has already been highlighted by Michael Bull's (2007) work—but more broadly changed the intimate material landscape of listeners' experience.

Now we will see how adopting a practice-based analysis allows us to develop a more articulated understanding of the processes of change and transformation within music listening practices, emphasizing the mutual articulation of meanings, objects, and ways of operating in relation to the appropriation and use of the iPod. In order to illustrate this point, I would like to consider an example that does not directly concern the practice of listening but is part of the ways in which students create groups and generate a sense of belonging within the context of a high school through the appropriation of Mp3 players. One of the most relevant contexts in which the iPod has been more readily adopted and incorporated into shared social practices is the teenage context. Teenagers interviewed in 2006 told me about the sudden and widespread adoption of the iPod and similar players among their schoolmates, as the following excerpt from the interview with Margherita—a 17-year-old high school student—clearly shows:

> This year [2005/2006] has been the year of the boom [of the iPod]. At the beginning of the year, only one person in 30 had a music player. But during the last year people asked to receive them as gifts for birthdays, anniversaries and other events, and I noted that this fact of having the iPod was . . . the iPod became a compulsory gift, desirable above all the others: "What can I give? I might just give an iPod!" Yes, I think that more people received an iPod as a gift than bought one. It's the perfect gift. (Margherita, F, 17 years old)

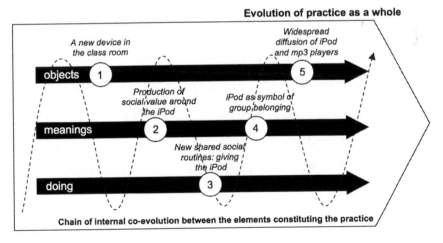

Figure 8.1 The process of performative integration of the iPod in the classroom as a gift visualized in form of chain of internal co-evolution of elements constituting practice.

A closer look at Margherita's short account reveals many interesting elements, which are useful in making sense of the socio-material processes involved in the adoption of the iPod among young students. We can articulate this account along the chain of co-evolution of elements constituting digital music consumption practices in order to explain the changing evolution of the relationship among materiality, representation, and way of doing. This is visualized in Figure 8.1.

The chain of co-evolution starts with step 1, when a new object, the iPod, appears in the context of the classroom. The process of socio-material appropriation of the iPod in the classroom produces different forms of value-production around that object, which are connected with its novelty and usage (step 2: meanings). The emergence of these social values among students consequently enables the development of new shared habits and practices, and, among these habits, Margherita traces the routine of giving the iPod as a gift on occasions of recognized social events such as birthdays (step 3: doing). The practice of giving the iPod as a gift helps re-produce a sense of belonging to the group of peers, in so doing establishing a new sign for group affiliation in the classroom (step 4: meanings). Finally, we can see the consequences of the socio-performative integration of the iPod in the classroom in terms of crystallization of the iPod's widespread presence in the school setting (step 5).

In this case, we see that the materiality of digital music seems to acquire a new constitutive role in redefining personal relationships. In particular, because the Ipod is seen as an ideal gift, which in turn has a constitutive role in social relations and organization. On this basis we are able to recognize that iPod gift-giving and possession represents a way through which new digital music devices and technologies have been socially integrated and re-materialized among the younger generations.

THE RE-MATERIALIZAITON OF AN EXISTING OBJECT BELONGING TO A DIFFERENT PRACTICE: THE CASE OF THE HARD DISK DRIVE

A second example regarding the way an object belonging to a different practice has been re-materialized inside the digital music world. It's the case of the hard drive used to store music. Indeed, digital music is not only used and stored in specific music devices such as the iPod, but more often in other and more generic kinds of devices, such as personal computers and external hard disk drives. One of the consequences of the increasing amount of music available for purchase on the Internet is the increased amount of music that one can possess and store: This makes it necessary to find new ways of storing digital music and, therefore, to often adopt and use an external hard drive, which was designed and produced primarily as a personal computer accessory.

The hard drive is an object that already existed in social practices, but it was not previously integrated into musical listening and collection practices. Indeed, the hard drive primarily belongs to the universe of IT and computers, and only recently, with the diffusion of digital music, it has been introduced into the practice of music consumption, often becoming an essential device. Thus, the following example shows what happens when a material object passes from one practice to another and how meanings and activities previously related to them are translated into another specific practice.

The integration of the hard disk drive into music consumption practices constitutes an interesting case in considering the trajectory of an object that previously belonged to a different practice and the processes by which this object has passed from one practice to another. As Alan Warde (2005: 143–145) stressed, the potential of adopting a practice-based perspective in consumption studies is also connected with the potentiality to understand how different and separated practices relate to one another. One case showing how devices previously only used for music are now, with the diffusion of digital music, transformed into objects useful for multiple purposes and practices, is the use of the Mp3 pen drive, which can be utilized to both store various files and reproduce music. Different users interviewed in the research reported that they actually use this device to both listen to music and store other kinds of files and information, thus showing how new material devices emerging in digital music constitute a crossroads between social practices previously separated. One specific example of the heterogeneous use of the Mp3 pen drive comes from the experience of Luciano:

> Yes, I have a player, one of those small pen drives that you can directly connect to the computer, which can also store files such as photos, word processor files, and emails as well, so that I can have them whenever I don't have my personal computer with me. In short, yes, I use it as a music player but, as far as I'm concerned, it has a double function. (Luciano, M, 28 years old)

For many music listeners, starting to use the hard disk for music purposes requires the development of new knowledge, strategies, and activities around the use of these devices. Hard disks are extremely useful for storing a large amount of music and also make it extraordinarily simple to share music with friends and other people; but unlike cassettes or CDs, hard disk drives are very sensitive and can be easily broken, damaged, or deleted. This sensitivity may depend on software problems, such as when a virus affects it, or on material and concrete flaws, when for example a hard disk falls on the floor and, in the majority of cases, becomes inoperative. The hard disk drive therefore not only represents a relatively "new entry" from outside the realm of music, but probably also constitutes the most evident example of the complex and problematic relationship, in a digital context, between the fragility of materiality and the persistence of immaterial and intangible contents. A concrete example of these kinds of issues regarding the fragility of music stored in the hard disk is provided by the account of Antonio, a digital music listener who told me that after he lost all his music due to a hard disk failure, he was compelled to develop new strategies involving the backup of his music:

> It was a gift for my graduation, I asked my friend to give me an external hard disk because once I lost all my data, all my data . . . so I need this hard disk drive to store a copy of all my 30 GB of music and some 40 GB of movies. And I'm very fond of this hard disk, because I have such a f. . . . . g fear of losing all my music. So, I use this hard drive as a sort of backup, containing a copy of all my music and also as a box to carry music around with me to share with my friends. (Antonio, M, 30 years old)

As in the previous case, we can understand more clearly and concretely the process of "performative integration" of the hard drive into Antonio's musical practices by considering this little experience in terms of the chain of co-evolution of practice. We can assume our point of departure is the material passage from CD to digital Mp3 and the digital storage of music (step 1), which produces a change in the subjective value accorded to the data stored in the hard drive (step 2), which is now perceived through the lens of the socio-cultural frame of the attachment and affection felt for one's personal music collection. This new feeling about the relevance of data, and the management of music as data, produces a development of new competence and knowledge for storing music as digital data (step 3), which

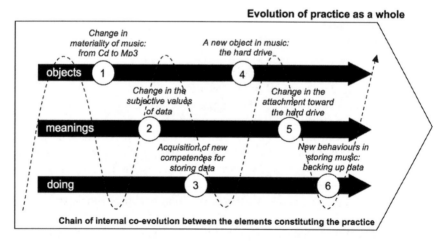

Figure 8.2 The process of performative integration of the hard drive in musical practice visualized through the chain of internal co-evolution of practice.

is the premise for the acquisition of a new musical object consisting of a hard drive especially devoted to backing up music (step 4). Consequently, we also see a reconfiguration of the meanings and affections toward this object (step 5) and a fully reconfigured behavior regarding music collection and storage (step 6) (see Figure 8.2).

In carefully considering the process of performative reconfiguration of music collections and storage practices, several issues emerge as relevant. One of the more evident is that the re-materialization of digital music has required the listener to elaborate an effective material strategy, which allows us to understand that the process of integration of a new material device typically brings about changes in the attachment and affection for an object, as well as in the ways this material device is embedded into a more complex shift of actions, behaviors, and forms of doings. Thus, the example of the hard drive shows us how the evolution of digital musical practices can be explained by looking at the re-adaptation of objects previously belonging to different contexts through which consumers develops processes of re-materialization.

RE-MATERIALIZING AN OBSOLETE MUSICAL OBJECT: THE VINYL RECORD

What happens to older existing objects when new digital material objects are introduced into the practice of music consumption? While an intuitive answer would suggest that existing materialities should lose relevance in favor of newer ones, the analysis of listeners' experiences can lead to a rather different conclusion. Indeed, the last example takes into consideration the process of re-materialization of an object that already existed in music consumption that seemed to have been marginalized in the practice of music listening: the long play vinyl record.

The historical trajectory of the long play vinyl record is quite a long one. It was introduced in 1948 and reached a high popularity in the 1970s, but since the 1980s it has been replaced first by the audiotape and then the digital compact disc (Millard, 2005). From the turn of the 1990s onward, the vinyl record seemed to have disappeared from shops as well as from common musical consumption practices and cultural representations. However, its continued use for both practical and symbolic reasons in different musical subcultures—such as alternative post-punk, ska-reggae, and especially in many dance-based musical genres—allowed vinyl to outlive the on-going process of technical innovation (Plasketes, 2004). Moreover, vinyl has remained the central focus of interest of many music collectors (see e.g., Milano, 2003).

Nevertheless, the use of vinyl records does not only concern older or more nostalgic listeners. For example, by using qualitative interviews focused on attachments to music, Haynes (2006) has shown that vinyl records and turntables have also come back into use in more widespread and newer consumption contexts. Young consumers adopt them in order to express a resistant attitude toward contemporary industry-regulated modes of music consumption and thus to enhance their personal agency (Haynes, 2006). On the side of music creation and production, the material interaction with the old vinyl disc is today at the basis of the development of new forms of use of music, for example, through the adaptation of some of the material features involved in the vinyl's manipulation into the new technology of the digital vinyl systems (see Attias, 2011; Lippit, 2006). Moreover, considering listening practices, here it is relevant to consider that the use and consumption of vinyl records is also connected with a whole reconfiguration in the materiality of listening enabled by these objects, which involves a different material activity in the moment of listening music. The different relationships established with music when listening to vinyl records in comparison with CDs is well illustrated by the 28-year-old Jacopo:

> The vinyl record is, in a certain sense, something that holds the attention. . . . You put on a record, and there is no way you can forget you have put it on, as it can happen with a compact disc, because after a while the stylus reaches the end of the record and you have to change side. . . . It does not last as long as a CD. . . . Maybe you were just about to forget that the vinyl was on, and it is already time to change side. It is like the vinyl asks for your attention when you are about to forget that the turntable is on. (Jacopo, M, 28 years old)

These kinds of accounts shed light on the role of vinyl in specific music cultures, which cannot simply be dismissed by the emergence of a new technology, and that the use of vinyl records, as in the case of Jacopo's experience, expresses a different pragmatic relationship with music and with the act of listening itself.

From the perspective of practice theory, we can add that the change of music into intangible data also produces a wider reconfiguration of existing materialities that can acquire a renewed role in expressing meanings as well as in serving as mediators for partially different activities and ways of doing. Indeed, in the same way that new music objects such as the iPod require the development of new meanings and practices, older ones can call for a similar process of reconfiguration, almost as if the whole reconfiguration triggered by the spread of digital music had produced the need for intense material relationships, which has to be reallocated to old and maybe obsolete objects.

In this regard, we can consider the arguments of Fabio, a 27-year-old guy, who had recently began buying and listening to music on vinyl. He tells us about the reasons and feelings that encouraged him to switch to this old music technology:

Because in my opinion [digital music] dehumanizes the relationship [of listeners] with the artist. Before, with the classical approach—I mean when we were teens—you were seeing music on television, then you would buy the CD and maybe read an article in a magazine. Today everything is on the computer screen, from music and videos to reviews, photos and everything else, and everything remains inside the screen. [. . .] Today there is the risk that bands could become a mere space occupied in a computer folder, and maybe it is for this reason that people like me have started to buy vinyl discs. Maybe it's because of the need to have human contact with the artist, even if this happens to be through fetishes. (Fabio, M, 27 years old)

What is particularly relevant here is the fact that the changes that affected music consumption when digital music activities began to pass through the computer screen have generated a sense of loss of meaning and cultural value around the musical experience. While Fabio defined this sense of loss as a "dehumanization" of music, we can regard it as a crisis of "authenticity" of the musical experience, which is one of the bases of the process of cultural value production in the realm of music. This loss of authenticity is perceived by Fabio not as a consequence of the digitalization of the music in itself, but as an outcome of the shift of the whole set of material activities and forms of doing in musical consumption, which also include, for example, the change in the way music magazines are read.

Once again, when we render the experience of this music listener through the chain of co-evolution of practice, we are able to show and make sense, in a more effective way, of the relationship between the construction of the experience and the change in practice and materiality of music (see Figure 8.3).

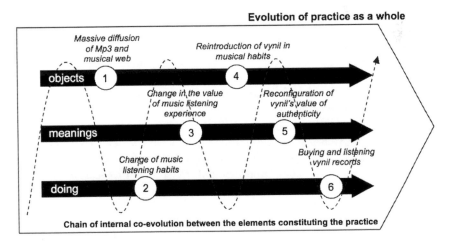

Figure 8.3 The process of performative re-integration of vinyl records in musical consumption practices visualized through the chain of co-evolution of practice.

Here, the chain starts from the spread of different forms of digital and computer-based musical objects and activities (step 1), which have an effect on listeners' habits and activities (step 2) that are now more and more often performed through the screen of a personal computer. These changes in the tools and activities used for familiarizing with, acquiring, and listening to music generate a change in the listener's approach to his music experience, which is now perceived as less authentic and significant (step 3). These feelings therefore produce a change on a material level, pushing the listener toward the adoption of vinyl and turntable (step 4), the appropriation of which is one of the elements that contribute to the development of a process of reconfiguration of meanings, values, and feelings around the use of the obsolete LP (step 5). Finally, the re-integration of vinyl records as socio-material music practices is the basis for the development of new activities and behaviors, which involve the buying, listening, conservation, and appreciation of the vinyl and turntable (step 6).

In short, this example can be interpreted as meaning that with the digital transition of music consumption, not only do materialities not disappear in consumer practices, but they can also find a renewed role through the process of re-materialization of old and obsolete objects. In this sense, the relationship between materiality and digitalization calls into question the whole set of material, cultural, and social elements constituting the practice of musical digital virtual consumption, even marginal or obsolete objects as in the case of vinyl records.

CONCLUSION: MATERIALITIES AND RE-MATERIALIZATION IN A DVC

When we look more closely at the changes in the listeners' experience as a consequence of the diffusion of digital music, the reduction of transformation only to the features connected with the de-materialization and digitalization of consumption is highly problematic. The material dimension of consumption, both in terms of material objects actually used and meanings ascribed to these objects by their users, reminds us of the embodied and material experience of social life. Whereas DVC represents a sort of liminal space between what is imagined and tangible objects, this liminality implies not only that the material and the symbolic are strictly interlaced and interwoven, but also that it is impossible to think of DVC without making reference to the changing forms of materiality in social life and to how this materiality contributes to shaping possibilities and constraints, opportunities and barriers of DVC.

This is particularly true when we think about the ways DVC experience is shaped and configured by the technical artefacts indispensable for interfacing with the Web and for inhabiting other digital virtual spaces of consumption. The more advanced and sophisticated personal computers and devices become the more relevant their role as material mediators of consumers' experience; hence our need to understand emerging patterns in the experiences of consumption.

This is not only true for music, but also for many different media products as in the more recent case of the digitalization of books and newspapers. Indeed, transition processes in written texts from traditional paper to digital objects have gained momentum only recently, when some specific material objects—first *Amazon's* Kindle and then, and more decisively, Apple's iPad—found a way to catalyze the attention of both cultural industries and consumers, allowing them to imagine a new attractive scenario of production and consumption of digital written texts. From the perspective advanced in this chapter, the recent success of iPads, ebooks, and emags can be easily seen as a process of re-materialization in the practice of reading texts in the digital virtual world. Similarly, we can expect that in the future we will probably witness many other forms of re-materialization in virtual digital consumption practices.

REFERENCES

Appadurai A. 1986. *The Social Life of Things: Commodities in Cultural Perspective*. Cambridge University Press: Cambridge.

Apple. 2008. *iTunes Store Top Music Retailer in the US*. Press release, 3 April.

Attias BA. 2011. Meditations on the Death of Vinyl. *Dancecult. Journal of Electronic Dance Music Culture* 3(1).

Bijker WE, Hughes TP, and Pinch TJ. 1987. *The Social Construction of Technological Systems: New Directions in the Sociology and History of Technology*. The MIT Press: Cambridge, MA.

Bull M. 2007. *Sound Moves*. Routledge: London.

Dant T. 2008. iPod. iCon. *Studi Culturali* 5(3): 355–373.

Denegri-Knott J, Molesworth M. 2010. Concepts and Practices of Digital Virtual Consumption. *Consumption Markets and Culture* 13(2): 109–132.

Douglas M, Isherwood B. 1978. *The World of Goods: Towards an Anthropology of Consumption*. Basic Books: New York.

Eisemberg E. 1987. *The Recording Angel: Music, Records and Culture from Aristotle to Zappa*. McGraw-Hill: New York.

European Union. 2009. *Consumers: EU Acts to Limit Health Risks from Exposure to Noise from Personal Music Players*. Press release IP/09/1364, 28 September.

Halkier B, Katz-Gerro T, and Martens L. 2011. Applying Practice Theory to the Study of Consumption: Theoretical and Methodological Considerations. *Journal of Consumer Culture* 11(1): 3–13.

Haynes D. 2006. Take Those Old Records off the Shelf: Youth and Music Consumption in the Postmodern Age. *Popular Music & Society* 29(1): 51–68.

Hesmondhalgh D. 2009. The Digitalization of Music, in *Creativity and Innovation in the Cultural Economy*, AC Pratt and P Jeffcut (eds.). Routledge: New York: 57–73.

Katz M. 2004. *Capturing Sound: How Technology Has changed Music*. University of California Press: Berkley, CA.

Kuzek D, Leonard G. 2005. *The Future of Music: Manifesto for the Digital Music Revolution*. Berkley Press: Boston, MA.

Latour B. 1987. *Science in Action: How to Follow Scientists and Engineers through Society.* Harvard University Press: Cambridge, MA.

Lippit TM. 2006. *Turntable Music in the Digital Era: Designing Alternative Tools for New Turntable Expression.* Proceedings of the 2006 International Conference on New Interfaces for Musical Expression (NIME06), Paris.

Magaudda P. 2011. When Materiality "Bites Back." Digital Music Consumption Practices in the Age of Dematerialization. *Journal of Consumer Culture* 11(1): 15–36.

McCracken G. 1988. *Culture and Consumption: New Approaches to the Symbolic of Consumer Goods and Activities.* Indiana University Press: Bloomington.

Milano B. 2003. *Vinyl Junkies: Adventures in Record Collecting.* St. Martin's Griffin: New York.

Millard A. 2005. *America on Record: A History of Recorded Music.* Cambridge University Press: Cambridge.

Miller D. 1987. *Material Culture and Mass Consumption.* Basil Backwell: Oxford.

Plasketes G. 2004. Romancing the Record. The Vinyl De-evolution and Subcultural evolution. *Journal of Popular Culture* 26(1): 109–122.

Reckwitz A. 2002. Toward a Theory of Social Practices. A Development in Culturalist Theorizing. *European Journal of Social Theory* 5(2): 243–263.

Rodman GB, Vanderdonckt C. 2006. Music for Nothing or, I Want My Mp3: The Regulation and Recirculation of Affect. *Cultural Studies* 20(2–3): 245–261.

Sassatelli R. 2007. *Consumer Culture: History, Theory and Politics.* Sage: London.

Schatzki T. 1996. *Social Practices: A Wittgensteinian Approach to Human Activity and the Social.* Cambridge University Press: Cambridge.

Schatzki T, Knorr-Cetina K, and Von Savigny E. 2001. *The Practice Turn in Contemporary Theory.* Routledge: London.

Shove E, Pantzar M. 2005. Consumers, Producers and Practices. Understanding the Invention and Reinvention of Nordic Walking. *Journal of Consumer Culture* 5(1): 43–64.

Shove E, Watson M, Hand M, and Ingram J. 2007. *The Design of Everyday Life.* Berg: Oxford.

Sterne, J. 2003. *The Audible Past: Cultural Origins of Sound Reproduction.* Duke University Press: Durham, NC.

Symes C. 2004. *Setting the Record Straight: A Material History of Classic Recording.* Wesleyan University Press: Middletown, CT.

Vannini P. 2009. *Material Culture and Technology in Everyday Life.* Peter Lang: New York.

Warde A. 2005. Consumption and Theories of Practice. *Journal of Consumer Culture* 5(2): 131–153.

Part II
Places and Practices

9 Online Investing as Digital Virtual Consumption
The Production of the Neoliberal Subject

Detlev Zwick

INTRODUCTION

Over the last decade or so, individual investing has become a mass phenomenon due to the virtualization of the stock market and the computerization of buying and selling (Zwick, 2005; Zwick and Dholakia, 2006a). Online investing has been hailed as the democratization of Wall Street and as a major factor in the spreading of the "ownership society." Impressively, the wide-spread adoption of online trading and the concurrent increase in the number of active stock market participants and owners of equities happened even as the individual investors have been faced with significant setbacks. Many of them became stock market enthusiasts and active investors during the market run-up of the late 1990s, a time of (irrational) market exuberance (Shiller, 2000) fueled by seemingly ever increasing stock prices. In those days, advertising time during a wide variety of television shows, ranging from the *Superbowl* to *Seinfeld*, were filled with commercials for any of the dozens of newly opened discount online brokerage services, illustrating the changing position of the stock market in the popular imagination of Americans. When the stock market crashed in the spring of 2000, the investment boom years of the late 1990s came to a grinding halt. Investors lost a lot of money in a very short period of time, and many online brokerages went out of business within a few months. However, the few years before the crash were enough to effect a profound transformation of how many Americans viewed self-directed and active stock trading. Certainly, many day traders fled the market, but they were replaced with even larger numbers of more long-term oriented investors. Hence, in 2005, only five years after the so-called dot com meltdown, more than twelve million Americans were trading stocks online, up six-fold from just a little more than two million in 1998 and up two-fold from the six million online investors in 2002 (Lee and Yongwoon, 2005).

Even the recent Great Recession, which effectively erased any gains investors had made over the seven years following the dot com bust, did not affect in a significant way the number of online investors trying their luck with the stock market. Three years after the worst economic crisis since the

Great Depression, commercials for online brokerage services are back on TV and business is brisk. Clearly, during the second half of the 1990s, a new online investor class of small, individual, do-it-yourself investors had formed at the intersection of information technological innovation and economic and social neoliberalization (experienced as a state of permanent economic insecurity and precarity as well as socio-economic individualization and responsibilization); an investor subject prepared to embrace as opportunities moments of serious economic crisis (Gagnier, 1997; Heelas et al., 1996; Sassen, 1999). In this chapter, I want to investigate what kind of investor subjectivities came into being at the turn of the century, when investing became popularized as a form of digital virtual consumption (DVC) (cf. Denegri-Knott and Molesworth, 2010). I draw on Foucault's (2008) critique of liberalism and his analyses of neoliberal governmentality to suggest that personal investment has become an important site for the (re)production of an entrepreneurial ethics of the self, where neoliberal theories of consumption and popular cultural representations suggest a specific mode of *subjectivation*[1] for the investor self (*qua* consumer) that is based on individualization, insecurity, competitiveness, and inequality. Hence, this chapter pursues three objectives. First, I show that from the perspective of neoliberal consumption studies, including the growing and diverse body of work produced by marketing scholars under the label of consumer culture theory, consumers are exhorted to fashion themselves as investors (here quite literally) and entrepreneurs. Hence, in extension, I suggest that the neoliberal turn exhorts the investor self to consider his or her investing activities as a form of consumption, rather than a collective and potentially socialized form of economic securitization (such as traditional pension schemes). Second, I analyze television commercials and interview data collected during the early days of online investing, specifically during the late 1990s and early 2000s, to argue that the virtualization of personal investing was accompanied by depictions of the New Economy online investor as an active, entrepreneurial, and voluntaristic market agent who embraces fiscal self-realization, competitive market logic, and the reality of individualized risk as personal freedom. In this context, it is important to recognize the effect on the investor subject with the transfer of stock trading from what could be called an analog world of phone calls, faxes, and trips to the local bank to the computer-mediated environment of the computer screen. Once the stock market has been reproduced on the computer screen as a virtual object, new kinds of individual experiences, practices, and subjectivities emerge at the intersection of the market and the screen (Zwick, 2005; Zwick and Dholakia, 2006b). Third, I caution against popular celebrations of personal investing as some kind of consumer democratization of Wall Street or the emancipation of the individual investor from the dependency of both the parasitic broker and any socialized forms of economic securitization. Instead, the popularization of investing-as-consumption should be scrutinized for the ways this practice enacts neoliberal governmentality, understood here as the strategic creation of social conditions that encourage and necessitate the production of the entrepreneurial consumer, a historically specific form of subjectivity constituted as a free and autonomous "atom" of self-interest implicated in, and accepting of, increasing economic inequality and insecurity, as well as the individualization of risk (Hamann, 2009: 37). More generally, my chapter aims at highlighting the role of the financialization of everyday life, often neglected by governmentality studies and critiques of neoliberalism, as a key site for completing, as it were, the transformation already well underway to an enterprising consumer society (cf. Lazzarato, 2009). Hence, if the project is to trace in practice the making of neoliberal subjectivities as the result of more or less strategic efforts of self-production and self-fashioning, the context of online investing as DVC, as defined by Denegri-Knott and Molesworth (2010), provides a useful starting point.

INVESTING AS CONSUMPTION/ CONSUMPTION AS INVESTING

In (neo) classical economic theory, investment has been characterized as an *act of creation* (of wealth), whereas consumption has been defined as the *act of destruction* (of wealth) (Allen and McGoun, 2000). However, as pointed out by cultural theorists and marketing and consumer researchers, consumption can also be an act of fulfillment, creation, and production (e.g., Belk, 1988; Firat and Dholakia, 1998; Firat and Venkatesh, 1995; Fiske, 1989; Kozinets, 2001). While generally unacknowledged, these scholars follow what Foucault (2008: 226) in his 1979 lectures on the birth of biopolitics called "a very interesting theory of consumption." This theory, articulated by neoliberal economist Gary Becker, regards the consumer as entrepreneur, an entrepreneur of himself, who is productive through consumption. He produces himself as a form of capital, which could include the production of identity, a lifestyle, a social network and community, and marketable skills, among other things. Hence, in practice as in theory, the stake in neoliberal analyses of consumption is the rejection of the consumer subject as a simple buyer and user of goods and services and the adoption of a notion of the entrepreneurial, agentic, and, indeed, producing consumer. Becker and his largely unsuspecting disciples in the marketing and consumer research field thus urge us to conceptualize consumption "as an enterprise activity by which the individual, precisely on the basis of the capital he has at his disposal, will produce something" (Foucault, 2008: 226; see also Zwick and Ozalp, 2011).

Etymologically, the double meaning of consumption—destruction *and* creation—is already embedded in the two Latin origins of the term "consumption." One origin is the word "consumere," which means "to use" in the sense of "to devour" or "to deplete." The second origin of consumption can be found in the term "consummare," which means "to consummate" in the sense of "to make perfect" or "to complete" (Knobloch, 1994). In classical economic theory only the first meaning gained currency. When we consume something we use it up. The second meaning, consumption as "building," never entered the economic discourse until the neoliberal turn in economics and the introduction of the concept of human capital (Becker, 1975; Schultz, 1970). Interesting here is that the neoliberals usher in a significant ontological transformation by proposing that consumption should be treated as a form of labor that enters the production of the individual as human capital. In other words, consumption is part of the self-production of the subject (which includes the ability to earn an income but extends to such things as identity, social networks, community, status, emotions, affect, etc.).

Especially the neoliberal camp of consumption studies, often referred to as consumer culture theory (CCT) by its proponents, has put forth a number of approaches promoting the productive moment of consumption (for an overview, see Arnould and Thompson, 2005). In a broad sense, we can identify four prominent socio-cultural theories of consumption, all of which follow Becker's theory of consumption by conceptualizing consumption as an active, productive, and valuable practice: (1) consumption as creative hedonism, (2) consumption as lifestyle, (3) consumption as communication, and (4) consumption as play. From these perspectives, it becomes clear that the distinction between investment and consumption makes little sense. For example, the consumption as communication theory postulates that consumers increasingly acquire things because of their sign character (Baudrillard, 1981; Douglas and Isherwood, 1979). In other words, products offer a set of symbolic meanings for the production of identity and social distinction. Equally productive, according to the neoliberal recasting of consumption and the consumer, are acts of pleasurable (hedonic) consumption as well as the performance of lifestyles for personal and public consumption. Traditionally, lifestyle analysis, a term that goes back to Max Weber and George Simmel, addresses typical behavior of social groups. Especially Simmel's remarks on "the role of style as a means of at once maintaining a distance and establishing the existence of shared attributes in an intensely individualistic and subjective culture, though written at the turn of the century, could have been composed with the 1980s in mind" (Callinicos, 1990: 190). What Simmel, Weber, and Veblen had in common was a belief in lifestyle as a social phenomenon. In other words, lifestyle is linked to the formation and existence of status groups. Consumption is the algorithm through which collectivities produce and challenge social distinction. As a member of a particular lifestyle grouping, the individual actively uses consumer goods—clothes, the home, furnishings, interior decor, car, holidays, food and drink, as well as cultural goods such as music, film, and art—in ways which indicate that particular grouping's taste and style (Lury, 1996: 80; see also Bourdieu, 1984). In sum, within the framework of lifestyle analysis, consumption plays an important role for the *production* of social realities. Lifestyle theory is thus an extension of the "hedonic" argument.

Viewed in this way, consumption becomes more than wasteful destruction, a mere accessory to the reproduction of labor, or a strategy to discipline the worker in the capitalist system of exploitation (for these well-known lines of thought, see exemplary Adorno, 1991; Horkheimer and Adorno, 1972; Marx, 1978). Consumption, then, becomes an ethical field of practice, in Foucault's sense, where consumers are asked to self-fashion themselves in specific productive, autonomous, and instrumental ways (see e.g., Binkley, 2006). It is here that we see the collapse of consuming and/or investing most clearly. Indeed, between the concept of human capital and the adoption, albeit not always consciously, of Becker's neoliberal theory of enterprising consumption by many consumer culture researchers, the hegemonic view of the active, autonomous, and productive consumer coming out of these bodies of literature is very well suited for conceptualizing the conduct of individual investors, especially when analyzed in conjunction with the rise of information and communication technologies (ICTs) such as the Internet (Knorr Cetina and Bruegger, 2002; Zwick, 2005).

POPULAR CULTURE AND THE MARKET ON THE SCREEN

Since the 1980s, market liberalism and economic individualism have become the dominant political and social frameworks in the US, Great Britain, and (with variations) Europe (Bourdieu, 1998; Comaroff and Comaroff, 2001; Giroux, 2004; Sassen, 2007). The socio-political discourse emanating from the neoliberal restructuring of national economies and the welfare state centers around the logic of the market and makes the nature of market conduct the paradigm for all forms of human conduct (Binkley, 2009a; Gagnier, 1997). Then, during the 1990s, individuals were flocking to the stock market in unprecedented numbers. Investors were getting younger, more technologically savvy, and—armed with the Internet and emboldened by a steadily climbing stock market seemingly void of risk—self-reliant. Toward the end of the millennium, online brokers were booming, and the number of individual investors using the Internet to conduct stock trades and other financial transactions was increasing. These autonomous "renegade capitalists," as a then popular commercial by online brokerage firm Ameritrade (now called Toronto-Dominion, or TD Ameritrade) called this new investor group,[2] were not trained investment professionals with business degrees and they tended to approach investing decisions and market dynamics from an emotional perspective, what Akerlof and Shiller (2009) refer to as "animal spirits." Clearly, at the turn of the century with the stock market at dazzling heights, new investor subjectivities were emerging at the intersection of complex economic, social, and cultural forces.

Investors are currently reeling from the second massive stock market crash in one decade that erased any gains made in the last ten years. Americans are especially disturbed by the market downturn because, historically, the perception of the stock market as a legitimate, if not required, place to create wealth and secure the future has formed particularly strongly among individual investors in the US. The US has more investors than any other country in the world (Staute, 1998), and the demand for stocks has been growing impressively for over a decade and a half now. It was hardly a coincidence that innovative companies and adventurous investors in the US were the first to challenge professional traders, financial investment advisors, fund managers, and other insiders for the right to trade stocks. At the beginning of the 21st century, individual online stock trading had established itself firmly as one of America's favorite pastimes, threatening the absolute monopoly of the Wall Street establishment. As one commentator remarked (Klam, 1999: 70):

> This is not about money-grubbing; it's a new democratic revolution. Day trading, like the right to own dirty magazines, the privilege of serving in our armed forces, is a fail-safe against the loss of individual freedom— which for Americans is the same thing as collective freedom—and for that matter is the only sure way to keep your soul intact.

New online brokerage firms were quick to pick up on this new *zeitgeist* of, as the *Wall Street Journal* slogan puts it, "adventures in capitalism" and understood the potential of the Internet to bring the global financial markets closer to everyone's living room (Steltzner, 1999). In a flood of TV commercials during the first heyday of online investing, the individual investor was directly challenged to "tear down the walls to Wall Street" (Datek), "beat the market" (E*Trade), and "outsmart the professionals" (Ameritrade). Their ads show a 12-year-old buying a helicopter with stock-market winnings and a 20-something loafer driving away in a Rolls-Royce towing a yacht. The message was this: In this age of online trading, the path to riches is not through the drudgery of productive work and slow, merit-based advancements on the corporate ladder. Rather, wealth depends on a will to be free, to take on the market like a high-tech soldier of fortune equipped with "swashbuckling fiscal adventurism, self-interest and self-responsibility" (Binkley, 2009b: 61). Instead of a conventional mindset that puts faith in cautious institutional progression and solid financial security, the new investor subject takes charge of his fiscal self-realization and instead of conventional education and sheepish work ethic celebrates the virtues of raw entrepreneurism, self-interest, and self-responsibility as a personal ethic (Binkley, 2009b). Consider the now famous reply by Ameritrade's TV ad character Stewart, a red-headed punk rocker, to the dismissive statement of his girlfriend's father, a "real" stock broker, regarding Stewart's online trading activities ("Give the kid a computer and he thinks he can beat the market"):

> I don't want to beat the market. I wanna grab it, sock it in the gut a couple of times, turn it upside down, hold it by the pants, and shake it 'til all those pockets empty out the spare change.

Further pushing the progressiveness of online trading as the beginning of a new era that requires a historically specific market subject—individualist, independent, and unencumbered capitalists freed from the shackles of corporate conformity and residual ideas of collective welfare—a series of commercials depicted goateed Gen-Xers with a calculating and assertive look. They proclaim "we're pioneers," and a 30-something professional female with a no-nonsense attitude seems to speak for her entire generation when she pronounces, "We're renegade capitalists." Finally, one ad shows how a classroom of immigrants studying English begins to rave about an Internet broker (Ameritrade): "They've mistaken it for the word America, they think their English teacher wants to talk about online trading and they all love this new country!" (Klam, 1999: 70). In their messages, online stock brokers promote neoliberal governmentality, which Binkley (2009a) explains as a way in which subjects are governed as market agents, encouraged to cultivate themselves as autonomous, self-interested individuals, and to view their resources and aptitudes as human capital to be maximized and brought to optimal profitability (Binkley, 2007; Foucault, 1991; Rose, 1996).

In no small part due to the advances in information technologies such as the Internet, which established as a technically effortless act the practice of investing, could something so complex and often consequential as the buying and selling of stocks become reduced to a seemingly straightforward act of online shopping. But perhaps more important than bringing to the individual investor's desk the hitherto unavailable power to buy and sell stocks in an inexpensive, autonomous, and convenient way has been the change in investors' perception of stocks and the stock market: No longer the Byzantine and exclusive playground for the masters of the universe, stock exchanges became places for everyone to enjoy and to feel at home, from the slightly juvenile college student to the technologically challenged senior citizen.

Put theoretically, new ICTs bring to the field of complex global financial flows an aesthetic quality that renders accessible, physically, emotionally, and intellectually, the market as a seemingly logical, *commonsense* entity

(Knorr Cetina, 1997; Knorr Cetina, and Bruegger, 2002). The computer screen is of particular importance here, as it assembles a geographically dispersed and usually invisible market and presents it to the trader as a cohesive and continuous consumptionscape (Zwick, 2005; Zwick and Dholakia, 2006a), not unlike the mall or the supermarket. The symbolic space generated by the screen assembles, contextualizes, and materializes "the market" as a place. "Finding the market," previously an imposing barrier to entry for masses of small investors, is no longer difficult. The screen now aggregates spatially dispersed and distanced information flows and subsequently visualizes them. The screen, in other words, becomes the gateway for investor-consumers to "enter" the market, and the image projected on the screen becomes the main stimulus driving his or her cognitive, emotional, and interpretative labor (Borgerson, 2005).

The notion that improvements in ICTs have played a part in turning individual investing into consumerist shopping and the investor into a shopper is certainly worth considering. Throughout the 1990s, ICTs made much larger inroads in the US than in almost any other part of the world, and this increase of Internet connectivity is paralleled by strong growth of the online investment market in the in the US (Carey, 1999). Yet it would be a mistake to reduce such a deep shift in individual investors' cultural and social imagination of the stock market to the ability to trade conveniently from your home computer. We need to be wary of the conceptual trap of technological determinism, which puts consumers in a profoundly passive relationship vis-à-vis technology, thereby producing reductionist explanatory models of social and individual behavior. Certainly, technology shapes human behavior, but it is equally the case that humans shape the use of technology (MacKenzie and Wajcman, 1999; Smith and Marx, 1994). Hence, in order to understand the growth of individual investing over the past fifteen years, and in particular its transformation into a prominent site of digital virtual consumption, a sociological rather than technological analysis is needed. The approach taken in this chapter recognizes that culture, including technoculture, is premised and made real on the basis of material subject-object relations that erect a web of "structured structures predisposed to function as structuring structures" (Bourdieu, 1990: 53), within which technology is designed, consumer subjectivities are constructed, and consumer action is taken. Specifically, I argue that the rise and the nature of the *investing subject* can only be fully understood within the larger context of the rise of neoliberal governmentality, which produces the conditions that encourage the individual investor to fashion oneself as an entrepreneur of the self (Foucault, 2008).

THE BIRTH OF THE CONSUMING INVESTOR

While the effect of popular culture and the Internet for the transformation of personal investing into a populist consumption activity can hardly be understated, we need to look at the larger social, cultural, and political structures within which the practice of individual online investing has been situated from its inception. With neoliberal politics firmly aimed at restoring the power of capital to determine the distribution of wealth and to establish the enterprise as a hegemonic social formation, its proponents understand that it is not enough to tweak some mechanisms of social organization and welfare (cf. Harvey, 2005). Neoliberal social policy aspires to reconstruct society as a whole by encouraging individual conduct conducive to the conditions of neoliberal market capitalism. Neoliberal social policy, then, has to do with making up and reproducing a new type of individual that aspires to make him or herself useful for the capitalist market. So what kinds of subjectivities are brought forth by the digital virtual consumption of stocks? In the following, I suggest that the popularization of investing as consumption should be considered an important social institution that creates conditions that encourage and necessitate the production of oneself as new *homo economicus*,[3] a subject that is morally responsible for navigating the social realm using rational choice and cost-benefit calculations grounded on market-based principles to the exclusion of all other ethical values and social interests (Hamann, 2009).

I argue below that in addition to the technologization of the stock market, recent socio-political transformations, such as the financialization and individualization of risk as well as the general insecuritization of the individual, are promoting a specific type of neoliberal conduct of the individual (entrepreneurial, competitive, self-reliant) while turning the digital virtual consumption of stocks into a site *par excellence* for the performance of this neoliberal self. Hence, the digital virtual consumption of stocks, by being linked in quite direct ways to the production of oneself as human capital, represents perhaps more than any other mode of consumption the strategic formation of a new type of individual, "the subject who is an 'entrepreneur of him/herself' who is meant to fit into the frame of society remade as an 'enterprise society' " (Lazzarato, 2009: 110).

INSECURITIZATION, INDIVIDUALIZATION, FINANCIALIZATION

The financialization of risk refers to policies and institutional structures designed to assert "the redistribution of risk and protection, leaving the individual increasingly at the mercy of the market" (Lazzarato, 2009: 111). Standardized, predictable, and collectively available life trajectories are being replaced with the vagaries of do-it-yourself career planning, institutional de-traditionalization, and socio-economic de-standardization (Bauman, 2000; Beck and Beck-Gernsheim, 1996). By design, the modern self no longer feels secure—socially, economically, and psychologically—and actively configures him or herself as what Giddens (1991) calls an ontologically insecure self. As a young German investor puts it, "that pension plan that my father got when he joined the workforce back in the 70s, well, that won't be there for my generation. These days, you have to secure ('absichern') yourself. I wouldn't trust government, or my company, to do it for me."

Not just collectively supported long-term financial planning schemes have become doubtful. Indeed, the world itself has become insecure (Beck, 1986; Giddens, 1990), and as traditional and institutional forms of security disappear, risk enters into modern lives from all directions (Bauman, 1991, 1996, 2003). Ulrich Beck (1986) calls this process "the democratization of civilization risk." Importantly, though, democratization of risk does not mean collectivization of risk for at the same time that risk becomes a universal condition the state withdraws collectivist forms of risk securitization (health care for victims of accidents and pollution, guaranteed retirement income regardless of the stock market performance, etc.), thus promoting individualized management of risk. Hence, insecuritization is central to the neoliberalization project. And as the neoliberal strategy of shifting responsibility onto individuals takes hold in the social body, if things go wrong—as they invariably do in a state-sanctioned finance capitalism that has been evacuated of democratic accountability and financial consequences for its actors and main beneficiaries—the individual expects to be responsible and left to his or her own devices in dealing with the personal fallout. The neoliberal subject, thus, embraces a perspective that risk and accidents are no longer the exception but the norm, and he is socialized into a world where stark ruptures and serious disruption are as common as they are revocable and (seemingly) repairable. But most importantly, macro-structural risk and ensuing crises that can move markets in often hysterical fashion are to be seized as the source of economic opportunity, even if based on the (undeserved) losses of others and exploited for individual profit.4 The invasion of Iraq by a US-led NATO coalition force in 2003, for example, drove up stocks of security, weapon and defense contractors, as well as heavy construction companies. As the statement of one of my American informants illustrates, configuring yourself as a consumer of market opportunity trumps any other consideration.

> It might not always seem fair or the right thing to do when you try to benefit from the misfortune of others but often that is how it works, isn't it? [...] I have done really well with defense related stocks since the invasion of Iraq. It's kinda ironic because I was against the invasion, actually, and still am. But when it comes to making money and making sure my wife and I can retire when we want to, as far as I am concerned, it's ok in my book. I'm taking advantage of an opportunity as an investor. It does not mean that I am a supporter of the war, either.

The individualization of risk, opportunities, costs, and benefits and the infusion of every aspect of social life with market values, such as competition and cost-benefit analysis, goes hand in hand with a retrenching welfare state where more and more of traditionally collective social systems, from health, to transportation, to education, to retirement planning, have been handed over to the market and made available for private choice and consumption. In addition, the dissolution of traditional life worlds is reflected in the erosion of religious worldviews, the end of highly stable and stratified social hierarchies, and the disintegration of social institutions (Giddens, 1991; Habermas, 1981; Weber, 1958). These changes combine to produce a modern self that is quickly finding itself emancipated from the collectivization of social expenditure, liberated from moral duties toward others beyond the letter of the law, and forced to adopt a mode of self-regulation centered on autonomy, flexibility, and instrumentality in professional and institutional life (Binkley, 2006). As Bauman (2000: 31) summarizes, " 'individualization' consists of transforming human 'identity' from a given into a 'task' and charging the actors with the responsibility for performing that task and for the consequences (also the side-effects) of their performance." Individualization and responsibilization, then, require a voluntaristic mode of life, the use of "techniques of the self" and the embrace of the ethico-aesthetic notion of making oneself as a work of art (Foucault, 1990). Many of the investors I interviewed expressed this sense of "self-made-ness" often related to making things happen in the market. As one informant put it:

> I'll be honest with you, buying and selling stock really excites me, doing the investing myself really excites me, and driving our financial future myself really excites me. And it scares me at times but so far, it's been really good. I think it's a control thing with me. I like to be in charge and even when I used a broker, I never liked it. Now, I am completely independent of others and that part feels really good.

The consequences of neoliberal social policy for the individual are two-fold: the loss of conventional support systems *and* the emancipation from social dependencies. In other words, the liberation of the subject is irreducibly connected to the requirement for individual self-reliance, self-provision, and autonomy. In concrete terms, this means that the end of predestined life projects and linear career planning (Wallulis, 1998) increases both the range of options available to the individual and the need to make decisions. Decisions about which school to go to, what career to choose, with whom to enter into a relationship, if and how to save for retirement, whether to get medical treatment and if so which one to choose, where to live, and so on are no longer predetermined by one's milieu or membership to a social class (Habermas, 1994) but must be made by the individual and always stand up to the question of "why?" In short, in individualized societies, the individual must learn to regard him or herself as the center of decision-making, as the only authoritative "planning office"—and hence the only one responsible for its effects—relative to his or her choices.

Under neoliberal social policy individual freedom therefore becomes anti-thetical to the notion of individual security. Free individuals are exhorted to approach life as an on-going project under construction, without lasting certainty (and perhaps even fleeting certainty) about the exact direction, let alone destination, of the life journey. Indeed, according to the new spirit of capitalism (Boltanski and Chiapello, 2007), any "buy-in" to long-term dependencies has the potential to become downright dangerous when individual plans about career, identity, residency, or social relationships must remain nimble, adaptable, and mobile in a world without certain-ties. Self-directed online investing, rather than state-sanctioned retirement schemes or company pension plans, embodies the new spirit of capital-ism by allowing the subject to fashion him or herself as an independent fiscal agent and a decisionistic market actor. Echoing the self-confident representations of the Ameritrade advertisements of the late 1990s, and in particular the swashbuckling attitude of punk-rock investor Steward, one US-based investor states, "I take care of my financial needs myself. I don't want to rely on some company or the government when I am older. I don't trust them, so, I'd rather do it myself. [. . .] It really is all about people taking responsibility for themselves rather than relying on others to do the work for them. And with the Internet, it's really easy to do."

Neoliberalism emphasizes individual liberty and freedom, in particu-lar as expressed through the market, where open and competitive supply responds to consumer desires through the individual liberties of market choice. The freedom of the market becomes the model of freedom *per se* (Brown, 2006). From this perspective, neoliberalism is a technique of government or governmentality (which with Foucault means both govern-ing and a mode of thought) that provides, through specific programs and initiatives, a climate that aims at bringing about the entrepreneurial self (Binkley, 2006; Dean, 1999; Rose, 1992). Hence, the freedom postulated by neoliberalism is not just individual but individual*istic* because, "rather than fostering social bonds, the target of neoliberal governmentality is to eliminate precisely those collectivist tendencies, which threaten to stifle self-interested, competitive economic behavior" (Binkley, 2009a). In other words, a new formula is taking shape to rule the conduct of individuals in the post-welfare state. This formula no longer governs through society in any traditional sense but through the regulated choices of individual con-sumers. Thus, investing as digital virtual consumption is the practice *par excellence* of neoliberal governmentality.

In sum, the social and political discourses that gained prominence after the post-war era gave birth to neoliberal subjectivities that fashion themselves as risk resilient, individualized, and self-reliant individuals. As authoritative voices are challenged and collective interests considered to stifle entrepreneurial, self-interested, and competitive behavior are increas-ingly dismantled, individuals are now responsible for governing them-selves as autonomous market actors and for exhibiting a mode of conduct conducive to market rationalities. The stock market—especially once made accessible by the personal computer—provided a "natural" playing field for individuals who are faced with a state that provides neither socialized forms of economic security nor the collectivization of social expenditures.

CONCLUSION

I am inclined to follow Tony Judt (2007), who states that today we live in an economic age where the new master narrative has abandoned the social for the economic. What he means by this is that there now is but one, however implicit, authority, which is the authority of a set of rationalities and technologies characteristic of the domain of economic conduct that individuals have been asked to accept. In other words, the only authority left is that of the market and of free individuals enacting choice. This disposition of the modern self, its neoliberal subjectivity, was met halfway by the individualizing, liberating, and empowering features of the Internet. It would therefore be inaccurate to reduce the popular rise of individual online investing to the emergence of the Internet. Rather, the emergence of individual investing can only be understood when linked to the broader philosophy, discourse, and practical rationality of neoliberalism centered on the maximization of profit and financial security as a form of self-government (cf. Binkley, 2009b).

Neoliberal governmentality, hence, is a political project that in its aspiration to control the conduct of populations focuses less on macro-structural, disciplinary forms of power imposed by the state and more on a growing emphasis on the practical activity of self-producing and self-fashioning oneself as a *homo economicus*.

Yet, under conditions of individual freedom, individuals are required to undertake the active, everyday practices of shaping, changing, or negating features of the self, which today is accomplished via consumerist yearnings for a life full of choices and opportunities. Therefore, having been put in a situation of freedom from social and cultural dependencies, thus a freedom to become anybody (Bauman, 2000: 62), the individual must become an entrepreneur of him or herself. He has no alternative but to configure him or herself in an on-going manner as human capital. Not amassing such capital would be irresponsible and show an ethics of the self based on dependence and bad habits. It is the market, then, where the neoliberal self has learned to enact responsible freedom and to look at consumption choices as the site for the subject to produce him or herself as a self-producing subject. From this vantage point, the strategy to confer more and more long-term planning tasks, including financial long-term planning, to the logic of the market in general and to digital virtual consumption in particular makes sense for neoliberal subjectivities, who on the one hand have seen traditional securities and long standing realities dissolve and, on the other, have acquired cognitive structures recognizing the "natural" importance of self-reliance and personal responsibility. The seemingly universal aspirations of agency, voluntarism, and autonomy bestowed on the investor by the digital virtual consumption model provided by the online brokerage puts the stock market, as a way of securing the future *qua* shopping for stocks, beyond criticism, no matter how ludicrous an idea it might be. Therefore, a market for stocks, just like any other contemporary consumer market, must be seen as a well adapted form of neoliberal social policy where the objective is no longer able to secure the future through collective social investment and mutualization of risk but to configure self-centered, insecure, and socially atomized consumer subjects.

NOTES

1. We follow the distinction made by Milchman and Rosenberg (2009) on Foucault's term "assujettissement." Milchman and Rosenberg distinguish between "subjectification" and "subjectivation," where the former refers to the mode of constituting others as subjects through processes of power (which often but not always include processes of subjugation and discipline) and the latter refers to the manner by which individuals are produced by power as self-producing subjects (see also Binkley, 2009b).
2. The term surfaced during an Ameritrade television commercial in spring/summer of 2000. In the ad, a determined, "professional" woman in her late 20s globally defines savvy Internet investors who take matters into their own hands rather than relying on traditional financial institutions as "renegade capitalists."
3. Foucault uses the concept of new homo oeconomicus as a form of subjectivation (Milchman and Rosenberg, 2009), where individuals are actively fashioning themselves as ethical subjects, and in this case an ethics of autonomy, decisionism, and individualism, the individual as an "entrepreneur of one-self," maximizing him or herself as "human capital" in competition with all other individuals (see Klein, 2007; Lazzarato, 2009).
4. As the godfather of American neoliberalism, Milton Friedman, put it (in Klein, 2007: 47): "Only a crisis—actual or perceived—produces real change. When that crisis occurs, the actions that are taken depend on the ideas that are lying around."

REFERENCES

Adorno T. 1991. *Culture Industry Reconsidered. The Culture Industry: Selected Essays on Mass Culture.* Routledge: London.

Akerlof GA, Shiller RJ. 2009 *Animal Spirits: How Human Psychology Drives The Economy, and Why It Matters for Global Capitalism.* Princeton University Press: Princeton.

Allen DE, McGoun EG. 2000. Hedonic Investment, in *Advances of Consumer Research*, SJ Hoch and R Myer (eds.). Association of Consumer Research: Provo, UT; 389–403.

Arnould EJ, Thompson CJ. 2005. Consumer Culture Theory (CCT): Twenty Years of Research. *Journal of Consumer Research* 31: 868–882.

Baudrillard J. 1981. *For a Critique of the Political Economy of the Sign.* Telos Press: St. Louis.

Bauman Z. 1991. *Modernity and Ambivalence.* Cornell University Press: Ithaca.

Bauman Z. 1996. Morality in the Age of Contingency, in *Detraditionalization*, P. Heelas, S. Lash, and P. Morris (eds.). Blackwell: Oxford; 49–58.

Bauman Z. 2000. *Liquid Modernity*. Polity Press: Cambridge.

Bauman Z. 2003. *Wasted Lives: Modernity and Its Outcasts*. Polity Press: Oxford.

Beck U. 1986. *Risikogesellschaft. Auf dem Weg in eine andere Moderne*. Suhrkamp: Munich.

Beck U, Beck-Gernsheim E. 1996. Individualization and "Precarious Freedoms": Perspectives and Controversies of a Subject-Oriented Sociology, in *Detraditionalization*, Paul Heelas, Scot Lash, and Paul Morris (eds.). Blackwell: Oxford; 437–446.

Becker GS. 1975. *Human Capital: A theoretical and Empirical Analysis, with Special Reference to Education*. Columbia University Press: New York.

Belk RW. 1988. Possessions and the Extended Self. *Journal of Consumer Research* 15: 139–168.

Binkley S. 2006. The Perilous Freedoms of Consumption: Toward a Theory of the Conduct of Consumer Conduct. *Journal for Cultural Research* 10: 343–362.

Binkley S. 2007. Governmentality and Lifestyle Studies. *Sociology Compass* 1: 111–126.

Binkley S. 2009a. *Governing Happiness*. Conference paper presented at the Schulich School of Business Consumer Culture Research Series.

Binkley S. 2009b. The Work of Neoliberal Governmentality: Temporality and Ethical Substance in the Tale of Two Dads. *Foucault Studies* 6: 60–78.

Boltanski L, Chiapello E. 2007. *The New Spirit of Capitalism*. Verso: London.

Borgerson JL. 2005. Materiality, Agency, and the Constitution of Consuming Subjects: Insights for Consumer Research. *Advances in Consumer Research* 32: 439–443.

Bourdieu P. 1984. *Distinction—A Social Critique of the Judgment of Taste*. Harvard University Press: Cambridge.

Bourdieu P. 1998. *Acts of Resistance: Against the Tyranny of the Market*. Polity Press: Cambridge.

Bourdieu P. 1990. *The Logic of Praxis*. Stanford University Press: Stanford.

Brown W. 2006. American Nightmare: Neoliberalism, Neoconservatism, and De-memocratization. *Political Theory* 34: 690–714.

Callinicos AT. 1990. *Against Postmodernism*. St. Martin's Press: New York.

Carey T. 1999. The Electronic Investor: Online and Outtasight. *Barron's*.

Comaroff J, Comaroff JL. 2001. *Millennial Capitalism and the Culture of Neoliberalism*. Duke University Press: Durham.

Dean M. 1999. *Governmentality: Power and Rule in Modern Society*. Sage Publications: Thousand Oaks.

Denegri-Knott J, Molesworth M. 2010. Concepts and Practices of Digital Virtual Consumption. *Consumption Markets and Culture* 13: 109–132.

Douglas M, Isherwood B. 1979. *The World of Goods*. Basic Books: New York.

Firat FA, Dholakia, N. 1998. *Consuming People: From Political Economy to Theatres of Consumption*. Routledge: London.

Firat FA, Venkatesh A. 1995. Liberatory Postmodernism and the Reenchantment of Consumption. *Journal of Consumer Research* 22: 239–267.

Fiske J. 1989. *Understanding Popular Culture*. Unwin Hyman: Boston.

Foucault M. 1990. *The Use of Pleasure*. Vintage Books: New York.

Foucault M. 1991. Governmentality, in *The Foucualt Effect*, Graham Burchell, Colin Gordon, and Peter Miller (eds.). University of Chicago Press: Chicago; 87–104.

Foucault M. 2008. *The Birth of Biopolitics: Lectures at the Collège de France, 1978–79*. Palgrave Macmillan: New York.

Gagnier R. 1997. Neoliberalism and the Political Theory of the Market. *Political Theory* 25: 434–454.

Giddens A. 1990. *The Consequences of Modernity.* Stanford University Press: Stanford.

Giddens A. 1991. *Modernity and Self-Identity: Self and Society in the Late Modern Age.* Stanford University Press: Stanford.

Giroux HA. 2004. *The Terror of Neoliberalism.* Paradigm Publishers: Boulder.

Habermas J. 1981. *Theorie des Kommunikative Handelns, Band 1.* Suhrkamp: Frankfurt.

Habermas J. 1994. Individualisierung und Vergesellschaftung, in *Riskante Freiheiten: Individualisierung in modernen Gesellschaften,* U. Beck and E. Beck-Gernsheim (eds.). Suhrkamp: Frankfurt; 437–446.

Hamann TH. 2009. Neoliberalism, Governmentality, and Ethics. *Foucault Studies* 6: 37–59.

Harvey D. 2005. *A Brief History of Neoliberalism.* Oxford University Press: Oxford.

Heelas P, Lash S, Morris P. (1996) *Detraditionalization: Critical Reflections on Authority and Identity.* Blackwell Publishers, Cambridge.

Horkheimer M, Adorno TW. 1972. *Dialectic of Enlightenment.* Herder and Herder: New York.

Judt T. 2007. The Wrecking Ball of Innovation. *The New York Review of Books.*

Klam M. 1999. Riding the Mo in the Lime Green Glow. *The New York Times.*

Klein N. 2007. *The Shock Doctrine: The Rise of Disaster Capitalism.* Metropolitan Books: New York.

Knobloch U. 1994. *Theorie und Ethik des Konsums.* Verlag Paul Haupt: Bern and Stuttgart.

Knorr Cetina KD. 1997. Sociality with Objects. Social Relations in Postsocial Knowledge Societies. *Theory, Culture and Society* 14: 1–30.

Knorr Cetina KD, Bruegger, U. 2002. Traders' Engagement with Markets. *Theory, Culture, and Society* 19: 161–185.

Kozinets RV. 2001. Utopian Enterprise: Articulating the Meanings of Star Trek's Culture of Consumption. *Journal of Consumer Research* 28: 67–88.

Lazzarato M. 2009. Neoliberalism in Action: Inequality, Insecurity and the Reconstitution of the Social. *Theory, Culture, & Society* 26: 109–133.

Lee H, Yongwoon, S. 2005. Do we need broadband? Impacts of broadband in Korea. Info -The *Journal of Policy, Regulation and Strategy for Telecommunications* 7: 47–56.

Lury C. 1996. *Consumer Culture.* Blackwell: Oxford.

MacKenzie DA, Wacjman J. 1999. *The Social Shaping of Technology.* Open University Press: Buckingham.

Marx K. 1978. *Capital.* Norton & Company: New York.

Milchman A, Rosenberg A. 2009. The Final Foucault: Government of Others and Government of the Self, in *A Foucault for the 21st Century: Governmentality, Biopolitics and Discipline in the New Millennium,* S. Binkley and J. Capetillo (eds.). Cambridge Scholars Publishing: Newcastle upon Tyne; 62–71.

Rose N. 1992. Governing the Enterprising Self, in *The Values of the Enterprise Culture,* P. Heelas and P. Morris (eds.). Routledge: London; 141–164.

Rose N. 1996. Governing "Advanced" Liberal Democracies, in *Foucault and Political Reason: Liberalism, Neo-Liberalism and Rationalities of Government,* A. Barry, T. Osborne, and N. Rose (eds.). University of Chicago Press: Chicago; 37–64.

Sassen S. 1999. Digital Networks and Power, in *Spaces of Culture,* M. Featherstone and S. Lash, (eds.). Sage: London; 48–63.

Sassen S. 2007. *Deciphering the Global: Its Scales, Spaces and Subjects.* Routledge: New York.

Schultz TW. 1970. *Investment in Human Capital: The Role of Education and of Research*. Free Press: New York.

Shiller RJ. 2000. *Irrational Exuberance*. Princeton University Press: Princeton.

Smith MR, Marx L. 1994. *Does Technology Drive History?: The Dilemma of Technological Determinism*. The MIT Press: Cambridge.

Staute J. 1998. *Borsenfieber: Was Anleger im Aktienrausch wissen sollten*. Campus: Frankfurt and New York.

Steltzner H. 1999. *Das Internet erobert die Finanzwelt. Frankfurter Allgemeine Zeitun*. Suhrkamp: Frankfurt.

Wallulis J. 1998. *The New Insecurity*. SUNY Press: Albany.

Weber M. 1958. *The Protestant Work Ethic and the Spirit of Capitalism*. Charles Scribner's Sons: New York.

Zwick D. 2005. Where the Action Is: Internet Stock Trading as Edgework. *Journal of Computer-Mediated Communication* 10. Available at www.jcmc.indiana. edu/vol11/issue1/zwick.htm> [accessed on 11 September 2011].

Zwick D, Dholakia N. 2006a. Bringing the Market to Life: Screen Aesthetics and the Epistemic Consumption Object. *Marketing Theory* 6: 41–62.

Zwick D, Dholakia N. 2006b. The Epistemic Consumption Object and Postsocial Consumption: Expanding Consumer-Object Theory in Consumer Research. *Consumption, Markets & Culture* 9: 17–43.

Zwick D, Ozalp Y. 2011. Flipping the Neighborhood: Biopolitical Marketing as Value Creation for Condos and Lofts, in *Inside Marketing: Practices, Ideologies, Devices*, D. Zwick and J. Cayla (eds.). Oxford University Press: Oxford and New York; 234–253.

10 Playing the Market and Sharing the Loot

Consumption Limits in a Virtual World

Sandy Ross

Consumption seems limitless in virtual worlds where tremendous amounts of digital goods are available to fulfill any desires or daydreams, unconstrained by finite resources. In game-oriented worlds—massively multiplayer online games (MMO) that emphasize achievement and character development—acquisition of sought-after equipment and items is limited by skill and patience. Given enough attempts to kill a powerful monster, each player will receive his or her desired items eventually. However, surrounded by myriad, fiercely desired commodities, players struggle to be patient. Impatience is expressed in various ways, but this chapter examines two common forms, interpersonal conflict and price instability, which are perceived as dangerous by players of the MMO Final Fantasy XI (FFXI). Preventing social and economic discord arising from competing consumption aspirations is considered a serious social problem by players, who have negotiated self-imposed consumption limits that balance personal desires with collective social and economic well-being.

This chapter examines some strategies for social and economic self-regulation explained by players of FFXI, a proprietary game-oriented fantasy world owned by Square-Enix, a Japanese company. Self-imposed consumption limits seem contrary to economic hedonic consumption theories (Hoch and Loewenstein, 1991; Loewenstein and Pralec, 2007) that suggest short-term thinking and conflicting preferences over time characterize consumer decision-making. Consumer societies in the North face sustainability challenges because of climate change, economic uncertainty, and diminishing resources, which necessitate less intensive modes of life with lower levels of consumption and waste. Convincing consumers that less consumption does not mean privation or poverty is a difficult proposition, yet within the limits of the virtual world of FFXI, individuals from consumer societies in the global north have not only accepted such limits, but negotiated and maintained them on their own initiative.

This chapter is based on six years of FFXI field work, from 2003 to 2009, including two periods of participant observation: August 2003–October 2005, with linkshells Yukikaze, Azalea, and OotakaraNakama; and May 2006–July 2008, with linkshells Sleipnir and Goobue. Thirty-two qualitative, open-ended interviews were conducted in 2005; and 37 one-on-one and 9 panel interviews from 2007 to 2009. Follow-up and correspondence continued with some interviewees in 2005–2006. Linkshell leaders and members agreed to participate and be quoted in publications; all names of persons and organisations are pseudonyms.

ECONOMIC LIFE AND MATERIAL ORGANISATION IN FFXI

Consumption limitations in FFXI can be arranged along a spectrum, but this analysis is limited to its two extremes. One end is characterized by affective accounts of "embeddedness of wealth and value in others" (Weiner, 1980: 73) or accumulating collective wealth in linkshells, closely knit social groups, equivalent to guilds in other MMOs. Linkshell consumption constraints include informal and routinized elements, and respondents emphasized social ties or fictive kinship (Lambert, 2000: 74–75) as reasons for accepting such limits. Social relations fostered in linkshells are believed to be more important than individual desires. Within linkshells, loot allocation is managed with an eye to maximizing collective power, transforming consumption into a collective activity.

At the other end of this spectrum are moral limits to market practices. Although some sharp dealings are acceptable, players avoid what Yoruba traders call *ajeju*, or "unnecessary profit" (Guyer, 2004: 104–105). Exploitative profit-making strategies—price gouging or undercutting—are believed to produce price instability, which players equate with economic instability. Economic flux threatens realization of consumption dreams (Campbell, 1987) and participation in economic life. For respondents, adherence to shared market behavior rules is a personal responsibility, narrowing consumption to a sphere of individual action. Yet even this personal consumption is linked to collective concerns because players connect economic stability with fairness and equal economic opportunities. Marketplace moralities are part of a shared quasi-utopian project. Although amoral market practices benefit only one person, acceptable market practices prioritize long-term stability beneficial for all players.

FFXI's Material World and Economy

Respondents' distinctions between shared consumption in linkshells and more individualized consumption do not re-iterate false "gift/commodity" dichotomies (Appadurai, 1988: 11). These distinctions reflect FFXI's material world and economies, which structure consumption opportunities and practices. FFXI is a virtual world where players create characters whose skills and attributes they strive to improve. The material world and economy of FFXI have become complex over the game's nine-year history, containing myriad non-circulating goods, spheres of exchange (Bohannon and Bohannon, 1968: 12; Guyer, 2004: 27–29), and monies.

Lame Deer, a long-time player, describes FFXI's economy as compartmentalized: "The economy is cut up into little pieces by all these monies and markets." This fragmented material world structures players' consumption. Digital consumption in FFXI consists of roughly three areas with different goods, monies, and consumption practices: player-to-player commerce in Auction Houses and bazaars using gil, discrete spheres of exchange with special monies and activities, and non-circulating items from battlefields and monsters. The first area is governed by self-imposed limits to profit seeking and consumption explained as instability avoidance strategies. Goods in this realm include less powerful equipment, consumables like food or medicines, and raw materials. The last, monster loot, involves linkshell participation and is governed by affective appeals to fictive kinship and regulation of individual desires and occasionally formal quantitative controls. This category contains the most powerful equipment in FFXI, most of which is non-circulating—it cannot be bought, shared, or sold. Such items are acquired by killing Notorious Monsters (NMs)—creatures that appear as infrequently as once every 72 hours or by completing arduous battlefields. The second area, discrete spheres of exchange, lies between the extremes, sometimes involving linkshell participation, sometimes undertaking individually. These consumption decisions and patterns occupy a middle ground and are beyond this chapter's scope, but they remind us that practices described here are part of a spectrum not a dichotomy.

SHARING THE LOOT: REGULATING CONSUMPTION AND DESIRE IN LINKSHELLS

Understanding players' self-restraint in FFXI's marketplaces begins with conflict avoidance in linkshells, where players develop a sense of shared interest in a collective project that impacts on their market practices. Consumption regulation in linkshells is a group effort involving negotiations outside the game, affective appeals in-world when conflicts arise and sometimes points systems. All members co-operate in these strategies; the rank-and-file police excessive consumption demands, defusing conflicts in early stages while leaders manage points systems and settle acrimonious disputes. Points systems become routinized, fading into the background of players' engagement with FFXI. Discussions on group websites and forums are the normative means through which consumption claims are negotiated.

Calculating and Negotiating Consumption Claims

Unlike *World of Warcraft* (Nardi, 2010: 75–76), where loot distribution conflicts arise at any point in raid cycles—preparation, mid-battle, and after—in FFXI disputes are rare in-game because players generally settle consumption claims long before raids through linkshell websites or over external voice chat. Such discussions produce a collective sense of fairness because decisions are debated over several days, outside intense battle situations, and most members can express their opinions. Claims are established through forum posts and supported by reference to points accumulated (where such systems are used) or according to qualitative criteria: contributions to the linkshell, willingness to relinquish claims by other members, or claims-making frequency/style.

Although not all linkshells use points systems, players believe they prevent greediness and help prioritize claims. Points systems are not part of FFXI's software; players devised them to organize wealth distribution. Members earn points for attending scheduled activities, some of which offer more than others. For example, killing monsters for items used to spawn powerful creatures is tedious and generates no loot, whereas dungeons are exciting and generate desirable items. Attending the latter expeditions earns fewer points than the former, incentivizing participation for boring activities. Points tallies are publicly listed on group websites, as are points values assigned to events and desirable items. Lair, Sleipnir LS member, explains points systems' regulatory effects:

> end game LS have a points system to make sure you worked hard to get the item you wanted, that's mostly to stop people from being greedy. really a LS needs to work as a group, and the game is more fun when you're all friendly than fighting over items.

According to Lair, points systems ensure members "work hard" to earn items, helping others by attending scheduled fights. Such schemes prevent players from being "greedy" by claiming multiple items at once or repeatedly claiming top loot. Points systems are quantitative consumption restraints, spreading claims evenly over time and minimizing competition when a player finally has enough points for long-awaited gear. Lair calls attention to desire regulation by mentioning how linkshells must remain "friendly" to effectively "work as a group." Regulating desire and consumption keeps peace in linkshells, ensuring members can have "more fun."

When the weekly event schedule includes fights providing equipment that a player desires, he or she makes a consumption claim by posting on his or her linkshell's website. Points accumulated and displayed on linkshell websites transform progress toward consumption goals into a shared project. Leaders accumulate larger tallies than rank-and-file members, so whenever new items are introduced, they always have enough points to claim exciting loot first. Yet this is not always what happens. Sherlock explains:

Sherlock: J [Sleipnir's leader] and I both had enough points for our first Novio [earring] drop but he passed it to me.

SR: Oh! J never told me that.

Sherlock: I've always been bl[ack] m[age][1] only, taking it to the utmost limit and he knew how much it meant to me so he passed. Plus as a leader he knows you have to keep your LSmates who work the hardest the happiest even if it means you pass on something at times. if a leader only thinks about themselves the LS will fail miserably.

Sherlock was the first interviewee to tell this story, but it became familiar as other Sleipnir members gave similar accounts of items forsworn by LS leaders. In this case, J could have used his privilege as leader (and massive points tally) to claim a Novio earring unopposed, but he chose to wait. When asked about these events, J said, "It's cool that they [LS members] remember it." By relinquishing his right to claim desirable items, J inspired loyalty and goodwill. In curbing his own desires, J shows that leaders too must by patient and accept consumption limits. As Sherlock suggests with his final comment, conspicuous non-consumption is an important strategy for social harmony.

Settling competing consumption claims and distributing spoils fairly is crucial to the continued functioning of a linkshell. Ashira, an FFXI player for more than five years and junior LS leader, identifies such conflicts as threats to group cohesion:

Drama over items can ruin a linkshell! Our old LS broke up over an Aristocrat's Tunic that was promised to one person but then the LS leader decided to give it to his girlfriend.

When competing claims are not settled fairly or when negotiated allocations are overturned, strife and group dissolution are difficult to avoid. Within a linkshell, members' desires are not regularly in conflict, but this is not because few players desire the same objects. Rather, players invest time and effort in sharing consumption dreams (Campbell, 1987) and re-prioritizing desires to avoid competition.

In Yukikaze linkshell, players used online forums and voice chat to discuss necessary or desired items for character development. Popular form threads concerned ideal equipment, with players debating which gear combinations provided optimal bonuses. Although such discussions are partly about demonstrating game world knowledge, they also facilitate sharing consumption dreams. An extract from Yukikaze members' voice chat from 2005 connects forum discussions and formal consumption claims and illustrates negotiation of conflicting desires. In the discussion below, Vivi tells Kasha about the new linkshell event schedule because Kasha posted about Byakko Haidate—called Kitty Pants because Byakko is a tiger—on a 'Want List' thread. Such discussions are not claims on goods. In Yukikaze, players must reply to weekly events schedules to officially register claims for items. Gilly also posted in the same discussion about Byakko Haidate.

Vivi:	Byakko is on this week, Kasha!
Kasha:	Kitty Pants MINE!
R2D2:	Doesn't Gilly want those?
Vivi:	Yea I think so. It's on the forum.
Kasha:	aww fuck.
R2D2:	Not in the schedule thingie
Gilly:	Haidate? Yea. My nin[ja gear] has to get good for tanking. . . . Gonna post that now.
Kasha:	D[amage] D[ealer] versus tank? Tank wins. Imma wait for kirin's osode.
R2D2:	We do Byakko regular
Gilly:	Haidate may not drop anyway, Kas.
Vivi:	We might wipe!

This situation could cause conflict. Both players desire Byakko Haidate and have valid claims. However, Gilly's job as a tank—in fights she absorbs attack damage—is more vital than Kasha's because Yukikaze has many fighters like him, but only two tanks. Putting Yukikaze's collective strength ahead of his own desires, Kasha decides to claim a different item later rather than competing with Gilly. In re-ordering his consumption desires—Kirin's Osode was on his "Want List," but ranked lower than Kitty Pants—Kasha also prioritized avoiding conflict. To soften Kasha's disappointment and positively reinforce his decision, R2D2 says the LS fights Byakko often while Gilly suggests the Haidate may not appear in the loot list. Vivi comically suggests Byakko might defeat the linkshell rather than the other way around. Although Gilly's claim was stronger, both her and Kasha's claims were perceived as reasonable, thus the friendly tone of the exchange. However, when excessive requests are made, negotiations become fraught.

Emotional Ties, Patience, and Collective Wealth

Affective appeals are used to counter consumption claims perceived as inappropriate or excessive. A claim can be unacceptable because of how it is phrased, as a demand rather than a request, or because it seems greedy. Such claims violate players' understandings of linkshells as social institutions that create what Weiner (1980: 73) calls "the build up and the embeddedness of wealth and value in others." In this view, goods generated and consumed by group members, although possessed individually, contribute to collective wealth and power. Rather than producing wealthier characters, a linkshell that shares loot well creates a stronger, more skilled community of players.

This 2005 exchange, taken from linkshell text chat in-world, shows an inappropriate consumption demand and its aftermath. Rick, a senior Yukikaze leader, announces that everyone must gather for an event, prompting an ultimatum from Dragonfly, a new member. Dragonfly will only attend if the linkshell helps him with Shikigami Weapon, a monster whose loot includes a powerful robe for Summoners, one of FFXI's combat jobs. The other speakers are K, a junior leader, and Kasha, R2D2, Pom, and Penelope.

Rick:	45 mins to Sky. meet at genbu[2]
Dragonfly:	Im only goin 2 Sky if u help me w/shikigami now
Kasha:	dont be a winy fag douchefly
K:	you cant ask like that dude
R2D2:	you've only been here 2 weeks
R2D2:	be patient. your turn will come
Dragonfly:	i helpd u last week
Pom:	ask nicely on forums
Pom:	its a fun fight but we cant do it this week
Dragonfly:	no i need that robe now 4 exp
R2D2:	but theres other ppl who need it
Kasha:	like u R2 lol
Kasha:	been waitin 6 months [. . .]
Penelope:	helping friends, being family yes
Penelope:	threats and drama no

Kasha perceives Dragonfly's demand as whiney and failing to uphold heteronormative masculine gender norms. His use of "douchefly" and "fag" reflects what Pascoe (2007: 54) calls fag discourse, a rhetorical technique for punishing failed masculine gender performances. K and Pom address the inappropriate framing of Dragonfly's request, highlighting the importance of treating fellow group members politely. Pom's injunction to "ask nicely" indicates that the current request is unacceptable; K expresses the same view. Pom directs Dragonfly to Yukikaze's forums, a more appropriate place for requests. Penelope argues that linkshells are about "helping friends, being family" not "threats." Her response links other speakers' appeals to consumption self-regulation to preservation of social ties and social harmony. Demanding compensation violates players' sense of linkshells as family, institutions producing and reproducing valued emotional ties and social networks. Excessive consumption demands transforming members from valued individuals into a "standing reserve" (Heidegger 1977: 17) of labor power.

Dragonfly says he needs the robe for experience points parties, but R2D2—a higher level Summoner—appeals to him to be patient in sympathy for others also stoically waiting. R2D2 suggests Dragonfly has not waited long, "only . . . 2 weeks." In response to these affective appeals, Dragonfly mentions his previous helpful activity, trying to evoke gratitude. Kasha states that R2D2 has been waiting six months for the same piece of equipment, tacitly implying that helping at one event is not sufficient grounds for consumption claims. The argument was eventually ended by Mushroom, Yukikaze's founder, who exiled Dragonfly from the group.

Controlling expressions of desire avoids conflict that many players, like Penelope and Ashira, call "drama." When Dragonfly says he needs the robe, R2D2 quickly says others also feel they need it. Although wealth and power in linkshells is believed to be collective, material possession and consumption remain individual. Claims disputes highlight tensions between an aspirational, utopian ideal and individual possession. Regulating consumption by controlling one's own desires and policing others' inappropriate expressions of desire is a protective strategy. Players are trying to preserve two highly valued things: continued access to challenging battlefields and desirable goods, and emotionally rich social ties and fictive kinship. These efforts obscure gaps between an emotionally resonant ideal and material realities. Protecting valued things through self-regulation is also fundamental to players' market moralities.

MARKET MORALITIES: SELF-REGULATION AND ECONOMIC STABILITY

In linkshells consumption regulation means patiently controlling desires, re-prioritizing consumption dreams, and situating individual consumption aspirations within a framework of collective accumulation of wealth and power. Players support and maintain these limits believing they ensure stable social relations and continuance of linkshells and valued aspects of the game. In FFXI's marketplaces, consumption regulation is equally bound up with concerns about maintaining aspects of the game world valued by all players. However, in this case, the fragile thing that players preserve is the virtual economy, which is framed as vulnerable and volatile. For players, FFXI's virtual economy requires protection through concerted efforts by all economic actors to make "responsible" decisions prioritizing long-term price stability over short-term virtual profits for individuals. For respondents, price stability is conceptually equivalent to economic stability. Practices described as "playing the A[uction] H[ouse]"—arbitrage, price-gouging, undercutting, market flooding, and crashing—highlight tensions and synergies between individual interests and price stability achieved through self-imposed limits. Such practices are ambivalent, potentially damaging *and* protective, selfish *and* responsible.

Activities described as "playing the AH" require heuristic economic decision-making, price trend knowledge, and lengthy periods spent at Auction Houses placing bids. In this panel interview extract, Mumitroll, Duck, and Ftpol give an overview:

SR: How do people "play the AH" in FFXI?

Mumitroll:	try to monopolize and manipulate prices is one option. arbitrage is another
Duck:	spend hours window shopping and memorizing patterns of buying/selling
SR:	Can you elaborate on arbitrage?
Mumitroll:	well that's old. dont know how well it works today but it used to be profitable to buy stuff in Jeuno and sell in the 3 [starting] cities AHs or vice versa
Duck:	people still do that
SR:	or buy from N[on]P[layer]C[haracter]s and sell in Jeuno?
Mumitroll:	yea
Ftpol:	i remember many pikas[3] used to get conquest points. then selling CS [Conquest][4] items
Duck:	i used to sell R[oyal] K[nights'] belts when i made it to rank 5 san d'oria

Mumitroll begins with supply manipulation, then mentions undercutting and gouging before explaining arbitrage with geographically restricted goods, or re-sale in central marketplaces of commodities purchased from vendors in distant locations. Ftpol describes another kind of arbitrage: selling items available only to characters with certain characteristics—fictive nationality in this case—in the Auction House where anyone can buy them. Duck agrees, citing his own experience selling Royal Knight's Belts, available only to citizens of San d'Oria, one of FFXI's fictive city-states.

Arbitragers seek out rapidly circulating commodities that are under-supplied—Duck's "hours [of] window shopping"—to generate reliable incomes. Respondents considered arbitrage useful and economically productive. Lame Deer said, "No one wants to run from Bastok to San d'Oria for [fishing] bait." Arbitragers expand consumption opportunities by bringing inconvenient or restricted commodities into general circulation. However, like Yoruba, merchants who must avoid accusations "unnecessary profit" (Guyer, 2004: 104–105), arbitragers maintain stable pricing to avoid accusations of price gouging.[5] For foods and raw materials, which are the staples of geographically restricted goods arbitrage, price increases are particularly appealing because small proportional increases accumulate quickly with large sales volumes. Cirdan, leader of a carpentry syndicate in FFXI, cautions against such temptations:

> Jacking up [the] price just rocks the boat. Going [it] alone and gouging means someone else will undercut you. Then we're all competing and losing money. Prices jump up and down, [it's] a big mess. [. . .] We try to keep prices fair [and] stable. We make decent profits but no gouging!

For Cirdan, price increases above syndicate limits constitute price gouging, or unfair profits. He identifies gougers as "Going [it] alone," prioritizing individualistic desire for quick cash over price stability, whereas sellers following syndicate prices help maintain a stable economy or at least minimize fluctuations. Cirdan argues that gouging incites undercutting, creating an "up and down" price cycle as sellers and buyers pursue their own ends rather than collective economic good. Cirdan's description of syndicate profits as "decent" is double voiced (Bakhtin, 1984: 185), meaning both morally upstanding and economically sufficient, linking moral framings and economic practices. For Cirdan's syndicate, economic stability is important enough to justify limiting virtual incomes and constraining consumption. Carpenters in Cirdan's group have varied levels of skill and ability. Some could undercut easily because of production or materials efficiencies, whereas others could drive down prices by selling large volumes of goods. Yet no syndicate members did so. Cirdan's woodworkers dominated carpentry-related commodity markets, maintaining stable prices during multiple cycles of inflation and deflation for several years. This co-operation ensured regular, predictable supply, at fixed prices, to vital consumables in FFXI, such as shihei, which are used in prodigious quantities by characters using the Ninja job to absorb monster damage. Players believe undercutting causes as much price instability as gouging. Qanael and Riddaraan, Sleipnir linkshell members, emphasize undercutting and arbitrage as playing the Auction House (AH):

Qanael: It's just [. . .] using the price differences in the AH.
Riddaraan: camping the AH, is people who just sit [. . .] and buy things for low amounts of gil, hoping someone puts some thing up for the wrong price, or a very low price in order to sell it fast.

For Quanael, "price differences" refer to arbitrage but also differences between sellers' threshold prices and buyers' bids, which can be large in cases of undercutting. Riddaraan's "wrong price" can be a mistake by sellers who drop a zero—inputting 100 instead of 1,000 gil as their minimum price—which can happen when listing many goods in haste, but can be a quick sale strategy. The former is an accident, the latter is perceived as undercutting because it manipulates Auction House sale priorities. A brief example with imaginary characters but based on common practices illustrates sales priorities manipulation. Harriet lists an Amemet Mantle in Jeuno's AH for five million gil, paying a proportional listing fee. Her listing remains in the AH for 72 hours. Marie also wants to sell an Amemet Mantle and knows there is another for sale. When multiple identical items are listed with the same threshold price, they will be sold in the order they were listed. Marie suspects the other seller has a threshold price of five million, matching previous prices. Amemet Mantles sell slowly. Marie does not want to pay listing fees twice, so she sets her minimum price at 4,599,999 gil so her mantle will sell first. Kim wants to buy an Amemet Mantle and sees two for sale. She suspects undercutting and bids four million, then 4.5 million. She tries 4.6 million and receives Marie's mantle. For players, Marie's undercutting is economically destructive because it costs Harriet her listing fee, subverts sales priorities in the Auction House, and could upset price trends, creating limited economic instability. In this view, undercutting prioritizes individual short-term gain—turning an item rapidly into cash—over price stability benefits for all players. Rain said, "When prices go out of control, no one can buy or sell anything. You can't play without eq[uipment] and tools!" Players' virtual consumption requires reliable virtual cash flow and economic stability. Being patient and not undercutting means accepting self-imposed constraints on income generation, thus limiting players' digital consumption. Yet players believe such self-restraint ensures continued viability of an economy in which they can participate by consuming goods. Self-restraint today constitutes a long-term consumption strategy.

Not everyone observes the same level of economic self-discipline. In this panel interview extract, Shukudai and Riddaraan explain what happens after "[p]rices jump up and down," suggesting desperate times call for desperate measures.

Shukudai:	I know a bonecrafter who was pissed at another bone crafter, who was constantly undercutting on Igqira Wes kits. so in return, he went out and raised the price of Dragon Talons by like 25k/ea. So if the guy wanted to continue to undercut, he'd take an even bigger loss . . . [6] He bought up all the stock on one character and sold it on another.
SR:	Didn't Sherlock do something like that with Cursed Mitts?
Shukudai:	Sherlock did something like that
Riddaraan:	People kept undercutting him during his duration of trying for H[igh] Q[uality].

Shukudai suggests gouging can be an acceptable response to undercutting. Dragon Talons are the most expensive components for making Igquira Weskits. Although Shukudai's friend manipulation supplies and price-gouged Dragon Talons, he was trying to repair undercut prices of Igquira Weskits. Price-gouging and undercutting are also ambivalent because these price rises—detrimental for bonecrafters buying Dragon Talons and players buying Igquira Weskits—provide better compensation for players generating income from raw materials. Many players do not practice a craft in FFXI, relying solely on sales of old equipment and basic crafting ingredients found while fighting monsters for income. When raw materials prices become unstable, these players may be unable to buy day-to-day necessities for parties or linkshell activities. FreakyBeaky, whose character is an archery specialist, observed, "If I got no arrows, I can't do nothin'." Accepting market constraints means lesser profits or more waiting, but it also safeguards economic and ludic participation.

Market crashing and flooding are equally ambivalent. Sherlock's Cursed Mitts affair, which Riddaraan and Shukudai referenced, is part of a longer story:

Sherlck: J and I have been trying to H[igh] Q[uality] Cursed Mitts for about 10–12 months now, finally did it the other night [. . .] Cursed Mitts, about .5 pairs sells a day, so 1 every other day. Normally players undercut 10k per sale. Now if the price is 80k on the A[uction] H[ouse] I'd rather shout sell for 50k than undercut lower than the other 5 pairs on the AH because in that case I'd have to undercut to 60k and then my 50k shout is not nearly as appealing. I can sell [. . .] while not lowering the AH price.

While Sherlock and J were trying to produce HQ Cursed Mitts they had avoided economically destructive selling tactics. Together they produced 144 pairs of Cursed Mitts, but sold them slowly in Sherlock's bazaar, which required him to shout and hawk his wares for hours. This strategy avoided AH fees and had no impact on prices, but it was quite inconvenient. Although Sherlock was selling Cursed Mitts for less than the AH price, his actions are not understood as undercutting because his sales did not change the prices other players could charge based on sales history listings. Meanwhile, another crafter flooded and crashed Cursed Mitts, decreasing the AH price. After making his HQ Cursed Mitts, Sherlock responded in kind, crashing the price far below cost. Although Sherlock's reaction resembles a fit of temper, he and Shukudai's bonecrafter friend were responding to perceived economic injustice.

A sense of fairness underlies framings of market moralities in FFXI. For players, fair prices are not established by what "the market" will decide, but by responsible selling decisions. Economic fairness is associated with price stability, which is achieved through individual economic self-discipline. Thus, economic instability—linked to decreased participatory capacity and diminished consumption aspirations—arises from poor decision-making that places personal short-term gain over collective longer term benefits. Only when prices are perceived to be unstable and unfair can ordinarily destructive practices—such as price-gouging or market flooding—be excused. Market moralities are ambivalent, simultaneously cramping income generation—reducing present purchasing—and enabling future consumption possibilities. Players' market moralities govern individual behavior but produce both collective and individual outcomes.

CONCLUSION

Whether sharing wealth in linkshells, pursuing commercial interests in FFXI's marketplaces, or something in between, players adopt consumption limits. Such constraints are accepted because it is believed that adherence to these rules ensures the continued existence of valued aspects of the game world. These treasured things range from the pragmatic—such as the virtual economy of FFXI, whose stability is needed for players to participate fully in the game world and in achieving individual consumption dreams—to the affective or emotionally engaging—like the networks of fictive kinship and social ties of a linkshell. Although self-imposed limits to consumption appear to primarily constrain players' acquisition of desired goods, they simultaneously enable future consumption. By preserving economic stability or social harmony in linkshells, players are working to facilitate future consumption of goods and of the game world itself.

Players' choices prioritize long-term benefit over immediate gratification, apparently contrary to what Hoch and Loewenstein (1991: 493) call "time-inconsistent preferences," choices reflecting momentary hedonistic urges rather than long-term considerations. Loewenstein and Pralec (2007: 434) suggest that consumer behavior is characterized by short-term thinking using the present as a frame of reference:

> the marginal utility of consumption at different points in time depends not on absolute levels of consumption, but on consumption relative to some standard or point of reference. Generally, the status quo serves as a reference point; people conserve on cognitive effort by evaluating new consumption alternatives in isolation, rather than by integrating them with existing plans.

For Loewenstein and Pralec, the "point of reference" is "the status quo," on which consumers rely as a cognitive heuristic. Players' consumption decisions are no less reliant on a "standard or reference point," but it is not the present. Respondents' reference point is temporally displaced in an idealized long-term where the virtual economy is more stable because of responsible decisions made by individual economic actors, where linkshell members enjoy fair wealth distribution and emotionally satisfying social relations. Rather than decisions made on the basis of immediate wants, players are engaged in a quasi-utopian project that protects shared and valued elements of FFXI.

We have built up a picture of what players are preserving by accepting self-imposed limits to consumption. If we want to generalize from these findings, we must consider how FFXI's design influences these practices. The most obvious condition is the structured nature of FFXI as a game world. Players are presented with a plethora of possible modes of achievement, but very few can be accomplished alone. From their earliest experiences in FFXI, players are forced to co-operate, which influences how individuals perceive their role in this virtual world. Dunes, who played FFXI for more than six years, speculated that this consensus-oriented pattern might be the result of a multi-cultural play environment:

Japanese players started this game first and set the standards. They're better at avoiding drama and keeping things fair.

There is a perception among many players that FFXI presents a more consensus-oriented social environment than that of other fantasy MMOs. Cultural essentialisms aside, achievement in FFXI does require reliance on others, and players quickly develop a sense of shared investment in the virtual world and a feeling of participating in a wider community with common goals. The size of this community is quite small, usually limited to a few hundred people with fuzzy extensions to the server population—up to 10,000 people—and weaker links to a wider group of all players of FFXI.

These common goals generate a sense of being invested in a shared project, another contributing factor in the development of self-regulating consumption strategies. Unlike public causes in everyday life where individual decisions are dwarfed by the scale of action required, players are able to see—and often even quantify—the consequences of their choices. FFXI is a small, almost simple, world compared with the enormous complexity of social problems on planet Earth. When a seller chooses not to undercut, she can see the influence of her decision in the AH sales history: Prices remain stable for a while. Links between actions and outcomes are shortened, making the results of players' decisions observable and their consequences immediate. Action not only feels as though it makes a difference, players are able to pursue what could be described as an evidence-based approach. In fact, the extent to which players develop nuanced and detailed lay theories of economic life supported by appeals to various forms of evidence—price trends, econometrics, carefully observed consumer behavior—suggests that economic life in FFXI at least is subject to a certain level of evidence-based lay analysis.

When players believe themselves to be invested in a shared project, to have common goals with others in the game world, which produces valued experiences, social networks, and ties, it is not surprising that they are willing to accept some temporary constraints to ensure long-term sustainability. It is indeed curious that suggestions for living on a finite planet are to be found in a realm of practically limitless digital virtual goods. Yet contributing factors in the development of players' consumption reduction strategies are relevant to continuing efforts to promote sustainable, lower levels of consumption. The experiences of FFXI players suggest that limits to consumption can be successful in smaller communities united by shared goals that seem achievable, as supported by observable change. In a very strange way, the globalized player base and digital political economy of a virtual world provide a compelling example of long-term thinking and local action.

NOTES

1. A damage dealing, magic using combat job in FFXI.
2. A monster whose spawn location is used as a rendezvous point.

3. Pikas is German slang for characters of the fictive Tartaru race.
4. Items bought with Conquest Points, a token money.
5. Arbitrage price setting rules are beyond the scope of this chapter. Briefly, acceptable prices vary according to vendor accessibility conditions, item supply restrictions, and item type.
6. Ellipses in original.

REFERENCES

Appadurai A. 1988. Introduction: Commodities and the Politics of Value, in *The Social Life of Things: Commodities in Cultural Perspective*, A. Appadurai (ed.). Cambridge University Press: Cambridge; 3–63.

Bakhtin M. 1984. *Problems of Dostoevsky's Poetics* (C. Emerson, trans.). University of Minnesota Press: Minneapolis.

Bohannon P, Bohannon L. 1968. *Tiv Economy*. Northwestern University Press: Evanston.

Campbell C. 1987. *The Romantic Ethic and the Spirit of Modern Consumerism*. Basil Blackwell: Oxford.

Guyer J. 2004. *Marginal Gains: Monetary Transactions in Atlantic Africa*. University of Chicago Press: Chicago.

Heidegger M. 1977. *The Question Concerning Technology and Other Essays*. HarperCollins: New York.

Hoch S, Loewenstein G. 1991. Time-Inconsistent Preferences and Consumer Self-Control. The Journal of Consumer Research 17(4): 492–507.

Lambert H. 2000. Sentiment and Substance in North Indian Forms of Relatedness, in *Cultures of Relatedness: New Approaches to the Study of Kinship*, J. Carsten (ed.). Cambridge University Press: Cambridge; 73–89.

Loewenstein G, Pralec D. 2007. Anomalies in Intertemporal Choice: Evidence and an Interpretation, in *Exotic Preferences: Behavioral Economics and Human Motivation*, G. Loewenstein (ed.). Oxford University Press: Oxford; 411–438.

Nardi, B. 2010. *My Life as a Night Elf Priest: An Anthropological Account of World of Warcraft*. University of Michigan Press: Michigan.

Pascoe C. 2007. *Dude, You're a Fag: Masculinity and Sexuality in High School*. University of California Press: Berkeley.

Weiner A. 1980. Reproduction: A Replacement for Reciprocity. *American Ethnologist* 7(1): 71–85.

11 Taking One—or Three—For the Team

Consumerism as Gameplay in Woot.com

Melinda Jacobs

INTRODUCTION

A Night Elf, a Dwarf, and a Human attack a ravenous beast in *World of Warcraft*; in *Anarchy Online*, new players gather together to fight off a powerful monster that has wandered over to the Newbie Island. Over in *Second Life*, a famous avatar singer performs in front of a group of adoring fans and friends who are working together to create a lively and interactive concert. Although this is only a tiny sampling of events that occur daily within the many virtual worlds available, by showcasing only a few aspects of their social and communal dynamics, one can see a major similarity across all examples: dynamics of teamwork. None of the activities described above could easily, if at all, be completed by a solo participant and instead require participants to band together to achieve the desired goal. Despite different virtual spaces having a different focus, the formation of communities of teamwork (both temporary and permanent) happens almost identically across the spectrum of worlds, varying often only in subject matter.

Scholars (i.e., Castronova, 2005, 2007; Chen, 2009; Jenkins, 2006; McGonigal, 2011; Taylor, 2006) have studied the formation of such communities within virtual worlds, analyzing how the structures of these worlds, especially within massively multiplayer online role-playing games (MMORPGs), such as *World of Warcraft*, *EverQuest*, and *Anarchy Online*, produce these communities of teamwork, both directly (Taylor, 2006) and more indirectly (Chen, 2009; Ducheneaut, Yee, Nickell, and Moore, 2006). Although a large amount of research has been done on these communities and the game design that structures, encourages, and, in some instances, demands the creation of them, up until recently few scholars had yet addressed the general motivation of people to enter these virtual worlds in the first place.

One of the first scholars to explicitly address this was Edward Castronova. In *Exodus to the Virtual World*, Castronova (2007) argues that it is not just the successful community-encouraging design of a virtual game world that leads to its popularity, rather it is a common longing for community derived from mistakes being made in the "design" of the physical world. He states, "The real world does not encourage people to band together. This must leave a yearning for community of meaning, a yearning that can be satisfied in the community of myth-making found in most virtual worlds" (Castronova, 2007: 205). Castronova continues to explain that he believes the game mechanics, the elements responsible for creating the structure of game-based virtual worlds, should not only be studied and modified within their own realm, but, instead, these mechanics (such as group challenges, intrinsic reward-based systems, and point-based leveling mechanics) should be adapted to the physical realm in the hopes of bringing the successes seen in the virtual worlds using these mechanics to the physical world as well (Castronova, 2007).

Jane McGonigal (2011) offers a similar line of reasoning, explaining that a lot can be learned from the structure of games that could help us create a better, more engaging "real life." Games, McGonigal argues, are better structured than most "real-life" situations, as games often can offer participants clearer goals, higher success rates, and more immediate feedback. Were these aspects of games to be adopted into situations within "real life," the same communal formations and meaningful attachments frequently seen within games (and the virtual environments in which they take place) could be replicated.

In summary, both Castronova and McGonigal argue that game design enhances the experience of the participant within the game environment by providing what could almost be called an inherent, wished-for structure, which is often lacking in the participant's "real life" or "real world." Therefore, were game design to be infused into everyday situations or instances that normally did not have a strong structure of goals and rules supporting it, the same benefits derived by the participant in the game environment could be derived from the situation or instance at hand.

In this chapter, I will build on Castronova's and McGonigal's argumentation, showing how the infusion of game structure (as described in general by Castronova and McGonigal) with the basic action of purchasing an item has led to a new form of consumerism, a game-inspired form, which I call "consumerism as gameplay." I will explore this concept by using a case study of the community formed around an American online wholesale outlet called *Woot*.[1]

In the first iteration of this research (Jacobs, 2009), I argued that we should look at how game structure, specifically of that frequently found in MMORPGs, can be used in non-traditional forms of play to create surprising new engaging opportunities, such as that seen in the *Woot* case study. At the time of the original research, the use of game mechanics in non-traditional applications was still relatively unheard of and undocumented. Gabe Zichermann had introduced the concept of "Funware" in mid-2008, but it wasn't until 2010 that the concept really hit the mainstream, especially through the marketing channels, and got a name that stuck: "Gamification." Gamification, in general, most commonly refers to the design process of "taking things that aren't games and trying to make them feel more like games" (Jesse Schell, quoted in Graft, 2011), but it also has seen more specific definitions such as "the art and science of turning your customers' everyday interactions into 'games' that serve your business purposes" (Zichermann, 2010: 20) or, as Ian Bogost puts it, "the easiest way to talk to marketers about games" (quoted in Graft, 2011). From the various proposed definitions, it's easy to see that the definition of gamification is far from universal, and it is most frequently this disagreement over definition that is debated as opposed to the methodology itself. Gamification is often referred to when discussing marketing or reward-based mechanic implementation, as opposed to the implementation of game mechanics in general. Therefore, although gamification is a noteworthy and important field of research, this chapter will not at any point go into the merits of the semantics of gamification because it is outside the scope of this research. The purpose of this chapter is not to weigh the advantages and disadvantages of the term itself nor to try and pin point an exact definition for the word. It is to address the use of game mechanics within non-game instances, which both Castronova and McGonigal address more aptly and specifically than Zichermann or Schell.

THE PRINCIPLES OF WOOT

The basic concept behind Woot is that it offers one item for sale every 24-hour period, and when it's sold out, it's sold out. In addition to the option to purchase one, two, or three of the daily items in the normal iteration of Woot, the website also offers an official blog run by the staff and a forum for community members to comment on the specific item offered for sale or compete in contests that are offered periodically by Woot, such as Photoshopping Woot products into photographs. As with most websites, in order to make a purchase or post in a forum, you must create an account. Although these aspects were unique to the market at the time Woot entered the scene (in 2004), it was not until the Woot-offs began to emerge (notably around early 2005) that the community began to develop into what it is today.

A Woot-off is based on the original concept, with one tweak: There is no default 24-hour waiting time. Instead, a new item will be placed the moment the current item is officially "sold out." The only available statistic showing the community how close the item is to selling out is a percentage bar; no exact amounts are given out until after the item has become sold out. This means two things: (1) if an item sells out quickly a new one will be placed much quicker than when Woot is operating on normal principles, and (2) if an item sells out slowly, there is no guarantee that a new item will be placed any time soon. This random variable makes it difficult to estimate when new items will appear, and strategies that work with the normal format (like waking up at a specific time to be ready for a new item) do not work for Woot in Woot-off mode. Woot-offs often last at least 36 hours (besides the newly introduced "happy hour" Woot-off, which lasts an hour) and are highly anticipated by the community as they, especially in the early years, only happened a few times a year.

In looking at the behavior surrounding the two forms of shopping experiences offered by *Woot*, one can see a few clear differences. On normal days, members are forced to wait the 24-hour period regardless of whether the item sells out; therefore, there is no incentive to do anything other than look out for the member's own needs (whether the user wants the item or not) and compete directly with other members to try and get the item before it sells out (with a limited amount of items, it's first come first serve). On Woot-off days, the solitary nature of purchasing items changes, shifting from a lone-wolf environment to an environment where team-work is proactive, as only the selling out of an item advances the site to the next product. Due to the limited amount of items a member is able to purchase, it often takes a large amount of people to make a purchase for an item to sell out. Therefore, the community has learned that it benefits everyone when items sell out, as it is only then that everyone gets a chance at a potentially bigger and better item. Through this one mechanic alone, the audience has gone from passive consumers to an active community of consumers, where everyone must do their part for the good of the community—in this case purchasing "their share" of items to help the group get to the next one. This communal drive can be seen within the official Woot forum, external fan blogs and sites, as well as within member-moderated IRC channels, which are often only active during a Woot-off.

The community itself is now not only kept together by the necessity of teamwork, but also by a culture that has emerged over time. Various items, while mostly useless at first glance—such as the Leakfrog, a water-detection alarm in the shape of a cartoonish-looking frog, or the much anticipated Bag-of-Crap, a bag with random items in it—have gained enough cultural value that those active in the community will often purchase the items for cultural status alone. What makes these items have social value varies. The Leakfrog, for instance, became popular in part due to its overuse in the Woot Photoshopping contest (where members could Photoshop a Woot item into a funny picture for a chance to win a gift certificate).

The Bag of Crap gained its value by the limited amount of bags sold in a Woot-off, the low price of one US$ per item (still maximum purchase of three), and the rumors that occurred at the beginning of 2006 that instead of the usual leftover items like cheap headphones, some members were receiving high-end prizes such as TVs. Because of the low price, high entertainment value, and low quantity, the Bag of Crap is a status symbol because it's very difficult to buy, often selling out in less than eight seconds with more than 3.1 million requests made by members.

These two core aspects—that members feel they have a clear goal with clear rules so they can complete satisfying work and that they feel socially connected—suggest that Woot can attribute the use of game mechanics for its success. But how does Woot do it? What mechanics does Woot use? And how does this all fit in to our previous understandings of consumerism?

EXPLORING THE FRONTIER

Before addressing the game-inspired structure of Woot and the Woot-off, it is important to consider an underlying factor of American consumerist culture that may drive consumption in general: frontierism.[2]

Shames (2003) describes shopping as a product of the ideology of the American dream of the frontier—the belief that the world contains unlimited possibilities and wealth waiting to be discovered. In simpler terms, frontierism is the desire of the American society for "more." Shames argues that the urge to invest in the unknown in the hopes of getting a better return, the original ideal of the American frontier, has created a society that is completely driven by the concept of more, leading to an America where "a sense of quality has lagged far behind a sense of scale" (Shames, 2003: 58).

I argue that Shames' observation that frontierism is still alive and well within American consumerism reigns true and is proven particularly true by the actions of the American consumers of Woot. Members *invest* money in products they may not need or even want in order to help the overall community unveil the next product (and have a chance to purchase it). In this instance, however, investment in a Woot-off purchase is often meant in a different sense than when referring to a general investment in a normal product purchase. Although some investments in items in the Woot-off are made for the item itself (wanting a product for one's own use and investing the money in having the product to use), other investments in items in the Woot-off are for the potential of a better option available next (wanting to purchase a product to have the product sell-out in order to unveil the next product).

In the discussion forums, members openly discuss purchasing the items for the community or "team" as opposed to purchasing them for the item itself. One member writes, "Might go in for 3 and take one for the team. Depends how much the charging station is" (12 May 2011, 5:49 a.m.) while another member remarks, "In for one . . . your welcome all!" [sic] (20 July 2007, 7:30 a.m.).

This common dream of "more" drives the community to achieve its goals (buying out the product) as the community wishes to see and have the chance to purchase not only the current product in the Woot-off, but what other riches may lie ahead in the Woot-off. The community does not know what item will come next (and toward the end of the Woot-off even if any item will come next), but the common desire to know what comes next, and to not miss a chance to get a good deal, bonds the community together beyond the inherent structure of the site itself and allows the members to successfully work together toward a common goal. The group works together to collectively explore the frontier, fully knowing not everyone will get their dream items, but still realizing that they cannot achieve anything alone.

THE BASICS OF CONSUMERISM

Before addressing the structural design of Woot, it is important to address *why* and *how* consumers are consuming. For this discussion, two main terminologies must be addressed: the definition of "product" and "consuming." To define the term "product," I shall use an economic definition, which states that products are "bundles of attributes that yield particular benefits" that are constructed as "vessels of meaning that signify similarly across all consumers" (Holt, 1995:1). Simplified, this means that products are something consumers want because of what they (the product) can offer a consumer, physically, socially, psychologically, and ideologically. Branching off of that definition, "consuming" itself can be defined as a "type of social action in which people make use of consumption of objects in a variety of ways" (Holt, 1995: 1). This leads to two major aspects of consuming: the structure of consumption and the purpose of consumption.

Using these definitions as a general outline, the consumerist characteristics of Woot can be analyzed using the categories of consumerism that Holt (1995) identifies in his article on consumerism typologies. The reason that I will focus solely on Holt's definitions and typologies of consumerism/consuming is due to the fact that his typology takes a psychological and sociological look at consumerism and, as such, not only touches on aspects of community in consumerism, but also on a basic level begins to address consuming in association with play as has been observed in the Woot community.

In his typology, Holt (1995) breaks down consumerism into four categories: consuming as experience, consuming as integration, consuming as classification, and consuming as play. In the following section, I will introduce each topic, showing how the structure of Woot has created a unique circumstance where not just one of the four forms of consumption is present, but all of them, and that this new structure has created need for a fifth category: consuming as gameplay.

Consuming as Experience

Consuming as experience is centered around the emotional state that arises during consumption based on how consumers experience the product through both cultural and natural frameworks used to interpret the experience of the product (Holt, 1995). Within Woot, this is the "natural high" as a result of purchasing an elusive and/or desired item before it is sold out.

Members know there is a limited amount of any specific item available for purchase, so for many items, members realize they are racing against other members who wish to purchase the same item. The joy experienced by the consumer is due to the structure and context of the purchase (the presence of competition against others) or, in other words, the moment of purchase itself, not simply the product.

An example of this is the Bag of Crap. Due to the fact that Woot-offs are of varied lengths, members often stay awake monitoring Woot for hours on end, waiting for the almost guaranteed appearance of the Bags of Crap near the end of the Woot-off. Once the Bags of Crap appear, the servers often become overloaded (making the purchasing of one of the bags even harder), leading to many posts of extreme happiness over a successful purchase:

OH YEAHHHHHHHHHHHHHHHHHHHHHHHHHHHH!!!!!!!!!!!!!!!!!!!!
Put me down for three! Confirmed! (18 July 2005, 7:01 a.m.)

I can die happy now, I finally got my craaaaaaappppp! (1 June 2007, 10:32 p.m.)

Consuming as Integration

Where consuming as experience deals with the effects of the moment of consumption on a personal level, consuming as integration deals with the effects of consumption on a communal level. Consuming as integration is defined as being "when consumers acquire and manipulate object meanings" during rituals and events that integrate objects into the community, allowing the objects to retain and hold symbolic properties (Holt, 1995: 2). In other words, this is the combining of object and culture, giving objects additional meaning beyond the basic properties the item may physically have and, as a result, changing the way the object is perceived within that specific community.

Although items often acquire their additional meanings and values through general socialization within the community on the official forums (for reasons such as appearing often despite the initial lack of interest or for being a very random and ridiculous item such as an Elvis shaped speaker), it has also been cultivated through Photoshop contests sponsored by Woot (as described earlier in the chapter). The use of Woot items in creative ways on a weekly basis offers a good foundation for the items to gain cultural value within the community, allowing some items to stand out for being able to be easily used in such contests.

Consuming as Classification

The purchases that a member makes through Woot are important to the community as a whole, as the community has its own social and cultural norms established through the process of working together. Therefore, the community also deals with consuming as classification. Consuming as classification occurs when objects "viewed as vessels of cultural and personal meanings act to classify their consumers" (Holt, 1995: 2). To simplify this definition in terms of the Woot community, the items a member purchases, the circumstances surrounding the items the member purchases, and the quantity of items the member has purchased all affect the status of the member within the Woot community.

Although an easy way for members to show at the time that they have purchased an item is to make a forum post stating so, the most common method of showing status within a community is through the member's forum signature, such as this example:

> TWENTY EIGHT WOOTS: SIXTY EIGHT ITEMS: TWO BROWN-EYE OF CAROLINES (Note: Browneye of Carolines is one of the community's terms for Boxes of Crap).

In this way the amount of items a member has purchased directly acts as a classification for the member as more purchases are seen as higher participation and more skill.

Consuming as Play

The final form of consumerism as described by Holt (1995), consuming as play, describes consumption with others, specifically concerning the social interactions that occur while consuming. Consuming as play is where friendships are formed and "inside inside jokes"—jokes not made obvious to even the majority of the community, but only to certain subgroups—are created. This is apparent in the example of Bacon Salt. In the Woot-off previous to the October 2008 Woot-off, Bacon Salt was the very last item. Although this fact by itself may not have upset the consumers, this was also the first recorded Woot-off where there was no chance to purchase a Bag of Crap; thus, the users were extraordinarily frustrated and began to take their frustrations out on the Bacon Salt—as it was the signifier of the end of the Woot-off. Only members of the community who are active understand where the joke about Bacon Salt comes from; those who are new or not as active are not able to engage in this aspect of consuming. As seen in this particular sale of Bacon Salt, some members recognized the humorous nature of the product:

> ITS BACONNNNNNNNNN!!!!!!!! (20 February 2009, 3:58 a.m.)

> And so begins the end. . . . (20 February 2009, 3:58 a.m.)
>   It was unexpected BACon IS BACKen (20 February 2009, 3:59 a.m.)

While others do not:

> Woot has reached a new low ladies and gentlemen. fragging Bacon Salt? You suck woot. (20 February 2009, 3:59 a.m.)

> Uhhh. . . . Huh. . . . (20 February 2009, 3:59 a.m.)

> Gah . . . wuh. . . . h . . . hey?? (20 February 2009, 4:00 a.m.)

So some even try to explain:

> In the past, Bacon Salt has been the tell-tale sign the flashing lights are soon to dim and go out. Sad. Very sad. (20 February 2009, 3:59 a.m.)

The socializing that occurs within the community provides an enjoyable aspect and is an incentive within itself to continue consuming within the Woot framework and community.

GAME DESIGN IN WOOT

What makes a game a game? Within the field of game studies, many scholars believe that a game is an instance where participants (players) attempt to achieve clearly defined objectives within the limitations of an artificial rule-bound environment. A game is "a system in which players engage in an artificial conflict, defined by rules, that results in a quantifiable outcome" (Salen and Zimmerman, 2004: 80) and "an exercise of voluntary control systems in which there is an opposition between forces confined by a procedure and rules in order to produce a disequilibrial outcome" (Avedon and Sutton-Smith, 1981: 7). Most simply, a game is play with goals and structures (Maroney, 2001). Despite minor differences, what all of these definitions have in common is one thing: The structure of a game is what makes it a game. As McGonigal (2011: 20–21) writes, "When we're playing a game, we just know it. There is something essentially unique about the way games structure experience." So what then is in the structure of a game?

Juul (2003) proposes a six characteristic approach to games after taking into consideration the work of Johan Huizinga (1955), Rogier Caillois (1961), Bernard Suits (1978), Avedon and Sutton Smith (1981), Crawford (1982), David Kelley (1988), and Salen and Zimmerman (2003). He argues that games must: (1) be rule-based; (2) have variable, quantifiable outcomes; (3) have outcomes with different values—in other words, some outcomes are positive and others are negative; (4) be structured so that the player needs to invest effort in order to influence the outcome; (5) be structured so that the player is attached to the outcome; and (6) have negotiable consequences, which may or may not have real-life consequences. McGonigal

(2011) also proposes a summarized structure for gaming based on many of the same scholars, coming up with four traits that a game must have: (1) a goal, (2) rules, (3) a feedback system, and (4) voluntary participation.

Before I continue analyzing Woot using the frameworks provided, it is important to note that I am not arguing that Woot is in fact a game. Rather I am arguing that Woot uses game mechanics within its structure, making it a form of game-infused design. As stated before, this is perhaps where the term gamification could be used to define what Woot is, but again, as gamification is still not solidly defined, I will use the term game-infused design as a neutral terminology referring to the use of game mechanics within non-game instances.

This being said, in looking at Woot and how it compares to game structure, the characteristics I address will mostly be based on Juul's (2003) and McGonigal's (2011) characteristics, as they are already most encompassing of the previous theories such as Caillois and Crawford: that games (1) are voluntary, (2) are rule-based, (3) require investment for success, (4) are goal-oriented, (5) are uncertain, (6) require risk taking, and (7) provide tangible feedback.

Structure of Woot

In this next section, I will take the seven characteristics defined above and look at the structure of Woot through the lenses of game design. I will show how Woot makes use of many of the mechanics (some stronger than others), and then in the following section, I will explain how the use of these mechanics forms a new kind of consumerism—consumerism as gameplay.

First off, Woot is voluntary. You do not need to participate in Woot. Even though Woot is voluntary, Woot also has rules. Woot has structured the availability of items. Under normal circumstances, a new item is offered for sale once every 24 hours. Under the special circumstances of the Woot-off, the previous rule changes and a new rule is put in place—that a new item is offered for sale once the current item becomes sold out, up until the end of the Woot-off. Building off of that rule, Woot has also structured the ability of consumers to consume. A member is only allowed to buy a maximum of three of any one item. These rules are defined in such a way that there is no negotiation possible; there are no exceptions during either of the two circumstances.

With these limitations in place, Woot has created an environment where goals can be created. Overall, there are two main goals that are closely connected for the participants in the Woot community. In both the normal mode of Woot and the Woot-off mode, the first goal is to watch the site in the hopes that one of the items a member wants will be offered for sale. The second goal is to then to successfully purchase the item. Whether the wanted item is a normal item, like a pair of headphones or a culturally special item like a Bag of Crap, the basic goal is the same: having the chance to successfully purchase a desired item. Naturally, within this overall goal, many sub-goals must be completed in order to have a chance to complete the overall goal, especially in the case of the Woot-off. In order to have a chance for the wanted item to become available (and thus have a chance to purchase it), all other items before it must be sold out. Therefore, the sub-goal during a Woot-off is to buy out the current item. Together in a Woot-off these three goals combine together to form three points of conflict: (1) waiting for the item while (2) working together with others to buy out the unwanted items that appear first, and then (3) once the item appears, competing against others to buy it first. It is important to note that although these are the three core goals in Woot, the reason a member wants to move to the next item is also a goal within itself, only that goal is often generated outside the structure of Woot itself (including the goal of purchasing an item that is defined by the community as having cultural capital) and therefore is not included when looking at goals created by the game structure in this way. This form of goal is constrained by the effect it has directly with the environment itself. Specifically purchasing a Leakfrog as opposed to another item (like a blender) does not affect a member's ability to get another item in purchasing any other items, while buying out an item to get to the next one does. In order to successfully achieve these goals, Woot requires an investment. In the case of Woot, this investment is both time and money. Members must invest time in waiting for items to appear to then have the chance to purchase it, and they must also frequently invest money in unwanted items in order to help the community as a whole progress to the next item.

Despite the fact the rules are certain and help to define the goals, the outcomes are uncertain. There is no guarantee that an item desired by a member will appear during the normal mode of Woot or during the Woot-off. The member may invest a huge amount of time in waiting for the item, only to have waited in vain and have the item never appear. There is also no guarantee that the member, even if the item appears, will be able to purchase the item before it is sold out. Even if the member invests a huge amount of time in waiting for the item and money in buying unwanted items in the hopes of getting to the current item, if the member is unable to be quick enough to purchase it before the others, the member will not get the chance to buy the item.

Due to all of these factors, the free participation, the rules, the goals, the investment, and the uncertain outcomes, the outcome then has a value to it, some outcomes being good (purchasing the item) and others bad (not purchasing the item). This then is where risk appears, the embodiment of the result of all of these aspects, which then generates the value and attachment to the outcome. As stated above, with uncertain outcomes, even if a member invests a huge amount of resources in getting an item, there is still the risk that he or she will not get that item. Thus, every decision within Woot is based on these principles of risk: is the member willing to risk the time and money and end up with nothing, and, if so, how much is the member willing to risk? Like with gambling, risk can also be a form of enjoyment. When the stakes are higher and the competition is stronger, a successful outcome can be that much more enjoyable, just as an unsuccessful outcome can be that much more painful.

Finally, Woot has tangible feedback. Members can see how many items they have purchased, how many valuable posts they have contributed to the community, and how they stand against others, but having access to a variety of statistics for each purchase. These statistics show, for example, how many people purchase one, two, or three of the items, which state in the US made the most purchases of the item, or who were the first and last members to purchase the item.

All of these characteristics show that Woot has a very similar structure to that of games. In the next section, I will break this analysis down further and introduce the concept of consuming as gameplay, which results from this game-like structure.

CONSUMING AS GAMEPLAY

Returning to Holt's typologies and considering the incredibly close similarities between game structure and the structure of Woot and the Woot-off, I propose that a new typology of consuming is required in order to explain this new gaming aspect of consuming that has emerged—consuming as gameplay.

I define consuming as gameplay as consumerism in which a challenge is presented as a roadblock to consuming, requiring perceived coordination or skill to resolve, in which the enjoyment of consuming stems from the solving of the original problem and in which, without completion of the challenge, consuming cannot occur. Consuming as gameplay is an extension of consuming as play, inclusive of the elements of consuming as experience, integration, and classification. Consuming as gameplay moves beyond simply the creation of community through consumption, as it is a community that evolves not only from the process of consumption, but from the need to overcome a conflict or challenge before consumption can begin.

In the case of Woot, this is consumerism where participation with other individuals is necessary to reach an end result of consuming individually. This environment is created by the basic desire of the consumer, the challenging structure of Woot and the Woot-off, and the ability for the community to communicate and be aware of the newfound common goal, allowing the community to emphasize the need to solve the challenge to meet the original desire, creating new desires in the process that, in some cases, replace the original desires.

The effect of consuming as gameplay in the formation of community can be seen within the official forums, specifically within three types of forum posts: (1) those that encourage action, (2) those that monitor and judge other's actions, and (3) those that promote self-accomplishments. Within consuming as gameplay, the goal of the community is to meet the challenges presented to them. Thus, the following actions of the community are necessary in order for the goal to be achieved: (1) encouragement of members to continue to consume (encouragement), (2) the weeding out of members making false claim or who are not actively participated but are still reaping the benefits (monitoring of behavior), and (3) members justifying their presence in the community by showing that they have contributed their part (promotion). This is, once again, where game theory proves to be strong, as these are the same logical steps needed to be successful within many cooperative game communities: (1) to challenge the players to perform, (2) to get rid of those players who cannot perform, and (3) players sharing achievements to claim their place within the community and environment.

First, we have the encouragement:

> Almost there . . . someone take one (or three) for the team. (19 June 2008, 11:44 p.m.)

> End it. End it now! Someone take one for the team. (19 June 2008, 11:43 p.m.)

> Come on wooters . . . we got five and already listed them on e-bay . . . you can do the same so we can move on to the next Woot. :-) (17 February 2006, 11:45 p.m.)

> 1gb for 60.00? Come on wooters . . . take one or three for the team. (29 July 2008, 9:52 p.m.)

In all of these posts (and there are hundreds if not thousands more like them on the Woot forums), the common theme is the emphasis on the team. This "take one for the team" mentality is exactly what consuming as gameplay is about; it is a group of consumers working together (as a team) against the obstacle preventing them from consuming, which ironically, in this instance, forces them to consume products that the members may or may not want in order to get to that final goal of consumption.

Second, we have the accusations:

> What I don't understand is why 11% of the buyers only bought 1? (28 October 2009, 3:53 a.m.)

In response to a user who said, "Cheaper here http://dealspl.us/product/silver-mini-cell-phone-light-excalibur-h102s-cs-sg," another user responded, "What are you doing!! Practice saying, 'I have one and love it.' WE need to move forward. You can go get one cheaper on your own time. It is not [cheaper] there for three of them and that item isn't available there anymore" (28 October 2009, 3:54 a.m.). In response to a user who said, "Hahaha I really hope you haven't been serious this whole time," another user said, "Dead serious. People need to get their posts accurate or else we have chaos. Otherwise someone might buy something based on incorrect information which could lead to unfortunate situations" (28 October 2009, 3:53 a.m.).

In response to a user who said, "Come on people, take one for the team and let's keep this woot-off going, I just bought three. :)," another user responded, "No you didn't: 95percent bought one 2percent bought two 0percent bought 3" (17 February 2006, 11:32 p.m.). These quotations are very interesting in the fact that there are two types of accusations: those who outright accuse others within the "team" (community) and those who defend the "team" against accusations given by a specific member. The second example is especially interesting, as a member had posted where to find the same product for cheaper (normally a valued bit of information when consuming); however, the member was then reprimanded by another member for posting such a site, explaining that it was not to the "team's" advantage to buy cheaper, as the task at hand required them to buy this specific product.

In consuming as gameplay, due to the context provided by the community within the challenge provided by Woot, an additional layer is added to consumption in an interestingly similar way to that of a baseball hit into a crowd by a baseball player. The ball that is hit gains a new value compared with other cheaper, yet identical baseballs, which one can find in a store at any point. The focus is not on what the item is, but what the item represents. In the case of the Woot-off, the point is not to find the item at the cheapest possible rate (although Woot often sells items for some of the cheapest prices available), it is to help advance the team, so buying an item through another channel devalues the item within the community, whereas buying the item within the Woot channel adds value to the item and to the members who "did their part" to purchase it. The third example is also a very interesting quotation because it too stresses the importance of accuracy in purchasing, taking, once again, emphasis away from the actual habit of personal consumption and instead placing emphasis on the solving of the problem and unlocking all the "levels" of the Woot-off.

Finally, there is the promotional: In response to a user who said, "I think anyone who buys this should be required to explain his or herself to the rest of us," another user responded, "They were willing to take one for the team. There was someone that just claimed they took three for the team. I hope it didn't hurt too badly" (27 October 2009, 11:26 p.m.). In response to a user who said, "Aren't we all fellow wooters??? I got 3, now you get 3! Take one for the team, or these will be on here FOREVER!! It's woot. You know they have a million of these!!! NOW, GO! BUY!", another user responded, "Pfft . . . I've taken ROOMBAS for the team (two at regular price and one in a b o c [bag of crap], so wake up some of the drunks, wil-lya?" (28 October 2009, 3:54 a.m.).

Although there are many "I bought 1" or "In for 3" posts, the two posts above represent a more detailed insight into the mindset of the community. The first post deals with the entire principle the consumers in Woot base their participation around, and the second post deals with the justification of participation within the group formed within Woot. It is a post where, on hearing a call to purchase things (of which the caller has also purchased), another member reinforces their status (despite not purchasing an item) by explaining that they, the member, have bought even more expensive items for the "team" and therefore they are not responsible for this round and that it's time for the others to do their part.

To move back to the first example, in this quote, a member questions the logic behind anyone buying a specific item; in fact, the member claims that they should "have to explain" themselves for making what is perceived as being a "stupid purchase." However, to accomplish the goal of the com-munity, the rules of the Woot-off require purchasing "stupid" items, and therefore the other member responds back to support his fellow members purchasing the item, explaining that those members were doing everyone a favor to take even just one and chiding the other member for challenging the system.

What is most interesting about these observations is that they only exist within this circumstance. During the normal Woot mode, there are post-ings of cheaper products, dissing of people who choose to buy the offered product, and mockery of the product. It is only during the Woot-off that this changes, and these posts become detrimental to the community's goal. I believe this is a very telling aspect that exemplifies the new form of consum-erism going on that only appears within a game structure environment.

CONCLUSION

As I have argued in this chapter, Woot is, in principle, a game-inspired design. It is founded on the voluntary participation of members within the consump-tion-centered, rule-based environment of which in order to achieve the goals of consumption, defined by the rules and goaded by the inherent presence of fronterism, members must make a steady investment of both time and money. Even with this investment, however, there are no guarantees as to the outcome as the results are always uncertain. With the presence of investment and the risk that naturally accompanies all of the other elements, members have great attachment to the outcome beyond the surface level, which then further invests them in the Woot community. Woot then provides tangible feedback to the members concerning their performance, as an individual and as a group, allowing members to track and showcase their progress, further attaching members to the site and the community surrounding it.

From this structure, the community has learned over time that the challenges presented during a Woot-off, the needing of an item to sell out before the next item is available, is only efficiently overcome through group coordination. This has since required the formation of an organized community within Woot. In this instance, a form of structure that has in the past normally focused on a participant versus participant mechanic has been transformed into a structure focused on a participant's versus challenge mechanic. The change of mechanics, from solo-participant able to consume with assistance to solo-participant being unable to consume without assistance, has created a form of community in which consumers must work together, due to the rules created by the structure of Woot, to overcome the challenges and then have a chance to consume on an individual basis. Unlike purely individualistic consumption, the group has evolved to expect those who reap the benefits, such as having the chance to purchase one of the wanted items (such as a good deal on an iPod or a Bag of Crap), will help the rest of the group, the "team," in return. Those who receive must give back to the community and help others to achieve the same goals by putting in their share of the work (which is monitored closely by the community).

For this reason, Woot is much more than just comparable to the structure of an online game; combining game mechanics with the consumption of items has led to a new form of consumerism, consuming as gameplay, where the consumer cannot consume without overcoming a challenge requiring a resolution, in which the enjoyment of consuming also stems from the overcoming of the challenge, and not just the moment of consumption. In the specific case of Woot, this is seen in a multiplayer, cooperative environment, where the consumer no longer has a selfish, solitary role, but is now part of a larger cause—consuming not only with the satisfaction of the self in mind but also the satisfaction of the group. This is consumption where the personal satisfaction of the pure consumption of a physical object is often secondary to the personal satisfaction of overcoming an obstacle to achieve the consumption.

In the end what is apparent is that the use of game mechanics in the case of Woot has created a successful game-based structure, of which one of the main enjoyments found by participants is not always the main purpose of the site, consumption, but rather the added layer of success and mastery of the challenge presented before consumption.

NOTES

1. Woot can be found at http://www.woot.com. Although Woot has many subsidiaries, such as Shirt.Woot, Kids.Woot, Sellout.Woot, and Wine.Woot, I will only be focusing on the main site. In this entire chapter, all quotes are taken from the official Woot forums found at http://www.woot.com/Forums/
2. American culture is singled out due to the fact that Woot targets and serves an almost solitarily American demographic

REFERENCES

Avedon EM, Sutton-Smith B. 1981. *The Study of Games.* John Wiley & Sons, Inc.: New York.

Castronova E. 2005. *Synthetic Worlds: The Business and Culture of Online Games.* The University of Chicago Press: Chicago.

Castronova E. 2007. *Exodus to the Virtual World: How Online Fun Is Changing Reality.* Palgrave Macmillan: New York.

Chen M. 2009. Communication, Coordination, and Camaraderie in World of Warcraft. *Games and Culture* 4: 47–73.

Crawford C. 1982. *The Art of Computer Game Design.* Osborne McGraw Hill: Berkeley.

Ducheneaut N, Yee N, Nickell E, and Moore R. 2006. Alone Together? Exploring the Social Dynamics of Massively Multiplayer Online Games. *Proceedings of the CHI 2006* (2006): 401–416.

Graft K. 2011. *GDC 2011: Time to ditch the term 'gamification'.* Available at: http://www.gamasutra.com/view/news/33315/gdc_2011_time_to_ditch_the_term_.php [accessed on 1 August 2011].

Holt D. 1995. How Consumers Consume: A Typology of Consumption Practices. *The Journal of Consumer Research* 22(1): 1–16.

Huizinga J. 1955. *Homo Ludens: A Study of the Play-Element in Culture.* The Beacon Press: Boston.

Jacobs M. 2009. Take One—or Three—for the Team: Consumerism as Play, in *Breaking New Ground: Innovation in Games, Play, Practice and Theory: Proceedings of the 2009 Digital Games Research Association Conference,* B. Atkins, H. Kennedy, and T. Krzywinska (eds.). Brunel University Press: London.

Jenkins H. 2006. *Fans, Bloggers, and Gamers: Exploring Participatory Culture.* New York University Press: New York.

Juul J. 2003. The Game, the Player, the World: Looking for a Heart of Gameness, in *Level Up: Digital Games Research Conference Proceedings,* M. Copier and J. Raessens (eds.). Utrecht University Press: Utrecht; 30–45.

Kelley, D. 1988. *The Art of Reasoning.* W. W. Norton & Company: New York.

Maroney K. 2001. *My Entire Waking Life.* Available at http://www.thegamesjournal.com/articles/MyEntireWakingLife.shtml [accessed on 8 July 2011].

McGonigal J. 2011. *Reality Is Broken: Why Games Make Us Better and How They Can Change the World.* Random House: London.

Salen K, Zimmerman E. 2004. *Rules of Play—Game Design Fundamentals.* MIT Press: Cambridge.

Shames L. 2003. The More Factor, in *Signs of Life in the U.S.A.,* S. Massik and J. Solomon (eds.). Bedford/St. Martin's: New York; 56–62.

Suits B. 1978. *The Grasshopper: Games, Life and Utopia.* University of Toronto Press: Toronto.

Taylor TL. 2006. *Play Between Worlds: Exploring Online Game Culture.* MIT Press: Boston.

Zichermann G, Linder J. 2010. *Game-Based Marketing: Inspire Customer Loyalty through Rewards, Challenges, and Contests.* John Wiley and Sons: Hoboken.

12 Creating Virtual Selves in Second Life

Handan Vicdan and Ebru Ulusoy

INTRODUCTION

With the increased recognition of the importance of co-creation in digital world (Baker and Curasi, 2008; Mukherjee and Venkatesh, 2008; Tumbat and Horowitz, 2008), consumer creativity has gained attention by scholars who explore consumption/production in the digital world. Scholars have explored consumer creativity primarily in terms of design (Moreau and Dahl, 2005), product co-creation (Vargo and Lusch, 2004), innovation (Hirschman, 1980), consumer intelligence (Hirschman, 1983), and meaning creation (Herd et al., 2009). Consumer creativity is mainly defined as " . . . the ability to engage in . . . productive thinking—the capacity to generate novel cognitive content" (Hirschman, 1980: 285), and is found to be influenced by situational and personal factors (Burroughs and Mick, 2004). Bonsu and Darmody (2008) also explored consumer creativity in virtual worlds and concluded that corporations exploit co-creative practices of consumers in these contexts.

In this study, we do not adopt a political approach that focuses on empowerment-exploitation dialectics between consumers and marketers. We aim to bring a different approach to the concept of consumer creativity as it relates to consumer virtual self-construction through the avatar in a virtual world called *Second Life* (SL). In doing so, we also focus on understanding consumer feelings and experiences and their perceptions of creativity as they construct alternative selves in SL. Consumer creativity in this context is utilized not only to create novel product designs, but also novel self-images and identities, fun and experience, and furthermore individual and social meanings. It is important to understand the role of consumer creativity from a neutral perspective in this context, as it is a very flexible environment that allows consumers both to imagine and realize many novel things they cannot in many other consumption contexts.

The body has also been an integral part of self-construction. Consumer researchers have conceptualized body (1) as a means of self-presentation and socialization (Thompson and Hirschman, 1995), and (2) as a project that modern consumers work on (Featherstone et al., 1991; Schouten, 1991).

In effect, with regards to the presence of the body in virtual worlds, some scholars argued that these technologies have enabled people to break out of the finitude of their embodiment and engage in disembodiment (Balsamo, 2000; Stone, 2000; Turkle, 1995; Ward, 2001), whereas others have advocated the essential role of embodiment in any human experience (Argyle and Shields, 1996; Flichy, 2007; Froy, 2003; Hansen, 2006; Mingers, 2001). The growing visual and semiotic potential of virtual worlds has allowed for the representation of one's physical self through images such as avatars and photos, and further complicated the embodiment/disembodiment debate.

Using netnography as our primary research methodology, we investigate consumer self-creation processes in virtual worlds. In doing so, we seek to contribute to the expansion and integration of insights regarding the self in contemporary life. Consequently, we aim to provide deeper insights into consumer creative processes, as they construct virtual bodily selves in SL. Findings of this research suggest that consumers engage in the creation of corporeal selves through avatars, and their creativity primarily focuses on creating experience and fun rather than managing a certain impression, and whilst experiencing transitions in between alternative selves. Most importantly, we draw attention to these paradoxes consumers experience in virtual self-construction, and that consumers create multiple virtual and real life selves that reflect upon each other. First, we provide some theoretical insights into consumer self-creation and the body concept in virtual worlds in order to provide the theoretical foundations that inform our netnographic research.

SELF-CREATION IN VIRTUAL WORLDS

The body has been an integral part of the self-concept, and body image has come to play an important role in contemporary society as a means of constructing, symbolizing, and expressing one's selves (Fisher, 1986; Schouten, 1991). Transformations in new technologies and culture also draw attention to the body concept in virtual worlds. For example, some scholars argue against the futility of body in the virtual world and advocate the importance of embodiment (Hansen, 2006; Madden, 1993; Takayoshi, 1994; Turkle, 1995) in any human experience and in identity processes (e.g., self-presentation) (Rook, 1985). Others emphasize the corporeal body serving no longer as a limitation in virtual worlds. The body concept becomes futile because virtual consumers break out of their corporeality and bodily constraints, and create for themselves new designations of gender, sex, and physical forms (cyborg, hybrids) (Haraway, 1997). Hence, virtual worlds enable consumers to engage in disembodied communication by breaking out of the finitude of their embodiment, overcome the limitations of their body to present their subjectivity in disembodiment, and serve as a playground for the liquid, shifting the postmodern self (Beetham, 2006).

Virtual worlds also allow for the visual representation of one's physical self through avatars, images, photos, and the like. Freed from the constraints of a physical body, virtual consumers playfully engage in novel forms of self-presentation and turn symbols into personal expressions (Schau and Gilly, 2003), hence presenting multiple selves (Schau and Gilly, 2003). In communicating their identities in virtual worlds, people manipulate signs (Wiley, 1994) at times to represent embodied presences and at other times experiencing a disembodied existence (Brewer, 1998). They can freely conceal the undesirable aspects of their actual physical and psychological selves or express their desirable aspects, aspects that are sometimes hard to convey in the physical realm (Schau and Gilly, 2003). They can reconcile their urge for physicality with the non-physicality of cyberspace in symbolic forms. Reid-Steere also (1996: 36) attracts attention to this characteristic of virtual worlds and suggests that "the boundaries delineated by cultural constructions of the body are both subverted and given free rein in virtual environments. With the body freed from the physical, it completely enters the realm of the symbol." As Cavallaro (1998: 13) also states, "If the body is not one fixed 'thing' but many possible 'bits' of things, the opportunities for play and experiment become virtually endless."

Avatars are among the most popular digital images or, in other words, symbolic forms used in the virtual world. They are "a representation of the user as an animated character" (Loos, 2003: 17), "graphic icons representing users through various forms" (Chung, 2005: 538), or "discursive or visual virtual selves" (Kolko, 1999). In virtual worlds, consumers can create and manipulate their avatars, constructing and reconstructing them with several attributes, gestures (using animated expressions such as smiling, winking, etc.), and physical appearances (humanlike, non-human, half-human, cyborg, animal, or other types of fantasy creatures). Consumers construct their selves in varying personas through these avatars and experience alternative lifestyles in virtual worlds. The use of avatars in creating cyber-"characters," participation in games or chat rooms on the Internet with personas other than ones experienced in "actual" life, and adventures in several virtual worlds are all providing people with possibilities of projecting selves constructed swiftly and temporally. There are many outlets on the Internet, in which present experiences can be constructed and shared, and different selves can be explored and experimented with. SL, described as "a 3-D virtual world entirely created by its residents,"[1] is one of these outlets where consumers can construct, reconstruct and experience multiple bodily representations.

SL enables people to experiment with and engage in creations of multiple selves. However, our observations on SL reveal that experiences generated with and through these bodily creations are in constant flux. Consumers experience several paradoxes in the processes of virtual self-construction and experience, which questions the embodiment/disembodiment debate among scholars. In the following sections, we detail our research method and articulate the paradoxes transitions consumers experience in virtual self-creation.

METHODOLOGY

Using netnography as our primary research methodology, we explored consumer involvement in SL, meanings they attached to their avatars, and their experiences lived through these avatar bodies. Netnography as a qualitative research method has several potential benefits. As Kozinets (2002: 61) states, "Netnography is ethnography adapted to the study of online communities and cultures." Netnography is also "an interpretive method devised specifically to investigate the consumer behavior of cultures and communities present on the Internet" (Kozinets, 1998: 366). Data compilation for this research was grounded in the collection of texts posted on SL consumer blogs, our observations as participant observers, and in-depth interviews conducted with SL consumers in both online and off-line contexts. Trustworthiness of the study was ensured through following the steps proposed by Kozinets (2002) in netnographic research.

Following the guidelines for participatory netnography (Kozinets, 2010), we started our research process by first becoming residents of SL. We created avatars that represent ourselves in SL by choosing from one of the default avatars and making modifications on them. Then we conducted participant observations as its residents. We became involved in some of our informants' virtual community called International Society for Technology in Education (ISTE) in SL. We videotaped most of our observations to provide deeper insights into the structure of SL. Accordingly, we developed a framework for possible questions to ask our informants.

In locating our informants, we used snowball-sampling method. We did not have limitations in finding informants only in First Life (FL).[2] Our objective was to conduct interviews with people in both SL and in their FL physical settings to gain deeper insights into the phenomena in which we were interested. We thought that the comparison of off-line data with online data might also be beneficial to our research as a means of articulating the strengths and weaknesses of our methodological approach.

As mentioned earlier, our major data source for this study was composed of our experiences as residents in SL, online and off-line interviews (only the interviews were off-line, but during these off-line interviews, the informants were online on SL, which enabled us to reflect both on their on-screen and off-screen aspects of SL experiences) with the informants, and textual data from SL consumer blogs. All of the interviews were in-depth and semistructured. However, a few of the earlier interviews were led more by the informants rather than by us. Thus, in the first few interviews, we started off with unstructured questions. As our understanding of the phenomena developed, we took the lead in conversations. However, we let the informants to express their selves as much as they wanted in the areas of inquiry. We followed an iterative approach, where we built our inquiry areas on all previous interviews for the next interview. Interviews lasted from 45 minutes to almost two hours. Our informants' ages ranged from 21 to 60. Four of our informants were female, and four of them were male.

We interviewed three people (Skyler, Jesse, and Fred) in physical everyday life settings, such as their offices or a computer lab at a university. These interviewees were also logged onto SL during the interviews. In addition, we interviewed five people (Raven, Esme, Spiff, Ginny, and Cecil) online in their SL settings. First, we asked informants to talk about their initial involvement in SL and their feelings when they first found out about SL. Then, we asked them to describe what an avatar meant to them and how having an avatar influences their SL experiences. Then we asked them to talk about the processes of their avatar(s) creation and re-creation and what influences them in these processes. The informants talked about the number of avatars they created, the reasons behind creating several avatars, and how they created and modified their avatar(s). Lastly, we asked them to talk about the characteristics of the avatar(s) they created and whether there are any similarities or differences when they compare the characteristics of their avatar(s) and their FL selves. In sum, the questions mainly focused on the feelings and motives concerning their lives in SL, the processes of the (re)creation of virtual bodies/avatars, the motives behind these processes, and the experiences with these avatars in SL.

We also looked for SL consumer blogs through keyword search method. Our search yielded several SL consumer blogs, and we randomly selected some of these blogs and read them over a period of one year. We specifically focused on the blog posts concerning consumer avatar (re)creation and experiences and downloaded approximately 200 pages of blog data.

After a two-year period of data collection, we proceeded in a systematic way to code and group findings. This involved many rereading of the data and discovering the main themes relevant to the topic under investigation through an iterative analysis. Textual data from blog posts and in-depth interviews, which are most pertinent to the research questions and offer rich and descriptive content (Kozinets, 2002), were included in the analysis after careful implementation of coding principles suggested by Glaser and Strauss (1967).

FINDINGS

We articulate findings from this research based on consumer bodily involvement and experiences in SL and the paradoxical nature of consumer virtual self-creation processes. We found that consumers in SL follow three steps (co-optation, co-production, and co-creation) in their co-production processes as defined by Lanier and Hampton (2008). Consumers' creativity level in the first stage is low as their involvement with the context is low. In this stage they co-opt the already available resources in SL. For example, in the creation of their avatars, they use some generic models. As they get more involved in the context, they start to use their creativity at a higher level but still depend highly on the readily found resources to enhance their fantasy engagement. As their involvement level increases further, consumers invest more of their own creativity resources in their self and body creations in SL, which further complicates the self-creation process, in which consumers go through numerous paradoxes. In light of our findings laid out in the following section, we articulate this multifaceted nature of consumer self-creation and bring an alternative approach to embodiment/disembodiment debate through efforts to analyze consumer created multiple virtual and real life selves that reflect on each other.

Bygones the Physical Self, Viva la "Avatar"(?): Possible and Proper Selves

Plenty of opportunities exist for consumers to create bodily selves and engage in multiple bodily experiences, all of which have been important motives for involvement of our informants in SL:

> You actually go ahead and live in your SL. I could do different characters, not just human, put whoever your mental image of yourself is onto the virtual world. There are abilities to make yourself to look exactly like how you are in real life, you can do make yourself a creature, or 20 feet tall. (Skyler, off-line interview)

Along with making gestures with their avatars, touching, flying, and involving in variousphysical activities in SL, people can experience various audio and visual elements of the body that they cannot experience in real life due to physical or social constraints. Skyler talks about the experience of such a possibility in SL:

> Something I really can't do in real life are tattoos and everything of that sort for future job instances. But I can do that on here, because you can place tattoos on yourself as well. (Skyler, off-line interview)

Skyler's motivation for involvement in SL is the ability to create and experience any possible bodily self that is desired. Whereas FL is limited in bodily creations, SL provides consumers freedom to (re)construct their desired bodily creations and experiences. This leads to higher involvement in SL.

> We're born with set bodies. They look a certain way; they will always look a certain way and that's it. My mind doesn't have those constraints.

> Raven is a woman that my mind projects as me. I guess if you're given the opportunity to be anything, to think outside the box like that, why stuck with what you are in real life, where you could be an animal you admire, a beautiful fish (Raven, online interview)

In SL, Raven expresses the move away from the bodily constraints experienced in FL and enjoys the bodily freedom and perceives it as a motive to get involved in SL and create multiple avatars to experience constraint free symbolic selves. Creation of multiple bodily selves is not only a motive for involvement in SL but also a motive for involvement in experiences without worries about appearance. Consider, for example, Spiff's experiences:

> I found in SL with, and I guess this is because of having an avatar, is you get to know people really quickly and easily, 'cause you're not so worried about your appearance as you might be in real life. (Spiff, online interview)

SL consumers engage in creative processes of virtual self-construction due to the ability, power, and freedom to be another self—a self that is symbolized in various ways. However, as consumers enjoy their freedom of constructing many bodily selves, they are still influenced by the gazes of virtual others. Despite the possibility to playfully engage in creating multiple avatars in SL (Reid-Steere, 1996), this freedom is attenuated by the gaze of the other (Gergen, 1991; Ricoeur, 1992). This suggests that the constitution of the body as a communicative medium (Domzal and Kernan, 1993) and as a project does not totally disappear in virtual worlds, as Esme reveals when she talks about her avatar creation process. This freedom to construct several bodily selves is also restricted by level of competence and skill (e.g., being a newbie):

> When I first came to SL, I adopted an avatar that was very plain, and I was steadfast about I wasn't going to spend any money to be very sexy or wear revealing clothes. But I saw that I actually stood out by being boring looking, so I spent a lot of time thinking about what kind of presentation I want to have. (Esme, online interview)

In our interview with Spiff, he talked about how he began to change the features of his avatar. He mentioned that he started to look for a secluded place on SL where others are not around and cannot see that he is transforming one virtual bodily self to another. His comments suggest that he experiences feelings of embarrassment that getting the avatar naked, changing clothes or the appearance of the avatar may not be a proper behavior.

> I usually start off here at the bottom of the stairs over there, and usually nobody is around. So, that's usually where I edit my appearance. (Spiff, online interview)

Our interview with Cecil, a half-human cyborg, also reflects on the urge to enjoy the possibility of constructing several virtual selves, yet with concerns for what he considers to be necessary to enhance his SL experience. For example, Cecil starts to read a poem from Sylvia Plath during the interview, and as he starts to read the poem he changes his voice (with a voice changer software used in SL) into a female voice because he thinks the poem sounds more beautiful when read with a soft, female voice rather than a deep masculine cyborg voice.

> One of the first things I learned as a newbie is that if you don't do a little bit of customization to your avatar, you'll continue to look (and potentially be treated) like a newbie. I don't know if I'll ever assimilate into the indigenous culture of SL (I may always be a colonial), but at least, I wanted to try to fit in. And to fit in, I needed a better skin (Katicus, mynameiskate.typepad.com)

In the blog post above, we observe a need to adopt a skin that is proper for the SL community. Although this avatar enjoys the quest for s second skin, the possibility of being different, being the "other" in SL, her or his imagination is still bounded by the presence of the "other" and the skills needed to (re)construct his or her virtual body.

Segregated and Integrated Selves

SL gives the opportunity to do things one cannot do in FL due to the ability to mask FL bodily appearances and increased freedom to (re)construct their desired bodies and experiences. Consumers engage in symbolic avatar creation and experience different bodily selves. Specifically, our findings reveal the excitement with experiencing completely different body features compared to the ones one has in FL. How Spiff constructed his avatar is also an example of the thrill in becoming someone else:

> Well, I guess I wanted to just make myself different than I was in real world, just to experience something different. I'm White, 41 years old, still have some of my hair in real life. Being black and bald looks pretty good in SL. (Spiff, online interview)

Nonetheless, SL consumers reflect their FL selves on SL selves (e.g., simulacrum of interpersonal behavior, keeping social distance in SL just like in FL), and vice versa (make FL self look like SL avatar, gain skills through SL, and reflect that self-esteem gained in SL on FL experiences) during avatar (re)creation. SL bodies are not freed from sensuality. Consumers engage in experiences they can(not) immerse into in FL because of physical/psychological constraints (e.g., flying, skydiving, death, suicide), which they react to in very embodied ways (e.g., having the sense of blood rush while the avatar is falling down). Consumers create several bodily selves in SL, yet these processes are full of refractions from both FL and SL. Avatars, for example, are still concerned about keeping interpersonal distance and making eye contact in SL. Esme explained the influence of physical distance on SL residents' feelings:

> Compared to real life, people stand much further apart in SL, unless the avatars are being intimate with each other. One day at ISTE, we all stepped forward, and we all commented on how much better we felt that we were closer. But then, I've noticed that since then those same people will stand far apart. (Esme, online interview).

Hence, we observe that similar variations that exist in FL can also be found in SL. Both the opportunities to create avatars and to live bodily experiences are abundant in SL. Yet SL is not free from some physical constraints, and it has its own construction of physical distance that influences the experiences of SL residents. Consequently, the construction of virtual selves and the experiences lived through them in this symbolic realm are nevertheless affected by consumers' FL selves and vice versa, which further intensify the body/mind dilemma in virtual worlds. Jesse's experiences reveal this interplay between FL physical body and the SL avatar:

> When I created my first avatar, I made sure she's brown skin, not thin, and average height and weight, which I am. Everything else is different. But I tried to make a little bit of myself in her. . . . I also make myself look more like the character; I straighten my hair, put make up on, and put contacts, just like her. So I can kind of make myself look like her, instead of her look like me. (Jesse, off-line interview)

Even though consumer experiences with their avatars take place in the virtual world, they may still feel some physical effects as a result. Ginny's statement below reveals such an impact:

> When I'm a human I go parasailing. My husband tells me I have a *symicidal* avatar, because I love to jump off the buildings, and just fly off wherever I wanna go. There is parachuting, where they get up in the air and just let go. That's pretty interesting because that free fall effect is, wow, you know, kind of gives you a blood rush there. (Ginny, online interview)

Interestingly, as SL consumers create their avatars that reflect their mental images of who they want to be, they build higher levels of empathy with their avatars, which strengthens the feeling aspects of their SL bodily experiences. Fred's explanation of his flying experience reveals this empathy and how this empathy enhances what he feels through his avatar experiences in SL:

I had a hard time landing at first and fell constantly, but I finally figured it out. I mean you can see the stress that he goes through . . . actually so every time I fly, I have this sensation of as if I'm doing it. It's strange cause I'm terrified of heights. But I like to do it. Isn't that weird? That's probably I enjoy the most, flying. (Fred, off-line interview)

Encore Mayne in the following blog post also draws attention to the utmost freedom to construct several bodily selves in SL, which are framed by our imaginations and FL bodily selves. For her or him, experiences are enhanced through developing tolerance to and gaining the ability to navigate between different orders and personas in SL:

SL allows us to express ourselves as freely as we wish, as much as our inhibitions and imagination allows I should say. Some people who are presented with a ultimately free platform to revel in that freedom are petrified. There are no boundaries of taste, no compass points. They maintain real life personas and shy from developing any other modes of thought. Embracing alternate realities is a must here. This is where the term tolerance has primary significance. It's a maxim we must all stand to defend. (Encore Mayne, blog post: http://maynewomen.blog-spot.com)

Presented and Constructed Selves

Our research findings of the meanings consumers attribute to their avatars reveal that preoccupation with body is also an essential part of virtual lives. In SL, "avatar" meanings expand beyond self-presentation and involve constant self-construction. Consumer creations of different avatars enable them to experience multiple selves in transition. Ginny's statement reveals meanings of "avatar" in the sense of possibilities of projecting selves that are constructed swiftly and temporally. As we carried out our interview with Ginny in her house in SL, Ginny constantly changed her avatar, from a mermaid to a human, and to a human with a leopard tail. In the avatar creation process, a few default avatars are given to consumers in SL as options to choose from. However, the avatar creation process usually does not end but starts at and continues from this point. This process usually becomes an on-going creation and re-creation process, as the options to choose from to create avatars are seemingly infinite. This continuing process is reflected in Ginny's questioning of having only one avatar:

I like to see how many different avatars I can make. There are so many things to choose from, so many different lifestyles you can lead. Why be restricted to one? Sometimes I get tired of being who I am and be something else. You wake up one day and say, "I think I wanna be a Neeko, or the next day a mermaid, a fairy. It just depends on what you

feel that day. I think it definitely extends the experience. You see different lifestyles, be somebody else for a while." (Ginny, online interview)

The process of avatar (re)construction is itself a core experience in SL.
Cecil's expression about his avatar construction process is an example to
this process being a focal and an on-going experience:

> When I was building the avatar, I don't know why I was attracted to
> that. I didn't actually seek out to become a half human, half borg. I just
> saw it when I was putting on clothes, trying on things, it just appealed
> to me. (Cecil, online interview)

Audio aspects of avatars in SL also enhance this constant avatar reconstruction, a transition that leads to more immersion into SL experiences. What
Cecil expresses with his two types of voices that he gets by using a voice filter
reveals how experiences are enriched in SL through these characteristics:

> [Using female voice] I think I can do more with the voice changer,
> make it a little bit more authentic and the characterization amusing. I
> like the female voice when I want to get in touch with my female side.
> Sometimes I read poetry in SL. I read Sylvia Plath and I think it helps
> to have the female voice, rather than my [using cyborg voice] "Hi, I'm
> Cecil Borg, you'll be assimilated" voice. (Cecil, online interview)

Consequently, bodily experiences through avatars in SL go beyond being
a medium of self-presentation (Schau and Gilly, 2003; Schouten, 1991;
Thompson and Hirschman, 1995). They also enhance immersion into SL
experiences involving symbolic (re)construction and experience of multiple
bodily selves. As mentioned earlier from our observations of avatars in SL,
a person can become a mermaid and all of a sudden grow a tail and experience the transition into a leopard; a half-human cyborg can change his deep
voice into a soft female voice while reading poems. Most intriguingly, online
self construction affects off-line self construction and vice versa, which also
reveals the ongoing self construction mediated by both SL and FL bodies:

> Both of my *SL* avatars still have their own set of friends and their Sec-
> ond Lives—which is as opposite as they are complimentary. After all,
> they would have to be complimentary since both of them are ME! . . .
> This avatar not only showed me (indirectly) the areas of my human'ness I
> needed to work on, but also taught me about *me*. His Real Life personality
> managed to find a way into my psyche and "heal" me. Was this planned?
> Absolutely not. (Maxine, asecondlifeconsciousness.blogspot.com)

For Maxine, alternative bodily selves she or he created through experiencing
SL have helped her or him enhance her or his real-life self. Another blog post

reveals that becoming a resident of SL helps consumers develop new skills that they never had before and that they will benefit from in their FL:

> I had the nerve to set up a counseling practice in SL and charge money for my services, while being up-front about the fact that I had no training at the start and only a little training later on. I've had a number of satisfied clients, and found it fulfilling to be able to help people in this way. The fulfillment was such that I am now in pursuit of a new career in FL as a counselor. (Veronique, vlalonde.blogspot.com)

DISCUSSION AND CONCLUSION

As observed in SL consumers' avatar creation processes and experiences, the construction of who one is and how one is constructed become user-generated processes that welcome multiplicity and change and subvert the oneness or singleness of the identity. Consumers can live "parallel lives" (Turkle, 1997: 1100), create multiple presentations and representations of their selves, and discover new aspects of their selves (Reid-Steere, 1998; Turkle, 1997). Hence, the Internet enables individuals to construct alternative lives and several identities that transcend the limits of embodiment (Venkatesh et al., 1997). Consequently, these technological and cultural transformations also draw attention to the debate of the non-resolvable fate of the bodily selves in virtual worlds.

Our findings reveal that in virtual worlds, the body concept is also a reflection of contemporary consumers' desire to experiment with different identities, experiences, and modes of life independent and free of nature and any particular way of being and living. This serves as an alternative to the perception of body as a "project," where the construction of the body and the associated body image served as a form of socialization and a means of signifying one's self-worth, status in social relationships and lifestyles, and exerting control over one's self (Thompson and Hirschman, 1995).

Our findings also reflect the momentous changes in consumer culture and technology, which enable increasing consumer involvement in creative consumption and production processes. We find a strong relationship between consumer involvement and creativity within the context of virtual worlds. These transformations further complicate consumer creative processes in virtual worlds as they relate to self-construction and bring particular modern paradoxes to further attention. Increasingly, we observe that consumers playfully and critically engage in experiencing different modes of being through these multiple selves and find meaning in the existence of the "other" (Caputo, 1997) rather than trying to find a resolution to the tensions derived from experiencing these different selves (Kellner, 1989; Kroker, 1992). In fact, tensions that arise in transition from one created self to another bring value to consumers' real and imagined lives.

As mentioned earlier, we specifically focus on consumer creativity in virtual self-construction and draw attention to the multiplicity of bodily selves created as well as the paradoxical nature of this self-construction. Our findings also articulate the dialectical nature of these paradoxes, through which consumers can transition into alternative selves without the concern for finding a resolution to these paradoxes. We articulate the nature of this dialectic (possible and proper, presented and constructed, segregated and integrated selves). The virtual body is also considered a resource for self-construction and can be modified and played with as a means to construct different meanings of the self (Callero, 2003). Virtual self-creation is in fact full of reflections from the "other(s)" (see Gergen, 1991; Ricoeur, 1992). In effect, despite the single corporeal body that consumers inhabit, construction of selves in transition is by no means completely distinct and independent of the other(s) and one's selves in both virtual and real lives.

Consequently, the construction of multiple selves in transition further supports the non-resolvable nature of embodiment/disembodiment debate concerning the presence of the body in virtual worlds. The corporeal body is always there, even when absent, but also always absent, even when present. We observe this inability to make a clear distinction between selves created in virtual worlds and selves in real life. Even selves created to have distinct experiences and lead distinct lifestyles come to stay constant flux, which enhance both virtual and real-life experiences and consumer creative processes as a result. Modern marketing's response to these paradoxes of life then should be not to find a resolution to the tensions, but to provide consumers with more venues to increase their creativity and further intensify these tensions for consumers to find deeper immersion into their experiences.

NOTES

1. http://secondlife.com/whatis/
2. Some of our informants also use the term Real Life when they refer to First Life.

REFERENCES

Argyle K, Shields R. 1996. Is There a Body on the Net?, in *Cultures of Internet: Virtual Spaces, Real Histories, Living Bodies*, R. Shields (ed.). Sage: London; 58–69.
Baker A, Curasi C. 2008. Consequences of Co-Creation in Fantasy-Based Consumption Communities: Netnographic Analysis of a Live Action Role Playing Organization, in *Advances in Consumer Research*, A. Y. Lee and D. Soman (eds.). Association for Consumer Research: Duluth, MN; 46–47.
Balsamo A. 2000. The Virtual Body in Cyberspace, in *The Cybercultures Reader*, D. Bell and B. M. Kennedy (eds.). Routledge: New York; 489–503.
Beetham M. 2006. Periodicals and the New Media: Women and Imagined Communities.*Women's Studies International Forum* 29: 231–240.

Bonsu S, Darmody, A. 2008. Co-Creating Second Life: Market-Consumer Cooperation in Contemporary Life. *Journal of Macromarketing* 28(4): 355–368.

Brewer B. 1998. Bodily Awareness and the Self, in *The Body and The Self*, J. L. Bermúdez, A. J. Marcel, and N. Eilan (eds.). MIT Press: Cambridge, MA; 291–309.

Burroughs JE, Mick DG. 2004. Exploring Antecedents and Consequences of Consumer Creativity in a Problem-Solving Context. *Journal of Consumer Research* 31(September): 402–411.

Callero PL. 2003. The Sociology of the Self. *Annual Review of Sociology* 29: 115–133.

Caputo JD. 1997. *Deconstruction in a Nutshell: A Conversation with Jacques Derrida*. Fordham University Press: New York.

Cavallaro D. 1998. *The Body for Beginners*. Writers and Readers Publishing Inc.: New York.

Chung D. 2005. Something for Nothing: Understanding Purchasing Behaviors in Virtual Environments. *Cyberpsychology and Behavior* 6: 538–554.

Domzal TJ, Kernan JB. 1993. Variations on the Pursuit of Beauty: Toward a Corporal Theory of the Body. *Psychology and Marketing* 10(6): 495–511.

Featherstone M, Hepworth M, and Turner BS. 1991. *The Body: Social Process and Cultural Theory*. Sage, London.

Fisher S. 1986. *Development and Structure of the Body Image*. Erlbaum: Hillsdale, NJ.

Flichy P. 2007. *The Internet Imaginaire*. The MIT Press: Cambridge, MA.

Froy F. 2003. Indeterminacy in Cyberspace, in *Indeterminate Bodies*, N. Segal, L. Taylor, and R. Cook (eds.). Palgrave Macmillan: New York; 139–151.

Gergen KJ. 1991. *The Saturated Self: Dilemmas of Identity in Contemporary Life*. Basic Books, HarperCollins: New York.

Glaser BG, Strauss AL. 1967. *The Discovery of Grounded Theory: Strategies for Qualitative Research*. Aldine Publishing Co.: Chicago, IL.

Hansen MBN. 2006. *Bodies in Code: Interfaces with Digital Media*. Routledge: New York.

Haraway DJ. 1997. *Modest-witness@second-millennium. Femaleman-meets-oncomouse: Feminism and technoscience*. Routledge: New York.

Herd K, Pew E, and Warren C. 2009. Product Meaning and Consumer Creativity, in *Advances in Consumer Research*, A. L. McGill and S. Shavitt (eds.). Association for Consumer Research: Duluth, MN; 875–876.

Hirschman EC. 1980. Innovativeness, Novelty Seeking, and Consumer Creativity. *Journal of Consumer Research* 7(3): 283–295.

Joy A, Venkatesh A. 1994. Postmodernism, Feminism and the Body: The Visible and the Invisible in Consumer Research. *International Journal of Research in Marketing* 11(September): 333–357.

Kellner D. 1989. *Jean Baudrillard: From Marxism to Postmodernism and Beyond*. Stanford University Press: Stanford, CA.

Kolko BE. 1999. Representing Bodies in Virtual Space: The Rhetoric of Avatar Design. *The Information Society* 15: 177–186.

Kozinets RV. 1998. On Netnography: Initial Reflections on Consumer Research Investigations of Cyberculture. *Advances in Consumer Research* 25: 366–371.

Kozinets RV. 2002. The Field Behind the Screen: Using Netnography for Marketing Research in Online Communications. *Journal of Marketing Research* 39(1): 61–72.

Kozinets RV. 2010. *Netnography: Doing Ethnographic Research in the Age of the Internet*. Sage Publications: Thousand Oaks, CA.

Kroker A. 1992. *The Possessed Individual: Technology and the French Postmodern*. St. Martin's Press: New York.

Lanier C Jr, Hampton R. 2008. Consumer Participation and Experiential Marketing: Understanding the Relationship Between Co-Creation and the Fantasy Life Cycle, in *Advances in Consumer Research*, A. Y. Lee and D. Soman (eds.). Association for Consumer Research: Duluth, MN; 45–46.

Loos P. 2003. Avatar, in *Lexiekon Electronic Business*, T. Schildhauer (ed.). Oldenbourg: Munich; 16–19.

Madden NE. 1993. Pseudonyms and Interchange: The Case of the Disappearing Body. *Wings* 1(1): 3–4.

Mingers J. 2001. Embodying Information Systems: The Contribution of Phenomenology. *Information and Organization* 11: 103–128.

Moreau CP, Dahl DW. 2005. Designing the Solution: The Impact of Constraints on Consumers' Creativity. *Journal of Consumer Research* 32(1): 13–22.

Mukherjee S, Venkatesh A. 2008. Co-Creating fun: Insights From Young Adults' Engagement with Video Games, in *Advances in Consumer Research*, A. Y. Lee and D. Soman (eds.). Association for Consumer Research: Duluth, MN; 44–45.

Reid E. 1998. The Self and the internet: Variations on the Illusion of One Self, in *Psychology and the Internet: Intrapersonal, Interpersonal, and Transpersonal Implications*, J. Gackenbach (ed.). Academic Press: San Diego, CA; 29–42.

Reid-Steere E. 1996. Text-Based Virtual Realities: Identity and the Cyborg Body, in *High Noon on the Electronic Frontier: Conceptual Issues in Cyberspace*, P. Ludlow (ed.). The MIT Press: Boston, MA; 30–42.

Ricoeur P. 1992. *Oneself as Another* (K. Blamey, trans.). University of Chicago Press: Chicago, IL.

Rook DW. 1985. Ritual Dimension of Consumer Behavior. *Journal of Consumer Research* 12(3): 251–264.

Schau HJ, Gilly MC. 2003. We Are What We Post? Self-Presentation in Personal Web Space. *Journal of Consumer Research* 30(December): 385–404.

Schouten JW. 1991. Selves in Transition: Symbolic Consumption in Personal Rites of Passage and Identity Reconstruction. *Journal of Consumer Research* 17: 412–425.

Stone AR. 2000. Will the Real Body Please Stand up? Boundary Stories About Virtual Cultures, in *The Cybercultures Reader*, D. Bell and B. M. Kennedy (eds.). Routledge: London and New York; 504–528.

Takayoshi P. 1994. Building New Networks From the Old: Women's Experiences With Electronic Communication. *Computers and Composition* 11(1): 21–35.

Thompson CJ, Hirschman E. 1995. Understanding the Socialized Body: A Poststructuralist Analysis of Consumers' Self-Conceptions, Body Images and Self-Care Products. *Journal of Consumer Research* 22: 139–153.

Tumbat G, Horowitz D. 2008. Culture Creators: Co-Production in Second Life, in *Advances in Consumer Research*, A. Y. Lee and D. Soman (eds.). Association for Consumer Research: Duluth, MN; 35–46.

Turkle S. 1995. *Life on the Screen: Identity in the Age of the Internet*. Simon and Schuster: New York.

Turkle S. 1997. Computational Technologies Ad Images of the Self. *Social Research* 64(3): 1093–1111.

Vargo SL, Lusch RF. 2004. Evolving to a Dominant Logic for Marketing. *Journal of Marketing* 68: 1–17.

Venkatesh A, Meamber LA, and Fırat AF. 1997. Cyberspace as the Next Marketing Frontier(?) Questions and Isue, in *Consumer Research: Postcards From the Edge*, S. Brown and D. Turley (eds.). Routledge: New York; 300–321.

Ward K. 2001. Crossing Cyber Boundaries: Where Is the Body Located in the Online Community?, in *Reframing the Body*, N. Watson and S. Cunningham-Burley (eds.). Palgrave: New York; 189–208.

Wiley N. 1994. *The Semiotic Self*. University of Chicago Press: Chicago, IL.

13 Consumption Without Currency

The Role of the Virtual Gift Economy in Second Life

Jennifer Martin

Enter the virtual world of *Second Life* (SL) with your avatar, and, even though you have not a virtual cent to your name, you can fill your inventory with clothes, accessories, pets, vehicles, furniture, and houses. While *Second Life* is known for having a virtual market economy valued at US$160 million (Linden Lab, 2010b), it also has a significant economy centered on gifts. With a wide selection of and easy access to a huge selection of virtual goods, avatars can easily outfit their second lives.

Often referred to as "freebies," the abundant free items available in-world represent a gift economy. In its most basic iteration, "the gift economy is a system by which members of a distinct community, joined through shared values and commitments create valuable artifacts and services for each other without using money, legal contracts, or other market mechanisms" (Bollier, 2002). This definition is straightforward but does not address some of the complexities of the gift economy as it pertains to virtual worlds. It does, however, set out the basic foundations of gift exchange: community, artifacts, services, and a lack of the more formal requirements and monetary concerns associated with market exchange.

SL's broader economy and consumption practices are frequently discussed in academic discourse (Boellstorff, 2008; Jones, 2008; Ondrejka, 2004) and among residents through forums and blogs.[1] While focusing on the economy in general is important, examining specific elements is also revealing. As Cheal (1988) suggests, "in case gift giving appears to be an unserious subject, it is important to realize that in it are reflected many of the important issues of modern times." Understanding the SL economy through gifts and their uses offers a clearer picture of elements that comprise the SL economy and their benefits, issues, and roles within the world and community.

VIRTUAL ECONOMIES

Almost all content within SL is user-generated, and the market economy is based on residents who have learned how to create and sell their goods to others. This economic system is based on the Linden dollar (L$), a virtual currency that trades at approximately L$250 to US$1. Virtual goods are frequently less costly than their off-line counterparts. A car, for instance, might range from L$500 (US$2) to L$2,000 (US$8). However, even given the relatively low cost of many goods, the market economy was valued at US$26 million at the first quarter of 2010 (Linden Lab, 2010b).

Despite this market activity, one noticeable feature of the SL economy is the availability of free gifts. While many sites are dedicated to consumption involving currency exchange, other stores and sims (simulations, SL's land) offer some or all of their goods as gifts. In-world stores like Amity Island Freebies and the Freebie Warehouse provide boxes of gifts, whereas other stores offer a smaller selection. With many thousands of items available in-world and over another 100,000 through SL's Web-based marketplace (Linden Lab, 2010c), almost anything a resident could want is available. The prevalence of freebies use is visible in the number of active participants in the world's economy. Estimates from SL insiders suggest that only about ten percent of *SL* residents are significant contributors (Au, 2007; Llewelyn, 2008a), with the availability of freebies making it possible to live virtually without spending money.

Given the existence of a sizeable market economy, the roles and effects of SL's large gift economy are especially important to consider. Because SL can be profitable for creators, the development of an accessible economy built on moneyless exchange and the giving of gifts is somewhat unexpected. It is therefore necessary to consider what makes such a gift economy possible, why residents are willing to contribute gifts, and what are the significance and consequences of the virtual gift economy are.

THE FEASIBILITY OF GIFTS

Beyond the immediate benefits to residents, a gift economy is feasible due to features associated with virtual worlds in general and SL specifically. While many elements of the world and economy mirror those found off-line, there are differences that make a gift economy possible. Freed from the burdens, limits, and costs of materiality, virtual gift economies become feasible, visible, and acceptable within the world.

The world's virtuality means that gift items are easily and inexpensively created and distributed. Creation is facilitated by the fact that all SL residents can build within the world and are equipped with the basic tools to make virtual items. Creating with these tools incurs few costs, and residents are able to develop any item they desire. Limited material costs also ease creation because goods can be produced inexpensively, making gift giving financially feasible. In-world costs can include textures, scripts, and animations. Outside of SL, creators can also use computer programs like Photoshop to facilitate the design and creation of their virtual items. These materials and programs do have initial costs, but they can often be used repeatedly, reducing the cost of gifts.

The availability and distribution of gifts is further facilitated by the fact that once items have been created, they are easily replicated and shared. Because items are code, replication does not incur on-going material costs. Producing a table off-line requires an initial outlay for the materials and tools. While tools can be re-used, new material is required for subsequent tables. The same is not true in SL, where there are no material costs associated with reproduction. Code is replicated, and a new table is brought into existence. Any item can be replicated and shared. Even when creating an item requires the purchase of materials for production, creating gifts can remain inexpensive enough to facilitate large-scale giving.

Gift giving can be a collective practice or can be conducted on a smaller scale, as within a group or between individuals. SL enables both forms of exchange. Large-scale giving is facilitated through the same system that governs paid transactions. An item can be put in the system used for monetary purchases and assigned a value of L$0. When selected, a small window asks if the resident wants to pay L$0 for the item. When the resident clicks "yes," the item is automatically delivered into his or her inventory. Purchases of freebie items through SL's Web-based marketplace also function this way. Transactions are completed as for purchasable items but with a value of L$0. Virtual items are also easily exchanged with individuals and smaller groups. The process can be as simple as handing an item to another resident through the user interface or as complicated as allowing only members of particular groups to acquire gifts at a specific location.

The feasibility of gift economies in SL is increased by the purposes that it serves and the value attached to these exchanges. Survival is not a concern in SL, where avatars do not have physical needs. Gifts are therefore not necessary to meet needs, although they do serve other purposes. For instance, they are useful to marketers looking to make sales, individuals looking to raise their status, and residents wanting to participate in the world without having to spend money. Because the gift economy serves many purposes, it maintains a significant place in the social life of the world.

THE SL GIFT ECONOMY

For Mauss (1970), it is rare to find an economic or a legal system in which exchange is simple. Complexity arises from what is being exchanged, how and with whom it is exchanged, and the spirit behind the gift. While these concerns apply to SL, the virtual world also further complicates elements of these exchanges. Between the structure of the world and its community, the scope of in-world gift exchange, and the anonymity of residents, virtual gift economies present new uses, benefits, and challenges.

Gifts afford residents an opportunity to become part of the world through receiving and giving. For the former, consumption can be an important personal and social element of virtual life (Boellstorff, 2008; Martin, 2008; Molesworth and Denegri-Knott, 2007; Taylor, 2009). Through the gift economy, residents who cannot or do not want to pay for virtual goods can participate and are able to find what they need or want in order to do things like customize their avatar or affiliate themselves with particular groups or activities. For the latter, they serve different purposes. Creators who give gifts can do so for a variety of reasons, from the more directly self-motivated to the exceedingly generous.

Direct Reciprocity

In gift exchange, gifts are frequently linked to reciprocity. According to Cheal (1988), "Since it is assumed that exchanges are conducted on the basis of a rational calculation of utilities given and received, repetitive interaction is thought to be characterized by balanced reciprocity. This arrangement has often been described as the dominant principle in gift transactions." In SL, as in other gift economies, some gifts are based on this expectation of reciprocity. While the return may not be directly comparable—exchanging one article of clothing for another, for example—the value or utility of what is exchanged should be equal.

Giving with an expectation of a return is visible in gifts used for marketing purposes. Many SL designers and content creators regularly give gifts. Gifts can be given to the community at large and made accessible in a particular store or through the marketplace. By going to Violette's Closet, Evaki, or Dreamscapes Art Gallery, residents can obtain a summery outfit, a windsurfing board, or a living room set. Gifts can also be limited to residents who have joined a particular group. After joining groups like Belleza and Glitterati, members receive gifts like hair and clothing that are not available to other residents.

Although these items are gifts, they help to develop reciprocal relationships in which the recipient is encouraged, if not obligated, to repayment (Hyde, 1983; Mauss, 1970). By providing a gift, it is hoped that recipients will make additional purchases. Designers offer freebies as a way to entice potential buyers to their stores or groups. A creator writes that, "I use gifts primarily to market my product. First and foremost, I want to get people into my store, to look around and maybe shop, and to remember the name of my product. . . . If they like it, they will come back" (Resident 1). These expectations are not misguided. Residents indicate that they are more likely to make purchases from designers who have offered gifts. For instance, one resident states that after receiving a gift, "I am both more likely to buy from them again and more willing to 'pay more' because there's no risk of getting a bad product" (Resident 2). By providing gifts, creators can build relationships with potential customers.

The reciprocal relationship can also be a result of the feeling that a gift that is accepted incurs an obligation to reciprocate (Cheal, 1988). Many residents believe that it is important to support content creators by buying their goods or giving tips when given a gift and advocate for others to do so too. SL Freebie Hunters, for instance, recommends that, "these places normally have great freebies out, but they are not required to have anything. If you like how a designer makes things, please go back and buy from their stores and give tips to the freebie makers out there" (Luik and Soderstrom, 2011).

What makes these offerings gifts rather than strictly marketing tools is that they are offered freely. While the hope may be for a reciprocal relationship, there is no built-in obligation within the exchange. These are not items given after a purchase has been made, nor is a later payment due. When groups must be joined in order to receive or acquire a gift—an action that could be considered to be somewhat reciprocal—residents are free to leave, even if they do so after a gift has been received. Without formalized obligations associated with giving, even goods intended as marketing tools remain gifts.

Despite the fact that they are freely given, gifts do generate reciprocity. When asked if it is acceptable to join a group for the gift and then leave, a resident writes that, "if the merchandise is good quality I keep the LM, often return and buy more of the products" (Resident 3), while another one recounts that, "I had joined a group, received the gift and then proceeded to purchase another L$2000, really loving the place" (Resident 4). These statements reflect the idea that reciprocity can be developed through giving based more on the idea that, "It is rude to refuse a gift, and ruder still to not return the kindness" (Liszkiewicz, 2010), rather than an explicit requirement to do so.

Gift economies are often associated with a redistribution of wealth through a group that creates bonds of reciprocity (Hyde, 1983; Mauss, 1970). Giving away or redistributing accumulated wealth in the form of virtual goods is a way to "create lasting relations of dependence" (Bourdieu, 1997). On the surface, virtual giving mirrors the sharing of wealth conventionally found in traditional economies. While giving in SL may not create reciprocity strong enough to be called "dependent," it can develop and maintain beneficial relationships.

While similar in some respects, gift exchange practices in SL that rely on reciprocity also remain somewhat apart from more traditional exchanges, in terms of both cost and necessity. Gift exchange conventionally requires wealth because a store of goods must be accumulated for redistribution. Wealth in SL, at least in the form of virtual goods, can be relatively easy to accumulate. The reproducibility and low production costs mean that virtual goods are not necessarily as representative of wealth as material goods. Furthermore, because residents are able to make goods on their own, there is less need for wealth to be redistributed.

The lack of physical needs in SL initially appears to make the abundance on which gift exchange is founded irrelevant. Avatars are not subject to physical needs that must be met. In as much as scarcity becomes extraneous in the virtual world, so too does abundance. However, the gifts distributed among SL residents have value, even though it takes different forms. With virtual goods, the individual giving the gift has put time, effort, skill, and possibly even money into its creation. The development of quality virtual goods worthy of sharing requires skills that not all residents are able or willing to master. By offering gifts to other residents, creators are forgoing any profit that could have been generated from their sale. As a result, virtual gifts still have value.

Indirect Reciprocity

While direct reciprocity is important, so, too, are the more indirect forms that are practical in large virtual environments. In a world with as large and varied a population as SL (Boellstorff, 2008), and with gifts readily available, reciprocity is altered. With thousands of gifts available and thousands of residents participating, the elements of obligation associated with giving, accepting, and reciprocating are difficult to pinpoint because direct interactions are infrequent, if not absent. In a freebie store like Freebie Warehouse or Nikita Freebie, with hundreds of items from different creators and thousands of visitors, tracking the relationships created through giving is problematic, necessitating new forms of reciprocity.

Rather than relying on direct relationships and the expectation of equivalent returns, reciprocity is engaged indirectly and linked with more intangible benefits (Andreoni, 1989). Indirect reciprocity takes multiple forms in SL. For those who give gifts, it may take the form of increased status or recognition, sales or land advantages, or even aesthetic benefits. Given that these less tangible forms are difficult to measure, the exchange relationship will not necessarily be equal. However, reciprocity does remain visible in ways that are more congruous with indirect forms of reciprocity.

Through giving, creators can increase their status as residents recognize and help raise their profile (Llewelyn, 2006). Stores and designers like Belleza and PixelDolls, for instance, are regularly mentioned in forums and on blogs as good sources for gifts. Status can also arise from the fact that gifts enable more residents to have particular goods, making them more visible throughout the world and in forums, where it is common to show virtual goods to other residents. One resident, for instance, details how they "put the LM [landmark] in a folder for newbs with instructions on how to get the free gifts" (Resident 5). This practice can raise awareness of givers and potentially increase sales or opportunities for further reciprocal relationships.

While no longer common due to Terms of Service changes, reciprocal benefits can be built into obtaining a gift. By coming to a particular place to acquire a gift, traffic—a measure of how many residents have stayed in one place for a period of time—is increased. These results determine where a place is situated in search rankings, making high-traffic areas easiest to find, which can attract more residents, further increasing traffic and possibly sales.

Traffic benefits are seen around lucky chairs and camping chairs. Lucky chairs display a random letter for a set period of time, usually between five and fifteen minutes. If a resident whose name starts with that letter sits in the chair, he or she wins and receives the gift. Camping chairs function similarly but offer residents a guaranteed result; those who sit for a designated period of time receive a gift. In many places, the reward is a small amount of money, but in some—especially stores—it is a gift. These gifts are often relatively high quality, and in exchange the recipient helps to increase the sim or store's traffic, benefitting the giver.

Ivalde, a store that specializes in vintage clothing, currently offers one lucky chair. Previously, the store has housed four lucky chairs that changed every fifteen minutes and two camping chairs that required sitting for an hour. Each chair was associated with a different article of clothing. With prices ranging from L$175 to L$400, chairs provide residents gifts they might not otherwise have access to or be willing to purchase. Because time must be spent at the store in order to take advantage of either type of chair, there is reciprocity here. The resident has a choice about whether he or she will spend the time necessary to receive the gift, and spending the time benefits the recipient with a gift and the giver with increased traffic and exposure to other goods.

While it is not a commonly espoused benefit, some givers hope for improved in-world aesthetics. Appearance is an important element of SL, and maintaining a reasonably well-appointed population is a concern among some residents. Providing access to gifts can help ensure the world's aesthetics. One gift giver explains that, "Oh WTH, I'm tired of new people coming onto SecondLife, all bleh, looking like newbies. I'm going to change that" (Resident 6). This topic is also raised among residents who view changing and improving avatar appearances as an important element of virtual life, a process that is facilitated through gifts. For those who are concerned, offering gifts can visually improve the world.

Altruism

Although it plays a role in giving, to suggest that residents give exclusively to further their own ends directly or indirectly is by no means a complete or an accurate assessment of SL's gift economy. Bourdieu (1997) suggests that there is tension between self-interest and generosity in the giving of gifts but acknowledges these practices can contain "a refusal of self-interest and egoistic calculation." Gift economies are founded on reciprocity, but this is not necessarily a conscious consideration when giving a gift. Virtual goods are also given away as gestures of goodwill, with no expectation of reciprocity or benefit on the part of the recipient. These gifts do not necessarily match with more traditional forms of the gift economy, which rely on reciprocity. They do, however, reflect more modern and open forms of gift exchange, such as those that exist within segments of the knowledge economy.

Within the gift economy, residents can and do distribute gifts simply because they want to. In some cases, residents want to offer gifts that are useful or helpful to the community. The Help Island Freebie Store and the Freebie Store at London City are shops known for helping new residents and providing a range of useful gifts. This type of place is a longstanding feature of SL (Rymaszewski et al., 2008). While frequently targeted to new users, they are open to all residents. In these instances, giving is a means of helping others.

Similarly, some residents want their creations to be available to anyone who wants them. When discussing why they make things, creators make clear that they enjoy the work and consider creating to be valuable in its own right. One creator asserts that, "We are just nice people, the vast majority of us; and working more for the love of the art and to help others enjoy their SL experience than for love of money" (Resident 7). Another writes that, "Most of us are just interested in making the grid a more interesting place to spend our free time, and are not twirling our mustaches scheming how to get another $100 out of some poor damsel by luring her into our evil clutches with some freebies" (Resident 8). These statements point to creativity as a motivator for giving that is not dependent on reciprocity.

Given its scope and function, the SL gift economy is similar to the open source movement, which is considered a modern form of the gift economy (Raymond, 2000). Not all who benefit from sharing software and knowledge must be known to the creators or developers or enter into a reciprocal relationship. Those who are able to contribute to the gift economy—be it software or virtual goods—do so, and those who can use their contributions take what they want. While there may be status associated with such giving—because status can accrue around altruism—it need not be linked to personal motivation and can instead be an expression of generosity by those who give their time, effort, knowledge, and creations for the betterment of the community.

GIFT ECONOMY CONSEQUENCES

In spite of its large gift economy, SL is not necessarily an idyllic paradise devoted to giving and sharing. The presence of a gift economy does not mean the end of economic or social issues within the virtual world. The SL economy has been beset at various times and to varying degrees by issues of intellectual property rights, theft of virtual goods, and questionable business practices. The gift economy has also seen its share of controversy both in its own right and with respect to its effects within the world.

With the availability of gifts in SL, some aspects of gift giving are perceived to be more of an expectation than would be preferred by many creators. Hyde (1983) suggests that one element of gift giving is the obligation to give. Some creators suggests that this expectation has gotten out of hand, with residents feeling entitled to a variety of quality gifts (Llewelyn, 2008b; Longcloth, 2008). These expectations are compounded by the use of gifts to attract customers and raise brand awareness. Giving is one way to get a foot in the door of the market economy (Llewelyn, 2006) and the world in general. However, the need to continually meet resident expectations and the subsequent influx of gifts can lead to greater expectations around the frequency and quality of gifts.

Content creators see the constant development of new and better gifts as a threat. Developers' continual supply of quality gifts means they may need to upgrade their goods or develop better products to surpass the standard set by freebies. In a debate, creators acknowledge that this can be an issue. A resident states that, "I can see the point of designers who don't like people creating reasonable quality freebies. It makes the marketplace more difficult for some" (Resident 9). In addition, when not all residents have the skill or desire to create, the burden of gift exchange is borne by a relatively small subset of the population.

Conversely, the gift economy is also criticized for lesser quality items that flood the market. Although gifts may be accepted, many residents make clear that the difference between purchased items and many gifts can be noticeable (Linden Lab, 2010a). In a debate on the quality of freebies, one resident states that, "Freebie clothing is generally awful. Don't fool yourself. Unless it's a give away from a good designer, freebie clothing is usually a vile eyesore. Bad for your self esteem and bad for the SL economy" (Resident 10). This issue is also tied in with a related consequence in which gifts are so abundant that they have less value, especially when they are not up-to-date. With the vast array of free gifts available, residents can access almost anything they need quickly and easily. Recipients still complain and criticize, however, suggesting that at least some gifts may not have the same perceived value as others.

Beyond individual experiences, SL's gift economy is criticized for its effects on the world's economy. With so many gifts available, it is not necessary for residents to participate in the market economy, and only about ten percent of the population contributes significantly (Au, 2008; Llewelyn, 2008a). Given that the market economy provides money with which many content creators support their virtual and even sometimes their offline lives, these effects can be detrimental to creators by raising expectations and allowing potential customers to acquire gifts rather than make purchases. While the SL market economy remains active, the establishment and growth of the gift economy has an impact on its activities by facilitating forms of consumption that are not based on market exchange.

Finally, these issues are linked to tensions between those who contribute to and depend on the gift economy and those who are opposed to it. The range of motivations for offering gifts in SL means that creators have a variety of different expectations about the role of the gift economy within the world and how it should be managed. Although those who give altruistically may hope that others will reciprocally do the same to make the world a better place, those who give for purely businesses reasons, or who do not give at all, may not appreciate the competition or effects. Consequently, this topic is regularly debated within related forums and blogs, although it is an issue for which there are few answers or resolutions.

SIGNIFICANCE TO SL

Given the gift economy's benefits and issues, it has significance within the broader virtual economy and in SL in general. While it is largely understudied, there is already some recognition of the presence of a gift economy. Anthropologist Tom Boellstorff (2008) invokes both the meaning of objects and the social relations created through their exchange in relation to gift economies. These social relationships are one of the areas in which the significance of the gift economy is visible, both in terms of the benefits gained by recipients and by givers. Givers are able to reciprocally meet needs ranging from increased sales to social recognition and status. Recipients, in turn, receive the virtual goods that they want. While these wants may be straightforward, such as desiring a car, they can also be linked to more intangible desires, like customizing the virtual body, creating a home, showing belonging or affiliation (Martin, 2008), or engaging in consumer fantasy (Molesworth and Denegri-Knott, 2007).

These practical elements of giving are not the only ways in which the gift economy is meaningful. Beyond the immediate receipt of gifts and the social relations created through these practices are other significant implications, especially around the acceptance, promotion, and normalizing of alternative economic forms. In-world gifts are not necessarily devalued as often happens when such gifts are given offline (Raghubir, 2004). While some residents are critical of their quality and effects, gifts are largely accepted and positively viewed (Linden Lab, 2010a; Pick, 2009). The place of free gifts within the world is established early. In many of the introductory sims, residents can access gifts for new residents that range from clothing and accessories to vehicles and houses. By providing gifts in introductory areas, not only are residents shown that they exist, but that they are an accessible and even acceptable way to gain virtual goods.

Acceptability is further increased by the relative quality of gifts. In the early days of SL, free items were rare and tended to be of lesser quality than items that were for sale. As the world has grown, more creators, competition, and tools have increased the availability and quality of gifts (Llewelyn, 2008a). The acceptability of gifts is also seen in the pride that residents show around gifts they have acquired. Rather than having negative associations, choosing or not being able to consume using money can be acceptable. Residents take pride in their ability to outfit an avatar without spending money. In this vein, a resident details that, "Personally I think it's fun to examine the outfits of other avatars and see something I recognize to have been obtained for free, and to see how interestingly it can be combined with higher priced items" (Resident 11). This acceptability is also seen through sites and groups like FreeStyle and FabFree that keep residents updated on available gifts. While some residents lament the relatively few residents who contribute to the market economy, not spending money remains acceptable to many residents and in some cases is actively celebrated.

Acceptability helps to normalize gifting practices. The gift economy is a longstanding and ordinary element of SL. Consequently, these practices are normalized within the world to the point where almost all residents are familiar with and many make use of or even expect them. This normalization has the potential to be useful. Awareness of other economic forms can be of benefit around issues like over-consumption and debt. SL has been explored in terms of its environmental benefits, as residents fulfill their shopping and spending desires in a way that uses few material resources (Lin, 2008). It is also a place where residents can affordably enact consumer fantasies (Molesworth and Denegri-Knott, 2007). Alternative economies, the giving and receiving of gifts, user-generated content, and the benefits that can arise from reciprocal relationships can expose residents to multiple and even alternative economic possibilities in ways that are beneficial in off-line as well as virtual life.

CONCLUSIONS

SL has attributes that facilitate the creation and maintenance of a gift economy that serves multiple purposes within the community. Traditional forms of gift exchange such as those based on reciprocity are possible based on the expectation or hope that by giving a gift the giver will later receive something of equal value. However, more modern conventions of the gift exchange can also be found in SL through indirect forms of exchange and altruism.

The consequences and significance of SL's gift economy are the subject of on-going debates among residents and scholars. There is no definitive claim that can yet be made regarding whether its effects are overwhelmingly negative or positive. However, this is not to say that certain conclusions cannot be drawn. Despite some similarities, the ways in which people interact with and rely on each other through gifts in an SL are not necessarily the same as in more traditional gift economies. Although elements of reciprocity are present, they are altered through virtuality and the scope of the gift economy. Moreover, these practices of giving alter perceptions of what is intended to be an important social act founded on obligation but also on generosity. Beyond the expected tensions between self-interest and generosity, SL's gift economy showcases concerns around expectation, entitlement, quality, criticism, status, gratitude, and altruism.

Although it is not without issues, the gift economy's strength lies in a functionality that is suited to the needs of the many residents who use it. Individuals are able to use it for markedly different ends. For those looking to benefit through giving, there are thousands of residents seeking gifts. For those who are looking for particular items, gifts are likely to be available. For those who simply want to be helpful and generous, giving is relatively easy. A thriving gift economy should meet the needs of its members, whether practical or social. Through offering a myriad of options for giving and receiving, the gift economy is used to meet the wants and needs of many of its residents, adding another dimension to their virtual lives and experiences.

NOTES

1. Although comments were published on publicly available sites, residents have been de-identified in this work.

REFERENCES

Andreoni J. 1989. Giving with Impure Altruism: Applications to Charity and Ricardian Equivalence. *The Journal of Political Economy* 97: 1447–1458.

Au WJ. 2007. *How Consumerist Is Second Life? Actual Economic Stats Say Not So Much.* Available at http://nwn.blogs.com/nwn/2007/09/how-consumerist. html [accessed on 25 July 2009].

Au WJ. 2008. *Are Freebies Hurting the Second Life Economy? Round-up of Thoughts on an Over-Saturated Economy.* Available at http://nwn.blogs.com/ nwn/2008/10/are-freebies-hu.html [accessed on 25 July 2009].

Boellstorff T. 2008. *Coming of Age in SL: An Anthropologist Explores the Virtually Human.* Princeton University Press: Princeton.

Bollier D. 2002. The Enclosure of the Academic Commons. *Academe* 88: 18–22.

Bourdieu P. 1997. Marginalia—Some Additional Notes on the Gift, in *The Logic of the Gift: Toward an Ethic of Generosity*, Alan D Schrift (ed.). Routledge: New York.

Cheal DJ. 1988. *The Gift Economy.* Routledge: New York.

Hyde L. 1983. *The Gift: Imagination and the Erotic Life of Property.* Vintage Books: New York.

Jones DE. 2008. I, Avatar: Constructions of Self and Pace, in *SL Gnovis* 6.

Lin AC. 2008. Virtual Consumption: A SL for Earth? *Brigham Young Law Review* 47: 1–74.

Linden Lab. 2010a. *Is Freebie Clothing Better Than Buying?* Available at http://blogs.secondlife.com/message/98425 [accessed on 15 October 2010].

LindenLab. 2010b. Second Life *Economy Hits New All-Time High in Q1 2010.* Available at http://blogs.secondlife.com/community/features/blog/2010/04/28/second-life-economy-hits-new-all-time-high-in-q1–2010 [accessed on 2 June 2010].

LindenLab. 2010c. Second Life *Marketplace.* Available at https://marketplace.secondlife.com/ [accessed on 21 September 2010].

Liszkiewicz AJP. 2010. *Cultivated Play: Farmville.* SUNY Press: Buffalo.

Llewelyn G. 2006. *Secrets to Success in* Second Life. Available at http://gwynethllewelyn.net/2006/12/18/secrets-to-success-in-second-life%C2%AE/ [accessed on 12 October 2010].

Llewelyn G. 2008a. *The Hard Facts About the* Second Life *Economy.* Available at http://gwynethllewelyn.net/2008/10/13/the-hard-facts-about-the-second-life%C2%AE-economy/ [accessed on 7 June 2009].

Llewelyn G. 2008b. *The Mighty Linden Dollar.* Available at http://gwynethllewelyn.net/2008/07/10/the-mighty-linden-dollar/ [accessed on 21 September 2010].

Longcloth B. 2008. *Marketing 101 and the Freebie.* Available at http://www.baileylongcloth.com/2008/10/page/2/ [accessed on 15 October 2010].

Luik S, Soderstrom T. 2011. *Freebie Info.* Available at http://slfreebiehunters.blogspot.com/p/freebie-info.html [accessed on 13 July 2011].

Martin J. 2008. Consuming Code: Use-Value, Exchange-Value, and the Role of Virtual Goods in *SL. Journal of Virtual Worlds Research* 1.

Mauss M. 1970. *The Gift: Forms and Functions of Exchange in Archaic Societies.* Cohen & West: London.

Molesworth M, Denegri-Knott J. 2007. Digital Pay and the Actualization of the Consumer Imagination. *Games and Culture* 2(2): 114–133.

Ondrejka C. 2004. *Aviators, Moguls, Fashionistas and Barons: Economics and Ownership in Second Life.* Available at http://ssrn.com/abstract=614663 [accessed on 10 May 2011].

Pick T. 2009. *The Best Things in Second Life Are Freebies!* Available at http://forums-archive.secondlife.com/327/f2/311704/1.html [accessed on 10 May 2011].

Raghubir P. 2004. Free Gift with Purchase: Promoting or Discounting the Brand? *Journal of Consumer Psychology* 14: 181–185.

Raymond ES. 2000. *Homesteading the Noospherer.* Available at http://catb.org/esr/writings/homesteading/homesteading/ [accessed on 15 September 2010].

Rymaszewski M, Au WJ, Ondrejka C, Platel R, Van Gordon S, Cezanne J, Cezanne P, Batstone-Cunningham B, Krotoski A, Trollop C, Rossignol J. 2008. *Second Life: The Official Guide.*Wiley Publishing, Inc.: Indiannapolis.

Taylor PG. 2009. Can We Move Beyond Visual Metaphors? *Journal of Virtual Worlds Research* 2: 1–7.

14 Eve Online as Meaningful Virtual World

Pétur Jóhannes Óskarsson

Over the course of history studies in anthropology and sociology have been conducted on both individuals and groups of people. Sometimes the groups have been volunteers, other times they have been studied from afar without them knowing, and people have even been studied up close in (what has been believed to be) an unobtrusive manner. Usually these studies are done on behavior, either that of an individual, the interactions between individuals, or some sort of a combination thereof. Definitions have been set in advance about groups of individuals in terms of culture, language, birthplace, or some other factors. This is all good and well, but with an obvious flaw: This method of observation requires the observer to observe his objects in close proximity in order to get accurate information. Thus, the danger of influencing the subject/s is great.

Things are getting better as the time goes by. Still, data collection was a problem in terms of volume until the digital age came along with all its wonders. In fact those wonders are so powerful that currently it could be maintained that the problem is moving in the opposite direction: There are too many data now, and although we won't go into specifics, this causes problems with interpretation, reliability, cross-checking, and other data manipulation. The point is that with digital methods individuals and groups can be monitored, with or without their knowledge, and thus the danger of influence has been reduced considerably—also giving more quality data in the process and a deeper understanding of how people behave.

Yet the commercial aspect of this type of data gathering is limited when it comes to online shopping. From a technical perspective it is possible to determine how customers got to a site and what they buy there then create a profile of the customers and suggest to them things they might like—suggestions based on other customers who behaved in a similar manner. The biggest gap in this type of customer profiling is the part that happens outside the online shop, which will still be shrouded in assumptions and guesswork. This is where virtual worlds come into play, specifically those that offer persistence of the user's achievements, actions, and losses. Granted, information such as whether a person brushes his or her teeth before or after showering will still not be available through monitoring of virtual worlds, but the context of the user's actions is much greater in there than with regular digital consumption on individual websites such as *Amazon* or *eBay*. Because of that context for actions, virtual worlds are very interesting for general behavior studies.

How relevant is this context? Does it form a solid ground from which we can learn something about individuals? In order to answer these questions (and other concerns that one might have regarding virtual worlds), I'd like to make a rather bold statement. Even though the environment is fabricated it does not mean that actions within that environment are fabricated. In fact, many things point towards the exact opposite (i.e., actions in a virtual world are just as real and meaningful as outside a virtual world). My excitement regarding my progress within a virtual world is just as real as my excitement with my progress at the gym. My sense of betrayal is just as strong whether a friend goes back on his word in the virtual world or in the real world. The interactions I have with the game-items seller are just as meaningful as the interaction I have with a clerk at the supermarket. My goal of getting item X in a game world is just as realistic to me as my goal to buy a car of type Y. In short, the "consumer game" in the real world is no less a game than the one in the virtual world.

It may be in order to explain two specific concepts—"meaningful" and "consumer game" When describing virtual worlds as meaningful, we mean the experience (emotional or practical) the person gains by participating. The difference between the skill required to manage and lead people inside a virtual world versus outside it is negligible. Learning how to organize a business is just as rewarding in a virtual world as it is outside of it: manufacturing plans, customer acquisitions, competition, and so on. All of these things exist in both locations, and the difference is a one of degree not of essence. When viewed in this light, virtual worlds are indeed meaningful.

The "consumer game" is not meant to be a negative judgment (there is, after all, more to games than just fun)—more to point out and emphasize the concepts of planned obsolescence and perceived obsolescence when it comes to products or services. Without going into a deep study of value engineering here, we can take the example of an imagined car. This car may be useful for seven to fifteen years or so, given that we define the end of usability as spending more time fixing a car than driving it. Thus, the planned obsolescence is seven to fifteen years for this car (i.e., its parts are not designed to last any longer than that). Of course manufacturers play with this, using cheaper parts to increase turnover of their products. That can, however, bite them in the rear so to speak, where people stop buying their products because they are of a subpar quality compared with other products.

Perceived obsolescence comes in when a product is no longer "cool" or part of the mainstream consumption behavior. In this case there is no mechanical or material reason to buy a new product (i.e., the product is working perfectly and does what it was designed to do), and the pressure to buy a new one is purely social. New clothing lines, new portable music players, or new computer hardware—these things (and others) are often switched out by us because we *feel* they don't serve their intended purpose anymore.

While I will not claim anything about this "game" and whether it is meaningful, I wanted to point out that we are all a part of it in one way or another—I wanted to tie this together in the same sentence to bring attention to it.

In my opinion, a sufficient doubt has been cast on the manner of thinking about virtual worlds as something less meaningful than the real world. Individuals inhabit and interact in both places, and all data collected in virtual worlds suggest that individuals are interacting. This is of course an age-old philosophical problem regarding what is real and what is not—and so far I've tried to maintain the thought that our experiences are real regardless of what causes them. With this in mind we will turn to the next subject of this chapter.

EVE Online (created by CCP Games) is a massively multiplayer online role playing game (MMORPG) set 23,000 years in the future. The story is that a giant wormhole named EVE opened near our solar system, an opportunity that sparked a mass exodus to the newfound region of space, New Eden. Events lead to the wormhole closing down, suddenly cutting all the new colonies from the supply and governance of Earth. Chaos and despair ensued, and only after 21,000 years did the surviving humans start to travel between the stars again and interact. This science fiction setting is very descriptive of the game itself—when you enter the virtual world of *EVE Online*, you are capable of going into whatever direction your ambition takes you. The atmosphere created with the back story strongly encourages the participants to develop and create, to forge their own destinies, to set their own goals. EVE is classified as a game, yet it does not provide the participants with a goal to achieve to "finish" the game; a player might decide to join EVE to rule the entire EVE universe. That is a perfectly acceptable goal for a user to set within EVE, although what he or she has to have in mind is that there might be another user with the exact same goal, which will cause problems for them both down the line when they finally meet. Clearly put, there is no way to "win" EVE or become the most "powerful" player in EVE because there are no predefined goals available in the game.

This lack of goals in a game environment is, to some, an alien concept. Most games have some sort of an end goal or a set of victory conditions. And in games where it is possible to argue that there are no victory conditions, the community that is playing said game usually comes up with a standard that can be used to declare a goal or victory condition: "If you kill The Dragon three times you have done it more often than anyone in the game." This isn't a predetermined victory condition within the game, but created by the community. Of course there is competition about who kills the dragon most often, but it is a clear enough goal. And most online games are updated or expanded, which causes the goals to change; yet they still remain within the game. EVE's game environment does not offer the

possibility of such unified goals or victory conditions. The people who practice piracy do not view the goal of owning ten space stations as something
worth striving for. And those who own ten space stations do not necessarily
aim to achieve the goal of being able to provide quality spaceship building
services to all those who ask for that.

This lack of goals coupled with the technical approach to *EVE Online*
makes it a unique online environment. It is called a game, by CCP the creator of *EVE Online* and everyone else, yet it is more like a virtual world than
a game—we will return to that a little bit later. Technically, *EVE Online* is
unique because of the single server approach that is used. All 360,000[1] sub-
scribers connect to the same server cluster. This means that a single player
can influence the whole of 360,000 people participating in *EVE* with his or
her actions. But why is this important? It is important because coupled with
the freeform nature of the environment, this is less like a game and more
like a virtual world where people behave in a meaningful manner. The
users of *EVE* have seen the need for banks within *EVE* and have simply
formed that social institution. Almost all trade in *EVE Online* is based on
goods manufactured by players. Other services that have been set up by the
inhabitants in this virtual world include media, information handling and
processing/analysis, transportation services, and even schools that teach
you how to participate and achieve your goals in *EVE*. In fact almost any
type of service you can see in a regular society has been tried and run in
EVE—some, of course, are successful and others less so.

One of the biggest steps taken by CCP in terms of interaction with the
population of *EVE* is to stop looking at it as a community and start looking
at it as a society. This small change in attitude opens up the world of sociology, politics, philosophy, economics, and other disciplines that are used to
studying "real" societies to *EVE* and the study of *EVE*'s society. With this
arsenal (if I may use that word), the health, strength, and growth of *EVE*'s
society are much more likely to increase than without it.

The strongest example to support the claim that *EVE* is a virtual world
(and not just simply a game), and currently the most studied example, is the
economy of *EVE*. In essence it doesn't matter to economists and economic
theory whether the systems they are studying are "virtual" or "real." In fact
it could be argued that all economic systems are virtual systems. The theorists (and ultimately the users of the system) don't care whether the data they
are looking at originate from a virtual world. They are looking at numbers
and processing those numbers with economic formulas with the aim of getting results. *EVE*'s economy behaves like a "normal" economy—and why
shouldn't it? People are using it to trade. There is actually (at least) one thing
that is superior when it comes to studying an economy like the one in *EVE*,
compared with a "real" economy: The amount and the quality of information that a virtual world contains, and the ease of which that information
can be stored and retrieved, is both vastly more realistic in practice than
doing that in the real world and much more reliable. Imagine having access to

literally every single trade transaction done in an economic system. It is then possible to track in extreme detail individual items or groups of items and how they flow in and out of the system—I'm not promising perfect information about the economic system in *EVE Online*, but it is approaching that status. With the information available to CCP, the maker of *EVE*, a detailed consumption behavior could be built and studied.

Another advantage that a virtual world offers (e.g., when studying the economy) is that most factors are known when it comes to the consumers' decision-making process. The exact emotional state of the person is of course not known, but the virtual world is finite, void of outside economic influences (as much as a closed economy can be), and the amounts of affecting influences are foreseeable.

Speaking of societies, there is one thing that all societies have besides an economy—a form of governance. The contemporary view on systems of governance is that a democratic model of some sorts is the preferred one. Since May 2008, a democratically elected council of nine players has been a part of *EVE Online*. The rules are kept as simple as possible; every valid subscriber who has no criminal record in *EVE* can run for candidacy on this council, and every paying subscriber can cast a vote in the election for the council. What is the purpose of this council? To have an official, formal conduit of communication between the society and the creators of *EVE* and to have elected representatives of the inhabitants available for consultation. Such a communication channel is a very strong and vital part of modern ideas about societies—the ability to affect and change your immediate surroundings through the means of an elected body. Claiming that *EVE* houses a society without a governance institution would make it a very poor claim.

The main topics of discussion between the elected council and CCP were initially technical *EVE* specific matters, such as whether this space ship should go faster than the other one or if a space highway should go between star systems A and B or between B and C. In short this was initially used to speak about the environment in *EVE* and how the inhabitants wanted minute changes done to it. As the institution matured and its users realized further how they could use it, the small matters gave way to broader discussions. Topics of the overall strategy of *EVE*'s development, customer service policies, and specific details of the implementation of virtual goods services have been discussed in meetings between the player council and CCP. Although the council doesn't have formal power in the sense that their suggestions have to be realized, they have been made a stakeholder in the development process. This status of being a stakeholder means that CCP has to take their wishes into account when it comes to prioritizing within the development process of *EVE*, just like the marketing team and customer service department within CCP are stakeholders. Thus, the players are on an equal footing with other stakeholders when it comes to representation within CCP toward the development of *EVE Online*.

Within the *EVE* society, the individuals, the avatars (or characters), are the smallest building blocks. With this in mind, a question can be raised: Let us assume that user A has two avatars in *EVE* with the names X and Y. No one within *EVE* knows that A is controlling both avatars unless that user decides to release that information. So, within the context of *EVE*, X and Y are two different avatars with two different behavior patterns—they could be sworn enemies, competitors on the market, voting for completely different candidates in the elections—but these two avatars are being controlled by the same user. The question is then, "Does this matter when we are looking at the behavior of the two avatars, X and Y?" Should the controller of the avatars be a part of our analysis?

It is clear that virtual worlds are suitable for studies of human behavior, whether it is consumer behavior, political behavior, or social behavior. A subject not mentioned above is the behaviors of groups of people in the virtual world, a subject that is well within the reach of study in terms of information available. The questions that arise with the possibility of a single user competing against him or herself do not necessarily complicate the matter if only the avatars are the object of study. It does, however, offer a unique possibility of studying a different aspect of behavior based on where the user's preferences truly are located. At the time of writing this text, this number was accurate. Historically *EVE*'s community has grown between years every year since the game was launched in May 2003. So this number will be inaccurate in the future; most likely it will be higher.

15 Conclusions
Trajectories of Digital Virtual Consumption

Mike Molesworth and Janice Denegri-Knott

We started this edited collection by noting a range of questions that immediately come to mind when exposed to the existence of DVC. Several themes emerge from the analysis and examples in the subsequent chapters, and in this final chapter, we want to review them. In doing so we may only highlight many of the questions raised by the work rather than close off or finalize what DVC is and does.

Questions like, What are the forms of DVC, where does it take place and how does this make it different from other types of consumption? Here we note that DVC may represent a range of activities related to the virtual (the imaginary or symbolic), the digital (technologies such as ecommerce sites, digital virtual worlds, and online and stand-alone videogames), and practices of acquisition, exchange, or use of digital *and* material goods. Many of these practices seem very new and even strange—they introduce words that capture new relationships and new practices. Others seem similar to established market behaviors and consumer sentiments, so we must resist a temptation to see DVC as radical or entirely removed from the rest of everyday life or from existing consumer practices.

As Lehdonvirta points out in Chapter 2, we might see DVC as a trajectory of established consumption practices that highlight consumption as meaning making more than the rational acquisition of goods, and that involve an increasing confidence and engagement with computer-mediated spaces by a range of actors, including consumers, programmers, and marketers. One result is that as consumers develop new practices, new digital virtual spaces emerge in an on-going cycle of innovation and transformation. The videogames, websites, and virtual worlds described here are contemporary examples, but it seems likely that even as we write, some of them may be fading in popularity just as others emerge.

If we accept that people consume for the pleasures of desire and that they therefore always demand novelty, DVC is a way for markets to respond with new and exciting opportunities for meaning making stripped from the alibi of utility, and in this sense we might see DVC as inherently "playful." In this regard, and as Óskarsson points out in Chapter 14, digital virtual spaces that are rich in consumption practices seem a good place to better understand the meaning of contemporary experiential consumption and market exchange more generally. In DVC we can rarely resort to "rational economic man" type explanations, even where material goods are purchased. Jacobs's explanation of Woot.com (Chapter 11) provides another illustration of this—what you buy from Woot seems much less important than what buying means to your relationship to the community. Her chapter may also remind us that in such an environment there are significant challenges to marketers who may feel more comfortable with long-term brand building and management strategies and who must now consider not just product innovation but innovations in the whole experience of consumption. However, we are also reminded that although DVC experiences seem to take place in a world behind a screen and in the mind, this does not mean we should ignore the materiality of DVC, including the body; we should resist "othering" these in any analysis.

The transformations we see are often subtle and nuanced, but they are still significant. This significance should be clear from the shear numbers of consumers now routinely using digital media within consumer practices. DVC then is already "normal" to many (see Venkatesh and Behairy's discussion [Chapter 3] on the pervasive use of technology by young people, for example) even if we see all sorts of new DVC practices emerging. This normality should also be obvious from the way the participants in many of the studies here talk about DVC as an important but routine part of their everyday lives, including their relationships with others. Yet the subtlety and complexity of changes resulting from DVC make understanding it hard. In this volume we have tried to mix necessary theoretical perspectives with detailed analysis of specific locations and practices in an attempt to both locate DVC within existing approaches to understanding consumer cultures and to illustrate the richness of the new experiences DVC can produce. Hence, well-established theories about consumer desire, identity, the meaning of goods in social relationships, play and its purpose, as well as established critiques of our consumer culture may all inform our understanding of DVC practices.

Once we have identified the scope and location of DVC, other significant questions present themselves, such as: Should we celebrate DVC and what are the potential sources of criticism? In this collection we see contributions to both. Moral positions are taken, but the ability to contest claims—the inherent ambiguity of DVC—means that we may not easily make final judgments as we ask whether more DVC would be good for individuals, businesses, or even the environment. DVC represents a negotiation among the use of digital technologies, the imagination, and consumer culture, and we might be invited to ask whether there are benefits to individuals in exploring their imagination and in a way that involves fewer material resources (the comparison of a digital car simulation to a material one is an obvious example). Yet, we can also note that DVC is sustained on ways of thinking that encourage the accumulation of "stuff" as a primary life goal.

Even where we see gift economies (see Martin, Chapter 13) or responsible and sustainable approaches to community consumption (see Ross, Chapter 10), we might recognize that resistance is more often to the terms presented by existing material markets and not necessarily to the endless accumulation of new things as a satisfying way of life. We can celebrate empowered communities of consumption (see Kozinets, Chapter 7) while maintaining criticisms that such struggles may do little harm to global technology and software corporations that may still dominate the way people live and think. Indeed consumer activism in this regard may be a rich source of business and marketing innovation as organizations find ways to make money from "free" services, from crowdsourcing, from contributions made by digital virtual communities of consumption, and especially from the sale of desirable digital virtual goods.

In some ways DVC represents the marketization of our digital virtual lives whether as consumers, entrepreneurs, or hybrids of the two. As consumers the digital virtual invites us to endlessly consume without many of the physical and financial restrictions experienced in our material lives. It presents us with the possibility to put aside or remove ourselves from that which we feel dissatisfied in everyday life and/or to think about experiences that are not actually possible in material form. In DVC consumption may also be accelerated both in terms of how much we can acquire in a given time and in the range of goods we interact with, including those that are previously only ideally possible, such as exotic fantasy and science-fiction quests, but that may now be actualized in the digital virtual. But it also suggests that in our digital virtual lives, we might primarily see ourselves as consumers (see Molesworth, Chapter 5) and therefore enter digital virtual spaces primarily as desiring and novelty-seeking individuals.

However, our desire for meaningful relationships with others, captured and concretized by consumption acts, means that we may also use digital virtual spaces to buy material things we don't need other than for this purpose, as in the case of Jacob's review of Woot.com. On the face of it, Woot.com is a novel retail site for a range of marginally useful commodities, but as Jacobs' analysis demonstrates, of far more interest to users is the symbolic value of the goods for sale as a context for various collaborative, competitive, and creative games. Engagement with DVC also requires us to become sophisticated consumers of material technologies, including high-definition screens, games consoles, computers, and smart phones, such that these things are not only necessities of modern life but desirable things to own and renew to get the latest DVC experiences. Our on-going commitment to and status within various multiplayer games and virtual worlds requires the purchase and update of a growing number of technologies. As Magaudda (Chapter 8) illustrates, DVC encourages a whole range of new material market activities (yet in doing so also suggests the possibility that older consumer practices gain a renewed purpose and attraction).

Alternatively, digital virtual spaces allows us opportunities to explore being entrepreneurs in a market made game-like. DVC is frequently about accumulating stuff or making money, and therefore it re-creates individuals in these ways. Zwick's analysis (Chapter 9) of the attractions of online stock trading is a good illustration of this—for online stock trading services to be profitable businesses, they must tap into a desire for "players" to be enterprising, responsible, self-interested individuals. This points to a compelling attribute of DVC spaces and possibly a concern. One of the attractions of the digital virtual world is that it is contained, knowable, and less complex than the messiness of life, and as such it provides a potential focus for our reflections on the self and our relationships to others. We see this elsewhere, such as in Ross's (Chapter 10) interviews with FFXI players who take responsibility for ensuring that the pleasures of the virtual world can be maintained for all. A necessary question, however, is whether people are ever able to translate what they learn from online worlds into the rest of everyday life or even if they would want to do so. Here we may see DVC as a form of escape from the demands of material life and perhaps compensation for its inadequacies as they are experienced, but in this volume, there is little to suggest that this might lead to any radical position on material market relations. So does engagement in such DVC allow us to see more clearly our responsibilities in the rest of our life or simply let us see the flaws and weaknesses in global markets before "othering" them as we re-enter the game world? DVC may suggest that people may simply find spaces where they can be more successful or satisfied worker-consumers, actualizing the roles that they have already internalized as ideal but given up on elsewhere. At least that's the critique.

However, an argument against the idea that DVC may *only* perpetuate and extend existing alienated consumerist ways of experiencing the world is the observation that it may encourage new and non-consumerist identity projects and therefore that the identities of the DVC are never entirely fixed and given. Indeed there is also little to suggest that current trajectories in DVC cultures will coalesce into something stable or routine; the invitation to endlessly play with who we are and who we might be seems strong enough to resist any final claims about the alienating aspects of DVC or the ersatz nature of any resistance, activism, or transformation.

Even if we take much of our existing consumer culture into DVC, it is currently a "sandbox" for new market relationships and consumer behaviors. Perhaps most interesting, explorations in DVC may invite users to think about the self, consumption, and markets more generally in different ways. This is what we mean by liminoid spaces. For example, we see sharing and socially responsible consumption in the digital virtual world as well as escapism and fantasy, spectacle and individualism. Kozinets makes a strong argument for the emergence of communities around consumption activity, and many of the more specific examples in Part II illustrate strong experiences of community. We might therefore be willing to claim that, for many, engagement with others in digital virtual spaces often leads to something we can call community and has powerful meanings for individuals involved. Digital virtual communities and DVC seem linked. A result is the sub-cultures that form around DVC in community enclaves, which are separated from the material world or partly outside it. These liminoid spaces generate their own norms and enforcement procedures based on informal and voluntary forums as much as legal structures or rules imposed by site owners. Acknowledging this can lead to co-operation and what we now call co-construction of value between organizations and consumers. Indeed, such approaches may be increasingly necessary for organizations. And these tensions and mechanisms require more research. Within these cultures, there are collective desires and moral actions that have the potential to change the relationships between groups of users and markets and/or marketers. Such groups of individuals can construct value with little help from marketers if marketers choose not to play. In the ownership of digital virtual things, we see the capturing of social relationships so that we can claim that for many the purpose of spending time on DVC is to be with others. Here then there is a more optimistic reading of what DVC practices might mean. Far from the selfish and alienating aspects of a consumer culture, DVC communities lead to "craft consumption," sharing, restraint, co-operation, gift giving, and attempts to build relationships with others that add meaning to life even if these behaviors remain within a market system most broadly.

Anonymity in digital space means taboo breaking of all sorts as part of the creative process. Imagination is the guide to what individuals and groups might do with DVC and its ultimate limit. The pleasures of the imagination are well established in consumer research, and in DVC we see the potential for these to be enhanced or exaggerated. Even if we accept that the rest of everyday life is already structured by the imagination, in DVC an experience of freedom may be possible. One way to see this is in a playfulness—role play, competition, chance and thrill—and when combined with a "safe" environment that carries fewer financial and no physical risks, DVC allows for experimentation that can easily be seen to re-enchant life through rich new cultures. In this sense it might be considered as a space where individuals can regain a control they feel they have lost elsewhere in life. Players seem to experience more control when within the constraints of a game but outside the more complex and unknowable constraints and complexities of everyday life. They may also reflect on this. Indeed the accelerated nature of DVC may aid reflections as people more easily see the outcomes of their actions on others and on the digital virtual societies that they inhabit (as in Ross's analysis), and here we may be reminded of the angst that our contemporary global society may produce in individuals. This in particular seems an important area for further study. It is where transformations in the individual and the cultures they maintain may be most significant.

Yet maintaining our important digital virtual things carries new risks that must also be controlled by the individual, as Denegri-Knott, Watkins, and Wood (Chapter 6) explain. As we come to treasure digital virtual goods, just as we would material things, we feel the need to protect them from loss, and here their lack of materiality can cause new angst. We also see the inevitable return to material concerns. Protecting digital virtual goods requires physical hard drives, memory sticks, and network services, and this again reminds us that physical markets are always present even for the most reflective and playful of consumers.

Overall we might consider that entrepreneurial, creative, and community aspects of DVC suggest an erosion of previously taken for granted categories of work and leisure or consumer and producer (or investor). This seems to be another important aspect of the transformations that DVC produces, or at least DVC may make the problems of such categories more transparent. It may even ask us to reconsider the term "consumer." Maybe we should talk more broadly about " virtual practices" and note how market relations seem to dominate many, but not all, of them. Although we have suggested that DVC is limited by the imagination, the willingness of individuals to engage in entrepreneurial activity reminds us that the imagination can be highly socialized so that we may end up using DVC to simply re-imagine ourselves as good workers, responsible individuals, and compliant consumers—perpetuating a capitalist, entrepreneurial orientation to the world and others. We might, for example, consider further why individuals would give up much of what might be considered precious and hard-earned leisure time to "play" at running a successful business in an online virtual world. Although this might remind us that "work" is not in itself unrewarding and indeed may be very satisfying; it may also remind us that for some or many, "real work is alienating and unsatisfying and must be compensated for by paying for satisfying work in a digital virtual game-world.

There is also the possibility of "free" goods in DVC or new types of market relationships that don't require money earned from alienated labor to be exchanged for goods—the disintermediation of whole markets even, as individuals create and share for the pleasures of a collective. Yet the market system still requires new hardware, online subscriptions to servers and growth in the knowledge economy. Again we can't easily escape either the materiality that is required to support DVC or the contradictions of escape from and then return to market relationships. Just as interactions, leaks, and take-outs from digital virtual worlds are also inevitable, existing material relations are required to sustain DVC, and whole new markets (and the appropriation of existing technologies) are involved in supporting DVC practices. New DVC practices emerge from the fabric of everyday life, from the gadgets we buy, to how we arrange the home, to how we organize our time, and to our relationships with others. What's important here is to avoid seeing DVC as something separate from everyday life and separated from the material world—to avoid idealizing DVC as we note its freedoms and meanings.

If issues of new freedoms may be contested by claims that a consumer orientation is perpetuated, claims for environmental benefits are also frustratingly ambiguous at best given the acknowledgment that DVC uses material hardware. DVC may be consumption without using up as much material resources, and here we might celebrate "guilt-free" consumption in an age of environmental sensitivities. Fashions in SL can be bought and discarded without concern for the energy in their manufacture. Cars can be built, raced, and crashed in videogames without concern for the environmental impact. Instead, as Myers (Chapter 4) points out, it is only novelty that is used up and ensures the on-going consumption of digital virtual goods. This also reminds us that the meta-game played is again consumption, and it is constructed that way to suit our consumer culture. Molesworth makes a similar point. Traditional games like chess are not enough for our consumer society, fascinated as it is by spectacle and novelty. Whatever the context for DVC and however satisfying the community it produces may be, the aim always seems to be a desire for something new—new symbols, new meanings, and maybe new relationships—which must be acquired and then replaced by something else.

It is also a mistake to assume the unquestioning and enthusiastic adoption of DVC as a replacement for other consumer practices and related material goods. A problem with presenting DVC as a trajectory is the danger that we see it as inevitably replacing other consumer practices. The transformations it produces seem more complex than this. For example, DVC can make certain material practices seem "more special," as is the case of vinyl records illustrated by Magaudda. Older material practices can be re-enchanted by their contrast with the "ease" of DVC. Awareness of and reflection on the "artificial" nature of DVC can lead to new searches for authenticity in material consumption practices. This also seems like a productive area for more research. Again we can link this to the accelerated nature of DVC. If some of the joy in it is that so much can be obtained so cheaply and easily (consider the ease of re-invention of the avatar as self suggested by Vicdan and Ulusoy in Chapter 12), where might this leave the desire that is meant to drive consumption? What happens when in DVC we find that acquisition is so easy that it may provide little pleasure in wanting? Can even the digital virtual craft consumer fully replace the desiring one? Might an online community also drive a desire to re-make physical ones? We are reminded here about the breathtaking pace of developments in DVC and so to think about where these multiple and accelerated consumer lives will leave people in just a few years. Will they crave ever-more elaborate, spectacular, and transgressive experiences? Or will fatigue and reflection on such things lead them to seek less complexity, more simple pleasures, and more direct contact with the material world, including other people?

What we see is DVC producing tensions in existing consumer practices. Probably these exist without DVC, although DVC highlights and exaggerates them. There are tensions in the relationships between the material and the imagination (meaning making and utility in consumption practice), between new freedoms and reflections and the perpetuation of consumer ways of seeing the world, and between old and new markets (tradition and innovation). Some or many established practices are easily carried into the digital virtual, but new practices are also formed opportunities to revisit what we think a consumer and market are and might be.

Contributors

Nivein Behairy received her PhD from the University of California, Irvine, and is completing a post-doctorate at the Center for Research on Information Technology (CRITO) at UC–Irvine.

Janice Denegri-Knott currently teaches Consumer Culture and Behaviour at the Bournemouth Media School. Since 2001, she has been researching and publishing in the areas of digital virtual consumption and consumer/marketing research. Her research interests span from conceptualizing and documenting digital virtual consumption and its practices, the emergence of media technology, the socio-historic patterning of consumption, and more generally the subject of power in consumer and marketing research. She received her PhD in Management from the University of Exeter.

Melinda Jacobs, MA, is a game designer and researcher. She is the co-founder and CEO of Flight 1337, where she specializes in developing game-inspired experiences that engage audiences with brands, concepts, and products. Melinda's main research interests are exploring the effects of social engagement in online communities (such as multiculturalism in MMORPGs) and the use of game structure to create engagement in non-traditional situations. More information about Melinda and her research can be found at www.melindajacobs.org or you can find her on Twitter as @melindajacobs.

Robert V. Kozinets is a globally recognized expert on social media marketing. He is an award-winning professor who has won top teaching honors at both the Kellogg School of Management in Chicago and the Schulich School of Business in Toronto. He has authored more than 80 research publications, including many in the world's top marketing journals, a textbook, and two books. He is frequently cited in the international press. An anthropologist by training, he is Professor of Marketing at York University's Schulich School of Business, where he is also Chair of the Marketing department. He is also an Affiliate Faculty member at MIT. His feed is available as kozinets on Twitter. Brandthroposophy, his popular blog on marketing and social media, is available at www.kozinets.net.

Vili Lehdonvirta is an Adjunct Professor of Economic Sociology at the University of Turku, Finland, and a Visiting Scholar at the Asia Research Centre, London School of Economics and Political Science. His research interests include virtual goods, virtual currencies and digital work. He is the principal author of the World Bank's 2011 Virtual Economy report and a Co-Founder and Editor of the Virtual Economy Research Network. In his research, Lehdonvirta collaborates with leading digital games and online communities (Angry Birds, Habbo, EVE Online) and frequently appears as a commentator on digital virtual consumption in mainstream media (Washington Post, Scientific American, Guardian). He previously spent over three years in Japan in visiting positions at the University of Tokyo and Waseda University. Lehdonvirta holds a Ph.D in Economic Sociology from the Turku School of Economics and aM.Sc (Tech) from the Helsinki University of Technology. Before his academic career, Lehdonvirta worked as a game developer, developing some of the web's first real-time multiplayer games.

Paolo Magaudda (PhD 2007 in Sociology) works as a researcher at the University of Padua (Italy) within the Research Unit PaSTIS and the research center on new and emerging technologies (CIGA). His main research interests are in the fields of science and technology, consumption processes, cultural studies, popular music, and art and creativity. He has published more than 30 articles and chapters in scientific books and international journals. He is part of the Board of Directors of *"Studi Culturali,"* the Italian Journal on Cultural Studies, and is also co-editor of *"Tecnoscienza: Italian Journal of Science & Technology Studies."* He has recently edited a book on the social representations of science & technology in Italian TV (with F. Neresini, in Italian; il Mulino, 2011) and has also completed another book on the consumption practices of musical listening technologies (in Italian; il Mulino, 2012).

Jennifer Martin is a lecturer in the Faculty of Information and Media Studies at the University of Western Ontario. Her current research focuses on interaction in virtual worlds and examines the practices, meanings, and effects of the consumption of virtual goods in these environments. In addition to this work, her research focuses more broadly on new media in society, including concerns around social justice through digital technologies, identity creation and formation, mobile technology use, psychogeography, and human-computer interaction.

Mike Molesworth is a senior lecturer at Bournemouth Media School, where he teaches and researchers in online culture and behaviour and consumer culture. He has a PhD in consumer culture and has published papers in international journals on topics relating to both consumer culture and videogames.

David Myers is the Rev. Aloysius B. Goodspeed, S.J./Beggars Distinguished Professor in Mass Communication at Loyola University, New Orleans. He is the author of *The Nature of Computer Games* (Peter Lang, 2003) and *Play Redux* (University of Michigan Press, 2010).

Pétur Jóhannes Óskarsson started as a customer representative at CCP Games in 2003, working on *EVE Online*, gathering a strong background in customer relations and the management of online communities. This background, coupled with a master's degree in Philosophy from the University of Iceland earned him a place in CCP's Research and Statistics department doing socio-economic research on a society living in the virtual world of *EVE Online*. He is the project leader of the Council of Stellar Management run at CCP Games, the first democratically elected player council for an MMO.

Sandy Ross is a doctoral candidate at the London School of Economics and Political Science (London, UK) and a recent Fellow of the Institute for Advanced Studies in Science, Technology and Society (Graz, Austria). Her dissertation research explores lay theories of economics as developed in two virtual worlds, Final Fantasy XI and Second Life. She is also working with Shahanah Schmid on gendered experiences of illness and online support groups, and she is preparing a new project on ICTs, energy consumption, and sustainability.

Ebru Ulusoy is an Assistant Professor of Marketing at the University of Maine, Maine Business School. Her research stream includes studies of experience marketing and consumption and the impact of cultural transformations on consumers' lives and consumption patterns. Her recent research specifically focuses on design issues and consumer behavior, feelings, sensations, and thoughts in experiential consumer environments.

Alladi Venkatesh is Professor of Management and Associate Director at the Center for Research on Technology (CRITO), University of California Irvine. His research interests are in the areas of technology diffusion, aesthetics of design, and cultural economies. His research has appeared in leading journals.

Handan Vicdan is an Assistant Professor of Marketing at Eastern Kentucky University. Her research stream includes studies of social, cultural, and technological transformations in how consumers (re)organize their lives—specifically issues of consumer freedom, body, power, resistance, the impact of social media on consumer-marketer collaboration, and the implications of social networking in healthcare.

Rebecca Watkins is a doctoral student at the Bournemouth Media School researching consumers' attachment to virtual possessions within the context videogames and online worlds.

Joseph Wood studied for a degree in Advertising and Marketing Communications at Bournemouth University. He now works as a Community Manager at an integrated agency in central London, where he manages the online communities and social presences of a range of brands.

Detlev Zwick is Associate Professor of Marketing at the Schulich School of Business, York University, Toronto, Canada. His research focuses on cultural and social theories of consumption and the critical cultural studies of marketing and management practice. His works has been published in communication, media culture, marketing and sociology journals, as well as in several edited collections. He is the editor (with Julien Cayla) of Inside Marketing: Practices, Ideologies, Devices (Oxford).

Index